The
EVERYTHING®
Blackjack Strategy Book

Dear Reader:

The fact that you are holding this book means there's a good chance that you're a beginning blackjack player. Or perhaps you've never played blackjack but you're intrigued by the game and you want to learn more about it. If so, you've come to the right place.

For centuries, gamblers have been drawn to blackjack's basic premise—seeing how close they can come to the magic number 21 without going over it or being beaten by a better hand held by the dealer. It's a fascinating challenge, and one that keeps players coming back time and time again.

For being such an old game, blackjack has lost none of its allure. Instead, it enjoys a larger audience now than it ever has. Today, blackjack is the most widely played card game of its type in the world, and it shows no signs of losing its top position anytime soon. Card games may come and go, but blackjack is here to stay.

We're glad you've decided to join us in taking a closer look at the great game of blackjack, and we wish you good gaming!

Tom Hagen

Sonia Weiss

The EVERYTHING® Series

Editorial

Publishing Director	Gary M. Krebs
Managing Editor	Kate McBride
Copy Chief	Laura M. Daly
Acquisitions Editor	Gina Chaimanis
Development Editor	Karen Johnson Jacot
Prodution Editors	Jamie Wielgus
	Bridget Brace

Production

Production Director	Susan Beale
Production Manager	Michelle Roy Kelly
Series Designers	Daria Perreault
	Colleen Cunningham
	John Paulhus
Cover Design	Paul Beatrice
	Matt LeBlanc
Layout and Graphics	Colleen Cunningham
	Rachael Eiben
	Michelle Roy Kelly
	John Paulhus
	Daria Perreault
	Monica Rhines
	Erin Ring
Series Cover Artist	Barry Littmann
Interior Illustrations	Argosy

Visit the entire Everything® Series at *www.everything.com*

THE
EVERYTHING®
BLACKJACK STRATEGY BOOK

Surefire ways to beat the
house every time

Tom Hagen and Sonia Weiss

Adams Media
Avon, Massachusetts

To my beautiful wife April and two great boys Bradley and Spencer.
They gave me their support during the writing of this book and
understood the attention and time I gave to it. —Tom

An Everything® Series Book.
Everything® and everything.com® are registered trademarks of F+W Publications, Inc.

Published by Adams Media, an F+W Publications Company
57 Littlefield Street, Avon, MA 02322 U.S.A.
www.adamsmedia.com

ISBN: 1-59337-306-6
Printed in the United States of America.

J I H G F E D C B

Library of Congress Cataloging-in-Publication Data
Hagen, Tom.
The everything blackjack strategy book / Tom Hagen and Sonia Weiss.
p.   cm. — (An everything series book)
ISBN 1-59337-306-6
1. Blackjack (Game) I. Weiss, Sonia. II. Title. III. Series: Everything series.

GV1295.H34 2005
95.4'23—dc22
2004026350

This publication is designed to provide accurate and authoritative information with regard to the subject matter covered. It is sold with the understanding that the publisher is not engaged in rendering legal, accounting, or other professional advice. If legal advice or other expert assistance is required, the services of a competent professional person should be sought.

—From a *Declaration of Principles* jointly adopted by a Committee of the American Bar Association and a Committee of Publishers and Associations

Many of the designations used by manufacturers and sellers to distinguish their products are claimed as trademarks. Where those designations appear in this book and Adams Media was aware of a trademark claim, the designations have been printed with initial capital letters.

This book is available at quantity discounts for bulk purchases.
For information, call 1-800-872-5627.

Contents

Acknowledgments

The authors jointly would like to thank the many individuals who made our work possible, including Jacky Sach and Jessica Faust at Bookends, LLC and the editorial team at Adams Media, especially Acquisitions Editor Gina Chaimanis and Development Editor Karen Jacot for their assistance during the course of this project.

In addition, Tom would particularly like to acknowledge the following individuals: Brian Bingales and Billy DeWolf, the two dealers who first interested him in getting a gaming license and going behind the table; George Picard, who gave him his first shot at managing a blackjack pit; Bob Del Rossi, who gave him his first real job in Las Vegas; and Rich Turbiville, Scott Roth, and Brian Carmichael, who gave him the chance to put his ideas about pit management into action. And, finally, the dealers and pit bosses who make it enjoyable to come to work every day.

Top Ten Things to Know
About Blackjack

1. Blackjack is one of the few casino games where the house advantage, or edge, can actually be in the player's favor.

2. Learning basic strategy is key to mastering the game. With basic strategy, it's possible to decrease the house edge to under 0.5 percent.

3. Basic card-counting strategies are what make blackjack a truly beatable game.

4. Some casinos will let you abandon or surrender your hand if you really don't want to play it, or if you think it's a good idea that you don't.

5. Doubling down is one of the most effective ways to slash the house's edge and help you come out a winner more often.

6. Splitting pairs can make good hands better, improve poor to marginal hands, and increase the amount of money you stand to win.

7. Insurance is almost never a good bet. The only time it makes sense is when you are counting cards and you know that a number of 10s still remain to be played.

8. Rule variations affect the amount of each bet you can expect to win or lose. When picking a place to play blackjack, it's a good idea to find out which rules are being used so you can plan your play accordingly.

9. The odds are against your being a big winner at blackjack.

10. You probably won't get rich playing blackjack, but you can have a lot of fun trying.

Introduction

▶ If you've ever spent time in a casino, or at an online gaming site, there's a good chance that you've tried your hand at blackjack. Blackjack is what's known as a "banked" card game—you're up against the bank (or dealer) rather than other players. Blackjack is the most widely played banked card game in the world. If you've never played, you're in for a treat. Blackjack is a great game. Not only is it a lot of fun to play, it's a fantastic mental challenge. Blackjack's basic premise—seeing how close you can come to 21 without going over it or being beaten by the dealer's hand—may sound easy. However, there are many different strategies that players use to get to that magic number. Learning these strategies and knowing how to use them correctly is what makes the game both intriguing and captivating, not to mention a blast to play.

There is nothing like the thrill you can get when you split pairs and play both hands out to big wins. There is also nothing like the suspense that builds when the dealer is showing a 10 as an up card and you beat him with lots of little cards that finally add up to 21. Neither situation might seem exciting to you now. When you're done with this book, they will.

Blackjack is one of the older table games in existence. As such, it typically doesn't grab the spotlight that some newer games do. What's more, it's simply not the sort of game that attracts the kind of attention that games like No-Limit Texas Hold'em do. However, when people discover blackjack, they rarely quit playing it. Even after they learn other games, they'll always enjoy the unique challenges that are part of the game of blackjack, and playing the game will always occupy some part of their gaming experience.

The Everything® Blackjack Strategy Book shows everyone—from beginner to seasoned player—what the game is all about and what you need to know to play it well. But blackjack doesn't happen in a vacuum, so we also included lots of information on what gambling in general is all about.

Beginners and experts approach the game differently. For the most part, these differences boil down to the strategies and skills that expert players often use to give themselves as much of an edge over the house—the casino—as they can get. This book teaches you the basics—including basic strategy, which all beginning blackjack players must master—as well as some of the more advanced techniques for mastering the game. What also sets this book apart from others is the backgrounds of the authors. You're getting a unique, dual-focus look at the game here—from the casinos' perspective (Tom's), and the player's perspective (Sonia's). As such, this book is not just an *Everything®* guide. It's also an insider's guide.

By the time you finish reading *The Everything® Blackjack Strategy Book*, you'll not only know how to play blackjack, you'll also have a feeling for what it's like to really play it in a casino, whether land-based or online. You'll know what to expect if you've never been in a casino and what to do when you're there.

You'll also know the basics of good gambling, and, most important, you'll know how to be a good gambler. Make these principles yours, and you'll always be a winner.

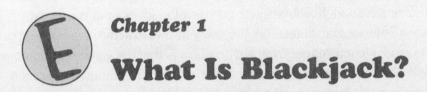

Chapter 1

What Is Blackjack?

Every year, millions of players sit down at blackjack tables in casinos, on riverboats—even at virtual tables in cyberspace. As they do, they have one purpose in mind: to see how close they can come to the magic number—21—without going over it or being beaten by a better hand held by the dealer. If you're wondering what's behind the game and why it's so popular, you've come to the right place.

History of the Game

To really understand what blackjack is all about, it's helpful to know something about the game's history and how it was developed. So let's start off with a short history lesson.

In spite of it being such a popular card game, we actually don't know that much about how blackjack was developed. Its origins and early history are a little unclear. In fact, no one really knows exactly where, when, or how it came into existence. What we do know is that the game originated somewhere in Europe. However, no fewer than three countries—France, Italy, and Spain—claim to be the birthplace of blackjack.

FACT

China gets the credit for being the home of the playing card and the card game, which both date back to roughly A.D. 900. Until the invention of playing cards, the Chinese used paper money, which they also invented, in their gambling games, both as the stakes they played for and as the elements of the game.

In France, it's believed that blackjack evolved from card games called *chemin de fer* and French Ferme, both of which have elements similar to blackjack. In Spain, a game called One and Thirty is said to be blackjack's forebear. Italians believe that blackjack is a modified version of two card games—Baccarat and Seven and One-Half.

How Blackjack Got Its Name

The first record of blackjack being played comes from early eighteenth-century France, where it was a popular casino game. Called vingt-et-un, which is French for "twenty and one," it paid out a special award to any player who got a jack of spades and an ace of spades as his first two cards. This hand came to be known as a "blackjack"—black, of course, being the color of the spades suit. Over time, blackjack became an alternative name for vingt-et-un.

Blackjack Comes to America

It took another hundred years for blackjack to come to the United States. When it did, in the early 1800s, it was welcomed in the wild and wooly frontier lands of the West, where gambling wasn't against the law. In the West, gambling was an important revenue source, as it previously had been in other parts of the United States. Some areas even licensed gambling parlors to raise money for civic and infrastructure construction and improvements—a practice that still goes on today in some parts of the country.

As the states joined the union, however, they were eager to shed their frontier-spirit personas and adopt new, more respectable images to reflect their new status. Since gambling was often blamed for promoting vice, dishonesty, and other social ills, cities and states began enacting laws against gamblers and gambling. By 1910, there wasn't a legal game of blackjack to be found in the United States. When blackjack was played, it was most often played as a private game at home.

FACT

Making gambling illegal didn't end it, it just drove card games and other forms of betting behind closed doors. Numerous gaming houses operated outside of the law in many parts of the United States. Some catered to specific clientele; in California, for example, certain gaming establishments were open just to Chinese gamblers.

There is record of blackjack being played in casinos in the Midwest around the turn of the twentieth century. Operating primarily as sport books, where gamblers could place bets on horse races, these casinos offered various table games—blackjack among them—to keep patrons occupied between races.

In 1931, the state of Nevada decided to make gambling legal again. While blackjack wasn't a hugely popular game for men, who tended to prefer games like craps and poker, the casinos did put a few blackjack tables in for the wives and girlfriends of their male customers.

Blackjack Gets Scientific

In the early 1960s, blackjack got a big boost in popularity when players began hearing about a new way to play blackjack. Based on scientific research, the new method of play was touted as one that could improve their advantage over the house and make them big winners.

Noted gambler, gaming expert, and games book author John Scarne takes the credit for what came to be known as the scientific approach (as well as for a great deal of blackjack's popularity) in his book *Scarne's New Complete Guide to Gambling*. According to Scarne, the first scientific analysis of blackjack appeared in the first edition of his book, which was published in 1961.

Skill, Not Luck

Whether Scarne's claims are legitimate can be disputed, as other sources date the first recognized effort to apply mathematics to blackjack back to the 1950s. In 1956, mathematicians Roger Baldwin, Wilbert Cantey, Herbert Maisel, and James McDermott published a paper called "The Optimum Strategy in Blackjack" in the *Journal of the American Statistical Association*. Based on three years' worth of analysis, it showed how probability and statistics theory could be used to give players a better edge over the house and formed the basis for what is known as basic strategy in the blackjack world.

FACT

"The Optimum Strategy in Blackjack" presented, for the first time, the theory that blackjack was a game of skill rather than luck. It also introduced charts that told players how to play their hands based on what the dealer was showing. Consulting these "basic play" charts took much of the guesswork out of playing blackjack, and gave players a better idea of what hands would win, and why.

What isn't in dispute is the fact that blackjack was a special kind of gambling game. It had elements that lent themselves well to scientific analysis of probability and play. As such, it posed an irresistible lure to others who liked to study such things.

The Beginning of Card Counting

Edward O. Thorp, while employed as a professor of mathematics at the Massachusetts Institute of Technology, expanded on the research published in "The Optimum Strategy in Blackjack" to prove there was a mathematical system for beating the game. In 1962, he published *Beat the Dealer: A Winning Strategy for the Game of Twenty-One*, a New York Times bestseller that refined the basic blackjack strategy presented by Baldwin and his associates and taught readers how to use it to their own advantage.

What Thorp advanced was a concept called card counting. Through computer-based research, he realized that unplayed cards in a deck affected play, with some combinations favoring the house and others favoring the player. The more face cards—jacks, queens, and kings, all of which carry the value of ten—that remained in a deck, the greater the player's chance of winning. The house had the edge when there were a preponderance of 5s and 6s.

At the time, blackjack was dealt from a single deck. By keeping track of which cards were played from the deck, players could better match their bets to their cards—keeping bets low when face cards were depleted, bumping them up when face cards remained. Thorp let the average person believe that he or she could easily beat blackjack and get rich quick. The reality is that while the average person could learn to count cards, it isn't easy. While Thorp's "Ten Count" method was touted as the key to unlocking great riches at the blackjack table, it actually wasn't quite that. For starters, many players found it difficult to learn, much less master. What's more, it had some flaws. However, another mathematician would soon straighten things out.

Blackjack on the Computer

Julian Braun, an IBM programmer, reworked Thorp's original computer program, wrote thousands of lines of new computer code, and played an estimated nine million games of blackjack on IBM's mainframe computers. When he was done, he had retooled Thorp's math and refined and improved his original calculations and strategies.

The second edition of *Beat the Dealer*, published in 1966, was based on Braun's research and presented the first correct version of basic blackjack strategy. Using it, players could reduce the house's edge to well below 1 percent.

Basic blackjack strategy charts are widely available. Some casinos even hand them out. If you're going to use them—many beginning players do—make sure to use charts that match the rules for the game you're going to play. Strategy varies between single-deck, double-deck, and multiple-deck games.

The second edition of *Beat the Dealer* sent shockwaves through the casinos. It made the game seem beatable, which greatly increased its popularity. While there might have been a small decline in the amount of money casinos realized from each game, volume more than made up for their losses. Still, the casinos felt they had to do something to regain their edge over players. They made changes to blackjack rules that affected players using basic strategy, and especially players who counted cards. These changes put blackjack players up in arms, and they showed their dislike of the new rules by ignoring the blackjack tables and spending their money elsewhere. Again faced with revenue losses, the casinos were forced to repeal the changes, and they reinstated the game's original rules.

Today, most of the changes made to foil card counting are history. One that remains in place, however, is the use of multiple decks. While you can still find some single-deck games, they're exceedingly rare. These days, it's not uncommon to see games played with four and even more decks, all shuffled together. Specially built contraptions called "shoes" hold the cards being dealt. Some shoes can handle as many as eight decks at a time. There is also something called an infinite deck shoe, which includes a shuffler that immediately recycles discards back into the unused portion of the deck.

Pushing the Edge in Card Counting

Hang around blackjack tables and around blackjack players long enough and you'll most likely hear someone talk about a man named Ken

Uston, one of the most colorful, successful, and controversial blackjack players of all time. It seems as if almost everyone who plays blackjack has a Uston story to tell.

The legendary Uston also used his mathematical and scientific prowess to beat the house. A magna cum laude graduate of Yale (he also held a degree from Harvard), he was a financial and mathematical whiz kid who worked his way into a vice president's slot at the Pacific Stock Exchange before he was forty years old.

In 1974, Uston received a call from a man named Al Francesco. A professional gambler, Francesco had heard of Uston and invited him to join a team of card-counting blackjack players. Uston, who was always looking for ways to make life more interesting, signed on and left the corporate world behind. The theory behind Francesco's scam was simple. He stationed card counters at several tables, where they played and placed minimum bets until the deck at their table was favorable. Then, they signaled the "Big Player," another member of the team who would join the action at the table and place big bets.

FACT

In efforts to thwart card counters, casinos often banned card counters, or "trash canned" them so they didn't want to come back again. Team play changed the blackjack scene by giving counters a way to disguise their play so they could continue to operate.

It took two years for the Las Vegas casinos to bust Francesco's team. By the time they did, the players had won approximately $1 million from the casinos, and Uston had become the team's best player. From there, Uston assembled his own teams, developed an advanced card-counting method, and began teaching it to others. Although the casinos were onto him, he continued to play, both under his own name and using a number of pseudonyms and disguises.

Ken Uston used computers to beat the house. He put the computers right on the playing floor, secreted in the shoes of his playing team. In 1977, Uston's team rapidly won more than $100,000, assisted by the shoe computers.

Then authorities confiscated one of the computers and sent it to the FBI. To the casinos' dismay, the government said the computer wasn't illegal, as it analyzed information that was freely available to the public. Uston also fought and won a successful legal challenge to prevent Atlantic City casinos from barring card counters.

In one interview, Uston said that blackjack's predictability was a main reason why the game appealed to him so much. It was, he said, the only game where it was possible to assess the mathematical expectations of winning or losing in advance, and know what those expectations are. For this reason, he saw blackjack as far less a gamble than investing in the stock market.

Ken Uston was found dead of an apparent heart attack in France on September 19, 1987. Given the life he had led, and the enemies he had amassed while doing it, many people suspected foul play when they heard the news, but none was involved. He died of natural causes. Uston was the subject of a movie, appeared on *60 Minutes*, and wrote several books about blackjack strategy, all of which drew even more players to the blackjack tables.

Growth of the Game

For many years, Nevada was the only place in the United States where gamblers could legally play blackjack. That changed in 1976 when New Jersey became the second state in the United States to legalize gambling. Up to 1989, Nevada and New Jersey were the only two states in the United States where casino gambling was legal. Since then, a number of states, including Colorado, South Dakota, and others, have joined suit. Today, approximately twenty states host casino gambling, either on the land or on riverboats on the Mississippi. Native American tribes also operate casinos in a number of states.

You can find some sort of gambling enterprise such as casinos, lottery, or riverboats in forty-eight of the fifty states. The only two states where gambling continues to be against the law are Utah and Hawaii.

Today, blackjack is played in virtually every legal gambling establishment (and some not so legal as well) in the United States, and in many of them around the world. It's also a popular game in private card clubs.

Why People Love to Play Blackjack

Why do players love to play blackjack? There are many reasons. If you were to ask a few players what they like about it, you'll get a variety of answers. Among them:

- **The rules of the game are not hard to learn.** All you have to do is hold a hand of cards that come as close to or equal to 21 as possible without going over and without the dealer holding a better hand than you do. This means that just about anyone, regardless of skill level, can walk up to a blackjack table, sit down, play a few hands, and have some fun without feeling intimidated or overwhelmed.
- **Players play against the dealer instead of other players.** Blackjack is what's known as a "banked" card game. You're up against a bank— the dealer—rather than other players. For this reason, how others play doesn't have a statistically significant effect on how well you're going to do, unlike some games (such as poker).
- **You can learn as little or as much about the game as you like and still be a pretty good player.** Basic blackjack strategy, which you'll learn more about in future chapters, isn't very difficult to learn.
- **It's a great way to exercise your mind.** Gambling on things like slots or keno is fairly mindless. While there are some theories behind each game that might help you win more often if you play them, there's not that much skill involved. Blackjack, on the other hand, is a strategy game. There are lots of ways to play a hand, and lots of variables to take into consideration. Because of this, being good at blackjack requires solid critical thinking, analytical skills, good decision-making, and a good memory.
- **It's fast-paced.** Hands are played quickly, making it an ideal game for players who like fast action.

- **It's possible to play big hands and win big.** In blackjack's early days, betting limits were fairly low, as were the payoffs. Some games had limits as low as a quarter. Even at a payout of 3 to 2 when a player hit blackjack, it wasn't enough to keep big players interested. The casinos realized this and began increasing their betting limits as well as their payouts. These days, if you want to play for big money, you won't have a problem finding a casino to accommodate you.

Perhaps most important, however, is that blackjack carries some of the lowest odds of any gambling game. This makes blackjack one of the best casino games you can play.

Why Casinos Love the Game

Why do casinos love blackjack? First, because people like to play it! To this day, blackjack ranks at the top of the favorites chart, as evidenced by the number of tables devoted to it in casinos around the world. Second, because it wins for them. Part of this is simply a numbers game: the more people who play blackjack, the more money casinos stand to take in. And third, as with other gambling games, when players wager on blackjack the house, or casino, wins a percent of every dollar they put up. This percentage, which varies depending on the game being played, is called the house advantage.

It can be a little hard to believe, perhaps, but in blackjack's early days players could actually have an edge over the casino. Over time, however, casinos made changes in how the game was played that allowed them to maintain an edge over the player. Today, the basic rules of blackjack are pretty much the same regardless of where you play, with only minor variations.

The house advantage is expressed as a percentage, which is based on known mathematical probabilities. The house advantage varies among different casino games. Play roulette, and the house has a 5.25 percent advantage over you. Baccarat? 1.17 percent. Craps? 1.414 percent. Keno? A whopping 25 percent.

Blackjack, however, stands apart from other casino games, as it doesn't have a set house advantage. There are a lot of long, involved mathematical equations behind this, some of which we'll talk more about in future chapters. For now, just know that many factors can affect the house's advantage when it comes to blackjack. Some of them are related to how the house sets up the game—in other words, the rules that govern how blackjack is played in a particular casino. For example, using a six-deck shoe can increase the house advantage by 0.54 percent. Allowing players to double down after splitting—a player option you'll read more about in future chapters—can give players a 0.14 percent advantage over the house. Surrender, a player option that you'll read about in future chapters, can give players a 0.02 advantage over the house. (These numbers assume that you are using these options at the correct times.)

The other variables that determine the house's advantage relate to the players themselves. Depending on how well—or how poorly—you play, you can increase or decrease the house's advantage over you. Play well enough and it's possible to whittle away the house's advantage to near zero.

ALERT!

While the basic blackjack game doesn't change, casinos employ a variety of rules that affect the house advantage. It's a good idea to find out what these rules are before you start playing. Some casinos—most notably those on cruise ships, where gamblers are a captive audience—have house rules that put players at a strong disadvantage. Unless you're a very good player, you might want to avoid these games, or bet very little if you do choose to play them.

So how can the house win if it doesn't have an advantage over its players? Most of the time, the casino has rules in place that give it an overall advantage. Add to this the fact that most players simply don't play that well, either because they don't know basic strategy or because they don't know it that well, and the house doesn't have much to worry about. Depending on how poorly people play, they can give the house as much as a 15 percent advantage over them.

All of this talk about mathematical equations, percentages, house advantages, and whatnot probably has you wondering if you have to be a mathematician or a Mensa genius to play blackjack. The short answer is definitely not! By mastering the basics, playing basic strategy, and playing it well, you can have a great time and come away a winner often enough to keep you coming back to the tables, which is a win-win proposition for both you and the casinos. However, the more you do learn about the mathematics behind the game, the better player you'll be, and the greater the chances are that you'll come away a big winner over time.

Who Plays Blackjack?

It's easy to assume that blackjack, like other gambling games, is traditionally a man's game. But this simply isn't so. While the history of this is a bit sketchy, it is known that men typically favored other games when Nevada casinos began offering blackjack in the early 1930s. Blackjack was seen as something that women could play while the guys were shooting craps. Then came card counting in the early 1960s, which attracted more players of both sexes to the tables.

FACT

One place where women gamblers dominate is online. According to AOL Games' "Casual Games Report," conducted by Digital Marketing Services, women who play games on the Web beat out both men and teens in frequency and length of play.

At today's blackjack tables you'll see lots of both women and men. You'll also see people of all ages playing blackjack. It doesn't attract any particular age group—young adults and seniors alike find a home at blackjack tables across the country and around the world. As they do, they join an ever-growing number of players who regularly pit their skills against the house, hoping to come away winners.

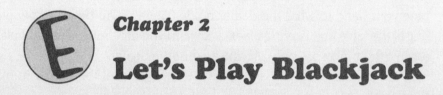

Chapter 2

Let's Play Blackjack

One of the reasons why blackjack is such a popular game is because it is so easy to play. However, newcomers to the game may find it intimidating at first, especially if they are unfamiliar with what gambling in general is all about. Let's take a look at the basics of the game and how it's played.

The Objective

At its most basic level, blackjack resembles other card games, as it is a comparison game—for the most part, an "I'll show you mine if you show me yours" kind of deal. However, unlike other card games, such as poker, where you compare your hand to other players', in blackjack you only compare your hand to what the dealer holds. There might be other people sitting at the table and playing blackjack when you are, but you are not playing against them. You are only playing against the dealer.

The goal in blackjack is simple. You want to beat the dealer in one of three ways, by:

- Accumulating a hand of cards that is better than the point total, or score, that the dealer has, without going over 21 points.
- Holding a hand with 21 points or fewer if the dealer goes over 21 points.
- Getting a natural 21, or blackjack. This is a hand with an ace and a 10-value card.

That's pretty much all there is to it. Depending on where you are playing, you might find slight variations in the rules of the game, but the objective will be the same.

If you're thinking blackjack looks like a pretty simple game, you're right. At its basic level, blackjack is amazingly easy to play. You can sit at a blackjack table and play a few hands without knowing much about it at all. If you are a real newbie, the dealer might even help you along by asking you if you're sure about making certain plays. And if you are lucky enough, you might even come away a winner. But luck only goes so far in blackjack. If you want to protect your investment, there are better ways to approach the game.

Game Gear

Because it is such a simple game, blackjack doesn't require an elaborate setup or lots of fancy equipment. All that you really need is a standard fifty-two-card deck of playing cards. If you're going to play a betting game, you'll need money or chips to indicate bet amounts.

Understanding Card Values

Blackjack uses a standard fifty-two-card deck. It contains four suits of cards—spades, clubs, diamonds, and hearts. Each suit has thirteen cards. Numbered cards run 1 through 10. In addition, each suit has three face cards—a jack, a queen, and a king. All face cards in blackjack are valued at 10. Each suit also contains an ace, which can count as either 1 or 11. Standard card decks typically come with a joker or two, which are not used in blackjack.

The Blackjack Table

Casinos use specially designed blackjack tables for their games. These semicircular tables seat from five to seven players. Blackjack tables are almost always topped with felt. This fabric, which has a soft, nappy surface, makes it easier for dealers to shuffle the cards and easier for players to pick up their cards.

Blackjack tables don't leave anything to chance when it comes to telling players the rules of the game. Gaming laws require gambling establishments to display the following information on the felt:

- What the house pays for blackjack (also called a natural)
- The point total at which the dealer is required to stop taking additional cards for his hand
- The insurance payout

Below this information are circles or other symbols defining the number of people who can play at any one time. These days, you will usually see six- or seven-spot tables, although there are tables that seat as few as five players.

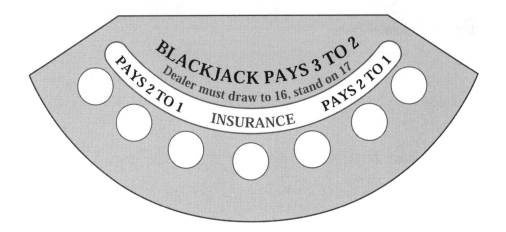

▲ Blackjack table layout.

Other Blackjack Gear

As mentioned, it doesn't take much to play blackjack. This doesn't mean that you won't see some other pieces of equipment when you play, including:

- **A shoe.** This plastic contraption holds the cards after they are shuffled before they are dealt.
- **A chip rack.** This holds the colored chips that indicate betting levels. They also hold silver coins—typically quarters—used to pay off amounts that are less than the minimum chip value (which is usually $1).
- **A discard tray.** Usually made of red plastic, this is where the dealer places the cards after they're played.
- **A shuffle machine.** This device, which shuffles the cards for the dealer, is becoming standard equipment in many casinos.
- **A peek window.** This is a small rectangular device in front of the tray that dealers use to check their hole (or face-down) cards.
- **A player card reader.** Also becoming standard equipment in many casinos, these devices accept player's club cards for rating play and determining comps.

The Order of Play

Again, given blackjack's simple setup, cards are dealt in a simple manner. Players at the table place their bets in front of them on the table. Everyone at the table—players and the dealer—receives two cards from the top of the deck. The deal begins with the player closest to the dealer's left hand, and goes around the table from there.

Table Position

You'll often hear the seat immediately to the dealer's left referred to as first base, as the person sitting there plays his or her hand first. And you'll sometimes hear the seat closest to the dealer's right hand (on the left side of the table from the player's perspective) called third base, as the player sitting here is the last to play his or her hand. Another term for third base is the anchor.

Gambling is not without its superstitions, and blackjack certainly has its share of them. Some people prefer to sit at first base because they believe they are more likely to receive a 10-value card. Others like third base because they think that seeing more of the cards before they play helps them make better decisions regarding their own play.

Running the Bases

Some people believe that the decisions made by the person sitting at third base control the dealer's hand, and, ultimately, the table's success. This simply isn't true. Of all the superstitions and beliefs surrounding blackjack, this is one of the most controversial.

Because of this, if you sit at third base and you don't play well, you risk the wrath of other players. If you hit (take a card) when other players believe you should stand, then you are taking the card that the dealer otherwise would have gotten himself. If this card would have busted him (made his cards go over 21), other players may blame you for taking that card and not letting the dealer bust.

The truth is—and this is explained further in future chapters—where you sit at the table doesn't have much effect on the outcome of the game. Over the long run, one person's play has no effect on the table's success. Bad players make decisions that help the table just as often as they make decisions that hurt it.

It is sometimes difficult to sort out fact from fiction when it comes to gambling, and especially when it comes to table position in blackjack. For every person who says it doesn't matter where you sit there's another who says it makes all the difference in the world. You have to decide what you want to believe, but most experts say that simply being a smart player is the best edge you can have as a gambler.

Getting the Game Started

Now that you know more about the basic mechanics of how blackjack is played, let's step through a game. To really get the flavor of what blackjack is all about, you've got to get to a casino. But this section can give you an idea of what the blackjack experience will be like. All of the aspects of play will be covered in depth in later chapters. For now, let's take a basic look at what happens at a blackjack table.

You can't play unless you are in the game, and being in the game means putting some money down on the table. If the game you want to join is already in progress, you might have to wait for the cards to be shuffled before you can join in. If not, the dealer will cut you in on the next dealing round.

If the table you chose is between rounds, play won't start until after the cards are shuffled. After this happens, the dealer will place the pack in front of one of the players to be cut. Cutting duty rotates clockwise from player to player after each shuffle. When it's your turn, the dealer will hand you a colored plastic card, called a cut card. You place the card in the deck, and the dealer cuts the deck and places it in the shoe. Then the dealer will place the cut card somewhere near the end of the pack to indicate the point at which he will quit dealing from that shoe and reshuffle the cards.

Does it matter where I insert the cut card?

Not really. All you're doing is splitting the deck in some way. You can split it high or low, your choice. Since the two parts are then reassembled, it just means that the order will be different. Gambling laws require players to make cuts a minimum of five cards in from either end. Casinos set their own rules from here, which vary from five cards up to fifty-two cards in from either side.

The dealer always discards the first card on top of the deck before the first deal. This is called a burn card. This move, done to protect against marked decks, is a gaming tradition. The dealer will slide the burn card across the table from his left to his right, and place it in the discard tray, which is where all used cards end up. You will sometimes hear players ask to see the burn card. If this happens at your table, the dealer will say something like "Showing the burn card," and turn it over for everyone to see before placing it in the discard tray. However, most casinos won't let dealers show the burn card. If a player asks, the dealer will politely decline.

Dealing the Cards

Next comes the deal. As previously mentioned, the dealer will start with the player to his immediate left and work clockwise around the table. Depending on the casino you're playing in, you will either get both cards face down or get both cards face up. Since you are only playing against the dealer, the way in which the cards face doesn't matter. If your cards are dealt face down, you may pick them up and look at them. If they are face up, however, you are not permitted to touch the cards.

The dealer deals himself one card face up. This is called the up card. His other card is dealt face down. This is called the hole card. Blackjack rules regarding hole cards can vary somewhat depending on where you play. At some casinos in Europe, for example, dealers don't draw their second card—the hole card—until all players finish playing their hands. You'll also see this rule on some cruise ships. Play begins after everyone gets his or her cards.

If the dealer is showing an ace or a 10 as the up card, he will act first, because if he holds a blackjack, the hand is over and all the players lose their wagers. If an ace is showing, the dealer will offer players the option to take insurance. Insurance is simply an additional wager on whether you think the dealer has a 10-value card in the hole. If you believe he does, you can take the insurance bet, which allows you to put down another bet of up to half of your original wager.

After everyone weighs in on insurance bets (if an ace is showing) or immediately (if a 10 is showing), the dealer will check his hole card. He does this by moving the corner of the card over the peek window. The cards are designed so that the markings for aces and 10-value cards appear in the corners in a different spot than other cards. He has only to check the mirror under the peek window to look for a marking. (In some casinos, the dealer may actually discreetly turn over the card to see its value.) If the card gives him blackjack (a 10 if he's showing an ace, or an ace if he's showing a 10), the dealer will flip over the hand to show the blackjack. If an ace was showing and any player took insurance, the dealer pays the insurance bets. At that point, the hand is over. If the dealer doesn't have a blackjack, the hand plays out as normal.

FACT

These days, most games are multideck, and cards are dealt face up from a shoe. If you should happen across a one- or two-deck game, which are dealt by hand, you'll get your cards face down. These games are becoming increasingly rare, however.

The only exception to this is when a player has a blackjack on the same hand that the dealer shows an ace. In this case, the dealer will offer the player "even money." This means the dealer pays the player 1:1 (instead of 3:2)—for example, a $10 bet pays $10, for a net win of $20—before the dealer checks his hole card. This gives the player the option of being certain of winning some money rather than winning none if the dealer does have blackjack.

If the player gambles and doesn't take even money, two things can happen:

- **The dealer has blackjack.** If so, the player's hand is a push, or a tie, and no money is exchanged. The player simply gets his original bet back.
- **The dealer doesn't have blackjack.** The player is then paid off at 3-to-2 odds—for example, a $10 bet wins an additional $15, for a total of $25.

Player Options

If you are the lucky one with an ace and a 10, you have a natural blackjack. If so, you should immediately turn over both of your cards so the dealer can see them. But most of the time you won't have a natural, and the dealer won't either.

There are several moves available to players. These are covered in detail in future chapters. For now, here is a quick peek at what players can do:

- **Surrender.** This option lets you turn in a hand without playing it. You forfeit half of your original bet when you do.
- **Hit.** If you feel your first two cards aren't close enough to 21 to win, you can ask for more cards—for as many as you need, in fact, until you reach a total you're happy with, or until you go over 21. To indicate that you want another card, tap your fingers on the table in front of your cards (or scratch the surface of the table lightly with your cards, if you're holding them). Each time you tap, the dealer will give you an additional card, face up. If the cards you receive push you over 21, you lose or go bust. The dealer then removes the cards and takes your bet.
- **Split.** If you are holding two cards with the same face value, you have the option of splitting them up and making them into two separate hands that you play independently of each other.
- **Double down.** This option lets you double your wager on the chance that you will win with just one (and no more) additional card.
- **Stand.** If you think you have a good enough hand, you can simply

stay where you are. To indicate this, wave one hand over your cards, or place your cards under your original bet.

FACT

An ace can be either 1 or 11. If you have an ace and a 7, for example, you can have either a "soft" 18 or 8. Once you have enough cards that its value is no longer optional, the hand then has a hard total. As an example, a hand with an ace, a 5, and a 6 would equal either 12 or 22. However, since 22 would be a losing hand, the ace can only be counted as a 1, so the hand is a hard 12.

After all the other players are done playing their hands, the dealer plays his hand in accordance with the rules of the house. First, he will turn over his hole card. If the two cards total 16 or less, he will hit. He will continue hitting his hand until the point total is 17 or more. This is the only option he has. He can't split, double down, or surrender. If he is holding a soft 17—an ace and a 6—he might be required to hit his hand. Some casinos allow their dealers to stand on a soft 17, others require them to hit these hands. (This rule is usually indicated on the table.)

After the dealer's hand reaches 17 or more, he will compare it to each player's hand. At this point, there are three possible outcomes:

- He busted (went over 21), and you didn't. You win, no matter how good or bad your hand is.
- He does not bust, but has a lower total than what you are holding. You win.
- He does not bust, and his total is higher than yours is. You lose.

The dealer pays the bets (if there are winners) and takes the losing bets, and the hand is over. That's it. Doesn't seem so intimidating now, does it?

Chapter 3

Understanding the Odds

To be a good gambler, you have to understand what you are up against. In other words, you need to know the odds. This is true whether you play blackjack or any other game where you're betting on what is going to happen. Knowing how the odds factor in blackjack takes a little education in how odds affect gambling in general, and in the basic mathematics that govern casino games, which is what this chapter is all about.

Why Do I Need to Know Math?

Understanding how the odds work both against you and for you in black-jack plays a huge role in becoming a successful player. Blackjack is one of the few casino games that players can beat—if they know how to do it. For this reason, it is one of the most player-favorable games you can play, if you learn the skills necessary for swinging the odds to your favor. If you do, you greatly increase the chances of coming out a winner.

QUESTION?

Do I need good math skills to be a good blackjack player?
Good math skills make it easier to understand why things happen the way they do when you play. Not having them might make it harder for you to get really good at blackjack, but you don't have to be a math-ematical whiz to play the game well.

No skills or strategies can guarantee that you'll win every single hand. But you can learn the specific mathematical principles that govern your chances of winning. Depending on the game you play, and the mathematical formu-las on which it's based, the odds of your winning at gambling range from slightly in your favor to very much against you. Understanding these princi-ples can help you make decisions about how to play that help you win more money than you lose, which is, of course, the ultimate goal of gambling.

The Heads and Tails of Probability

Gambling on games is based on probability, the branch of mathematics that focuses on calculating the likelihood of a specific occurrence, such as a coin landing face up or a roulette wheel landing on black. Probability is expressed as a number between 1 and 0. Something that is certain to hap-pen—such as the fact that a coin will land face up or face down—has a probability of 1. An event with a probability of 0 is considered an impossibil-ity, while one with a probability of .5 has—you guessed it—equal odds of occurring or not.

Simple Probability

To illustrate probability, let's take a very simple example—tossing a coin. Coin tossing is easy to analyze, since there are only two ways a coin can land—heads or tails—when it's tossed. No matter whether you call heads or tails, there is one chance out of two that you will win the toss. Expressed another way, there is a 1 in 2 chance that the coin will land in your favor. This is a probability of ½, or .5.

A coin toss is known as an independent event, because the outcome of one toss has nothing to do with what will happen on subsequent tosses. (A dependent event, as the term implies, has outcomes based on other factors, such as what happened before the event.) Let's say you were to toss a coin 100 times, and you're going to bet $1 on each toss that the coin will land on heads. If it does, you win a dollar plus your bet, doubling your money. If it doesn't, you win nothing and forfeit your bet. Will you come out ahead? Let's do the math.

You know there is a 50/50 chance, or a .5 probability, that the coin will land heads-up on each toss. Every time it does, you win $2. $2 times 50 is $100. However, you are also forfeiting $1 on every toss you don't win. On a .5 probability, out of every $100 you put up, you stand the chance to lose fifty tosses, or $50. Theoretically, you would not lose or gain anything on your original bankroll. You'd end up even.

FACT

Flipping a coin to determine who gets the ball first or to settle a dispute really isn't all that fair. Human-generated flips introduce factors that affect probability, as the coin isn't launched the same way twice. Researchers have also found that when a tossed coin starts out heads, it ends up heads when caught more often than tails.

We say theoretically because probability theory tells us that this is what *should* happen. Does this mean that in 100 coin tosses, exactly 50 percent of those will be heads? Definitely not. But the odds are that they will even out, over time, based on the theory of the law of large numbers. This theory states that a large sample of a particular probabilistic event will tend to reflect the underlying probabilities. In layman's terms, what this means is that the more times you flip a coin, the closer you get to coming up with 50 percent heads and 50 percent tails, or hitting 50/50 odds.

Going Against the Odds

Sometimes probability theory doesn't seem like it really works. If you toss that coin and it lands heads-up a number of times in succession, it may seem like you are going against the odds. You might be for a short time, but you won't be over the long haul. The .5 probability will hold. In other words, the odds remain at 50/50 since a coin—or mathematics, for that matter—has no memory. The next toss could result in heads. Then again, it might not.

Unfortunately, this kind of thinking gets some gamblers into big trouble. They get on a winning streak and start betting big because they believe the streak will continue. Or the opposite happens. They get on a losing streak and start betting big because they think the odds favor an end to the streak. They might, but it could happen long after they lose all their money.

Thinking that a run of luck—good or bad—will influence the odds of winning or losing in the future is called the gambler's fallacy. It misapplies probability theory, as the assumption that the odds have changed is wrong. In gambling, there really is no such thing as luck, although it might sometimes seem as if there is. But it is really all mathematics.

Probability vs. Odds

Now that you've got the basics down, let's take things up a notch. For this example, we will play a simple card game, using a standard deck of fifty-two cards to which we have added four jokers. You are betting on the chance that you will pick a joker from the deck, and you are going to pay $1 every time you try. If you win, you get $10.

Is this a game you should play? Let's shuffle up and do the math. We are starting with a deck of fifty-six cards, of which four are jokers. This means your probability of pulling a joker out the deck is 4 out of 56, or 1 in 14.

Probability represents the ratio of the number of times an outcome occurs (in this case, four) to the number of times the experiment is conducted (in this case, fifty-six). Another way of expressing your chances is by stating the odds against your successfully pulling out a joker, which represents the number of times an outcome does not occur to the number of times an outcome does occur.

To factor the odds, compare the number of other cards in the deck (the outcome not occurring) to the number of jokers (the outcome occurring). Your odds of picking a joker would be 52 to 4, or 13 to 1 against.

Not great odds, right? Let's keep going. Keep in mind that these odds are in place for only the first pull. After each card is dealt, it is discarded, which means that the total number of cards you have to select from decreases. Let's say you lost the first hand and pulled something other than a joker. Here's what the probability and odds look like on your next hand:

Probability: 4 out of 55, or 1 in 13.75
Odds: 51 to 4, or 12.75 to 1 against

Now the odds are more in your favor, although not significantly so. Just for fun, let's say you pulled a joker the first time. How does that affect the odds on the next pull?

Probability: 3 out of 55, or 1 in 18.3
Odds: 52 to 3, or 17.3 to 1 against

Would you win any money at this at all? Maybe. If you were to pull a joker the very first time, you'd win $10. But you paid $1 in, so you really only win $9. Still, you've won some money, and you've beaten the odds handsomely. However, statistics show that you would probably have to play more than one hand to win. As you do, the odds of your winning will change depending on the cards you pull. Because of this, you might end up pulling more than ten cards before you hit a joker, which would put you at a loss. Or you could pull two, three, or even four jokers in pretty short order, and come away with lots more than you put down. Over time, as you eliminate cards other than jokers from the deck, the odds continue to improve in your favor. Eventually, you're bound to win. Or are you?

FACT

Casinos use a variety of methods to keep their coffers full. The difference between real odds—the actual odds related to a game—and payoff odds, which are calculated at something less than real odds—also contributes. Certain games, such as craps, baccarat, and poker, require players to pay a fee, called vigorish, or the vig.

The House Always Wins

If everything ended up about even in gambling, there wouldn't be much reason for casinos to stay open. But they do, and they make huge money doing so.

How do they do it? There are lots of factors involved, but the simple answer is that, in the long run, all gambling games are set up to favor the casinos. Casino operators factor things in such a way that there is a percent of profit on virtually every bet. For this reason, the casinos are always winners in the end.

In the gambling world, the fact that the house always wins is known as the house advantage, or house edge. The house advantage represents the biggest odds you face in gambling, other than the odds created by your own skill and level of play. You will read and hear a lot about house advantage when you gamble. Understanding the house edge can help you decide what games to play, and, as in the case of blackjack, can help you play in ways that decrease the house edge to its smallest and increase your chances of coming out ahead.

How much of an advantage—or edge—the house has over its players can vary quite a bit. Different games have different house edges. What's more, for certain games, like craps and blackjack, how you play the game can have a big effect on the house edge, and the edge can vary from one hand or one bet to another.

TABLE 3-1 illustrates basic house advantages for some of the more popular casino games, and what the casino stands to keep out of every $10 you bet on them (over the long term).

Game	House Edge	What the casino keeps from every $10 bet
Baccarat	1.2%	12 cents
Blackjack	0.0% to 2.0%	0 to 20 cents
Craps	0.6% to 1.4%	6 to 14 cents
Let It Ride Poker	3.5%	35 cents
Pai Gow Poker	2.5%	25 cents
Slots	5% to 10%	50 cents to $1
Video Poker	0.5% to 3%	5 cents to 30 cents

TABLE 3-1: Typical House Advantages

You can use the house edge to determine how quickly you'll lose money when playing certain games. For example, if you are playing a game with a 3 percent house advantage, you'll lose your money twice as fast as when playing one in which the house has a 1.5 percent advantage.

Should you always avoid playing games with large house advantages? Not necessarily. Here are some reasons why you might want to play them:

- Some are simply enjoyable, and you'd be missing out on some fun if you didn't play them.
- There are ways to reduce the house's edge on some of them, such as knowing which bets to place (and which ones to avoid).
- Casinos often offer promotions that improve the odds for players and sometimes even give players the edge.

That said, it is generally a good idea to focus on games that give players the best possible edge. If you do decide to play games that aren't as favorable, you can minimize your risk by playing less. Still, it's important to remember that over time, with everything being equal, you'll lose at these games. The casinos, in fact, count on it.

Player Expectation

Another way to look at the odds is from the player's perspective. This approach is called the player's expectation or expected value. It represents the amount of money you can reasonably expect to win or lose from every dollar you wager.

There are some long and involved formulas for figuring player expectation, but you can come up with a basic idea of what it is simply by reversing the numbers on the previous chart. In other words, if a game has a 1.2 percent edge for the house, this means it has a −1.2 percent expectation for the player, or that you can expect to lose 1.2 cents for every dollar you bet on that game.

If you go back to the chart that shows the casino edge for various games, you'll note that almost every one of them shows the casino making money. The only exception is blackjack. Video poker comes close.

FACT

Casinos are regulated based on fairness and honesty. Fairness relates to the house advantage, which sometimes might not seem very fair. Honesty relates to games not being fixed in the casino's favor. Most regulatory bodies require casinos to conduct some type of mathematical analysis to determine house advantage and confirm random outcomes for games played, and this information is available to anyone who asks for it.

This is an important point to note, as it proves that, in the long run, it is impossible for a player to play a game with a negative player expectation and come out ahead. But this doesn't mean that it's hopeless, or that you should stay completely away from these games. Other variables also kick in. And, as previously mentioned, casino owners know that it's not much fun to play games that you always lose at, so they sometimes do things, such as run special promotions, to make it easier for you to win, or that reward you for playing whether you win or not.

Chapter 4

Understanding Basic Strategy

Thanks to mathematics and computer simulations, experts have been able to evaluate the probabilities of winning in every possible situation in blackjack. And you can take advantage of this knowledge to help you win. Learning basic strategy and using it well can significantly reduce the advantage that the casino has over unskilled players. Sounds great, doesn't it? Let's take a closer look at what basic strategy is all about.

Evening the Score

In technical terms, basic strategy maximizes the player's average expectation playing one hand against a full deck of cards. It is a complete set of decision rules covering all possible choices that the player may encounter, without consideration for other players' cards.

In plain English, this simply means that basic strategy is a set of decisions governing the moves a player makes. These decisions are based on certain rules that take into consideration all the possible choices that a player encounters. The rules are not dependent on any other player's cards or on any other cards used on a previous round before the deck was reshuffled. In a nutshell, players who learn basic strategy, and use it well, can lower or eliminate the edge that the house has over them.

By now you should know that blackjack, like all other gambling games, is set up so that the house—the casino—always wins. Unlike other games, however, blackjack is a game composed of many variables that can affect exactly how much of an edge the house has. Of these variables, basic strategy is the most powerful.

Many of the better casino blackjack games in the United States employ rules that give the house an advantage of around 0.5 percent when you follow basic strategy. Every so often you'll come across a casino that offers games where using basic strategy will give you the advantage over the house. Single-deck games, for example, can be very player-favorable. However, they tend to be few and far between, and the casinos typically put other rules in place—such as low maximum bets—that minimize how much you can win when you play them.

If you take the time to learn just the rudiments of basic strategy, you can break even, or come close to it, even when you're a rank beginner at blackjack. If you learn basic strategy well, and hone your skills at it, you can come out a winner in the long run in two ways: you can increase your winnings and you can cut your losses.

Note, however, the word "can." Basic strategy, in and of itself, isn't a big moneymaker for players. Yes, it can reduce the house advantage against you to 0.5 percent or less. In real money, this means you'll only lose a half cent for every dollar you wager, or 5 cents for every $10 bet. However, there are plenty of other factors that can—and do—affect the house's advantage over you. Another big factor affecting player expectation is casino rules. Here are some common casino rules, ranked from the worst to the most positive for players, and how they affect player expectation:

House Rule	Effect on Player Expectation
Dealer wins ties	−9.00%
Natural pays 1 to 1	−2.32%
Double down only on 11	−0.78%
Eight decks	−0.58%
Six decks	−0.54%
Four decks	−0.48%
Two decks	−0.32%
Dealer hits soft 17	−0.20%
Double down only on 10 or 11 (no soft, no 9, no 8)	−0.14%
Double down only on 9, 10, 11 (no soft, no 8)	−0.14%
No re-splitting of any pairs	−0.03%
Late surrender	+0.06%
Re-splitting aces	+0.06%
Double down after splitting pairs	+0.14%
Draw to split aces	+0.14%
Six-card winner	+0.15%
Player 21 pushes dealer's 10-up blackjack	+0.16%
Double down on any number of cards	+0.24%
Early surrender	+0.62%
Natural pays 2 to 1	+2.32%

Wise players keep these factors in mind when choosing a casino (or Web site) to play at. Some house rules don't give the casino a huge advantage, but they can add up. For example, play at a casino where dealers win ties, shoes hold eight decks, and players can only double down on 11, and you've got a total statistical disadvantage of –10.36. In casinos like this (it's best to avoid them, by the way), playing basic strategy will help you cut your losses, but the house will still maintain a tremendous edge regardless of how well you play.

Understanding the Strategy

The premise of basic strategy is amazingly simple: the dealer's up card provides all the information you need to make a reliable prediction about what will happen with his or her hand. This prediction will then determine what you do with yours.

Let's take a closer look at this and why it works as well as it does. A standard fifty-two-card deck, which is what blackjack uses, has a total of sixteen cards that carry a value of 10. This is slightly more than 30 percent of the deck.

QUESTION?

Is using basic strategy considered cheating?
Definitely not! It's always a good idea to learn as much as possible about the basics of any game you're going to play. Since basic strategy is based on information that is available to any player of blackjack, it can hardly be considered cheating.

This is where the predicting comes in. If a dealer is showing an up card with a low value—2, 3, 4, 5, or 6—he or she will need at least two additional cards to reach 17 (and remember that the dealer has no choice but to hit until he reaches at least 17 or busts). Given the preponderance of 10-value cards in a deck, there is a greater chance of dealers busting when they have low-value up cards.

Now, let's take a closer look at what happens if the dealer is showing a higher-value up card—a 7, 8, 9, 10, or ace. Given the percentage of 10-value cards in the deck, with these cards it's more likely that the dealer will have a pat hand—in other words, won't have to draw another card. Therefore, he is less likely to bust.

So there are two situations: one in which the dealer is likely to bust, one in which he isn't likely to bust. Based on this information, you need to decide what you are going to do with your own hand. What should you do? In a nutshell:

- If there's a good chance that the dealer is going to bust, you should avoid busting your own hand. Remember, if the dealer busts and you bust, this isn't a push. You lose your bet. For the most part, you'll want to stand on the cards you already hold, or hit if you hold very low cards with no chance of busting. Your goal is to win simply by letting the dealer go bust. In situations like this, you can be more aggressive about maximizing your play by employing options such as doubling down or splitting, which you'll read more about in Chapters 6 and 7.
- If the dealer's up card indicates that he's less likely to bust, you can be less cautious about busting your own hand. You should hit with the intention of trying to reach a winning total.

Many times basic strategy is used to lessen a certain loss. As an example, let's say you're holding a 16 into the dealer's 10. The odds are against the player winning this hand no matter how it's played. Over time, however, you will lose less if you hit than if you stand.

Simple Basic Strategy

Now that you know what basic strategy is all about, let's take a look at some basic strategy tables. **TABLE 4-1** represents the simplest possible basic strategy. It takes into consideration fairly standard playing conditions of the kind you'll find at most of the larger casinos. The table starts with a hand of 12 since with any total less than 12 no single card can bust you and you should always hit.

TABLE 4-1: Simple Basic Strategy										
Dealer's Up Card	**2**	**3**	**4**	**5**	**6**	**7**	**8**	**9**	**10**	**Ace**
Player's Hand										
12	H	H	S	S	S	H	H	H	H	H
13	S	S	S	S	S	H	H	H	H	H
14	S	S	S	S	S	H	H	H	H	H
15	S	S	S	S	S	H	H	H	H	H
16	S	S	S	S	S	H	H	H	H	H
17	S	S	S	S	S	S	S	S	S	S
18	S	S	S	S	S	S	S	S	S	S
19	S	S	S	S	S	S	S	S	S	S
20	S	S	S	S	S	S	S	S	S	S
21	S	S	S	S	S	S	S	S	S	S
A-2	H	H	H	H	H	H	H	H	H	H
A-3	H	H	H	H	H	H	H	H	H	H
A-4	H	H	H	H	H	H	H	H	H	H
A-5	H	H	H	H	H	H	H	H	H	H
A-6	H	H	H	H	H	H	H	H	H	H
A-7	S	S	S	S	S	S	S	H	H	H

H = Hit, S = Stand
With A-8 or A-9 you should always stand. There is no occasion to hit or double on a soft 19 or a soft 20.

Remember, there are many different variables that can affect how you play the game of blackjack, and there is no one table or set of tables that apply to every situation. But this one will work more often than not. If you master it, you'll be a better player than 80 percent of those who sit down to a blackjack table.

More Complex Basic Strategy

The next two tables show basic strategy that's also based on fairly standard playing conditions. However, these tables reflect a couple of player options, double down and splitting—two strategies that can be very much to the player's advantage. You'll find more information about them in Chapters 6 and 7. But we're showing you tables that include them now to demonstrate how things can change when certain rules come into play.

TABLE 4-2 is for hard hands—hands that don't include an ace. TABLE 4-3 is for soft hands, which do include an ace. In the latter situation, hit any hand lower than an 8.

TABLE 4-2: Basic Strategy for Hard Hands, Including Doubling Down										
Dealer's Up Card	**2**	**3**	**4**	**5**	**6**	**7**	**8**	**9**	**10**	**Ace**
Player's Hand										
8	H	H	H	H	H	H	H	H	H	H
9	H	D	D	D	D	H	H	H	H	H
10	D	D	D	D	D	D	D	D	H	H
11	D	D	D	D	D	D	D	D	D	H
12	H	H	S	S	S	H	H	H	H	H
13	S	S	S	S	S	H	H	H	H	H
14	S	S	S	S	S	H	H	H	H	H
15	S	S	S	S	S	H	H	H	H	H
16	S	S	S	S	S	H	H	H	H	H
17	S	S	S	S	S	S	S	S	S	S

H = Hit, S = Stand, D = Double down

Dealer's Up Card	2	3	4	5	6	7	8	9	10	Ace
TABLE 4-3: Basic Strategy for Soft Hands, Including Doubling Down and Splitting										
Player's Hand										
A-2	H	H	H	D	D	H	H	H	H	H
A-3	H	H	H	D	D	H	H	H	H	H
A-4	H	H	D	D	D	H	H	H	H	H
A-5	H	H	D	D	D	H	H	H	H	H
A-6	H	D	D	D	D	H	H	H	H	H
A-7	S	D	D	D	D	S	S	H	H	H
A-8	S	S	S	S	S	S	S	S	S	S
A-A	P	P	P	P	P	P	P	P	P	P
T-T	S	S	S	S	S	S	S	S	S	S
2-2	H	H	P	P	P	P	H	H	H	H
3-3	H	H	P	P	P	P	H	H	H	H
4-4	H	H	H	S	S	H	H	H	H	H
5-5	Treat as 10, never split									
6-6	H	P	P	P	P	H	H	H	H	H
7-7	P	P	P	P	P	P	H	H	H	H
8-8	P	P	P	P	P	P	P	P	P	P
9-9	P	P	P	P	P	S	P	P	S	S

H = Hit, S = Stand, D = Double down, P = Split

There are variations on basic strategy for one deck, one deck with double after split, two decks, six decks, you name it. However, for the average player, the statistical differences these strategies provide are so slight that it's not really worth the effort to memorize them.

Getting Good at Basic Strategy

As with all skills, you have to learn basic strategy to get good at it. This takes some effort, but just about every blackjack player you'll ever meet will tell you it's worth it. Not knowing basic strategy is like eating at a fine restaurant when you have a cold. You can get whiffs of all the wonderful aromas before you, but your stopped-up nose will keep you from fully enjoying the dining experience.

Getting good at basic strategy involves memorizing the tables. Yes, you can take them to the casino with you, but you'll never gain true proficiency as a player if you rely on pieces of paper forever. Once you're able to commit the basics of basic strategy to memory, you can practice it and become proficient at it. You'll find suggestions for how to do this, and drills you can do, in Chapter 13. Mastering basic strategy is also a key element in being a good bettor, which you'll read more about in Chapters 11 and 12.

Disadvantages to Basic Strategy

Basic strategy can seem intimidating at first glance. There are a lot of charts involved, or, perhaps better put, there *can be*. Simplified basic strategy only uses one set of rules. However, because these rules can be affected by the rules in place in the casino, no one strategy will work in every situation. If you're really keen on playing perfect basic strategy, it involves seeking out the rules that reflect the exact playing situation and memorizing them.

If memorization isn't your strong suit, this alone could be enough to make you wonder if playing blackjack by instinct and gut feeling isn't good enough. (It's not, so don't even go there!) If you're not good at memorizing things, most casinos let you bring basic strategy cards to the tables. It's important to remember that basic strategy consists of a specific set of actions that are exactly the same for a number of possible hands, as you'll soon learn more about. So there really isn't a huge amount to learn. While there are charts available that take into account any number of specific situations, you can simply learn the one that works in most situations, and play with it.

Another possible disadvantage to basic strategy, and an argument that you'll sometimes hear against it, is that it is based on perfect and correct blackjack sessions played in sterile computer labs. In real life, of course, there are no such things. Because of this, some people believe that while basic strategy is a good strategy, it's not necessarily the way the game should be played all the time.

Let's take a closer look at the logic behind this belief. Yes, there is no such thing in real life as a statistically correct blackjack session. There are just too many variables to take into consideration. But it's also true that more games than not come very close to being statistically correct. If you were to take 100 games and rank them on a bell curve, with the center of the curve representing a statistically perfect game, you'd find more games coming closer to the center than not.

Basic strategy was developed mathematically and is based on statistically correct moves that have been tested millions of times. This doesn't mean, however, that what basic strategy tells players to do always seems logical. In fact, some of the strategies in basic strategy seem to go against logic. But they really don't. For this reason, most if not just about all experts recommend that players use basic strategy and adhere to it strictly. Especially if they're not counting cards.

Stick around blackjack long enough, and you'll find there are lots of different playing strategies, offered by experts based on their experiences and analysis. That's fine, but you should never try to change basic strategy based on your own experiences or hunches. When you deviate from basic strategy, you're ditching science in favor of gut instinct or intuition, and there is no scientific basis for either.

So why do people disagree about basic strategy's merits at all? For a couple of reasons. First, correct basic strategy hinges upon the exact details of the game being played. As you now know, how the game is played in any one casino can make a big difference in the correct strategy you should use to play it.

If you were to walk into a casino and use a chart that applies to most common games, but the game you're playing isn't governed by common rules, the decisions you make might be correct according to the strategy you learned, but incorrect for the specific situation you're playing in. If you're playing an eight-deck game, for example, and you've learned basic strategy for single-deck play, there's a good chance that some of the decisions you'll make won't yield results as good as you'd get in a single-deck game.

Finally, the biggest argument against it has to do with money. Basic strategy is free to anyone, so no one makes money off it. Offer people a better system, one that you guarantee will help them win, and you can line your pockets with cash.

ALERT!

Thinking about buying someone else's system? You might want to think twice. Some authors' charts are simply incorrect for any game. Others might offer good charts but they don't clarify which game the charts are matched to.

There are lots of beat-the-casino strategies, some of which you'll read about in later chapters. But basic strategy is better than all of them. The charts used for basic strategy were devised after millions of hands of computer-simulated blackjack. The actions they suggest are statistically proven to be the best possible moves for players to make. If you play according to the charts, you won't win every hand, but you will stand the best chance of winning that hand.

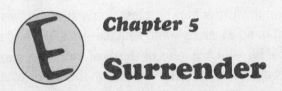

Chapter 5

Surrender

When you sit down to play blackjack, you usually do so with the intention of playing the entire hand through, come what may. However, sometimes your cards are just plain bad. Some casinos will let you abandon your hand if you don't want to play it, or if you think it's a good idea that you don't. This option is called surrender, and it is a little like waving a white flag, since you're telling the casino that you're giving up on this particular hand.

Giving Up

Sometimes, no matter what, you're just going to have a really bad hand, and the dealer is going to have a very good one. As an example, let's say you have a 9 and a 7 for 16, and the dealer is showing a 10. Your hand is about the worst you could hope to get. Statistically, there are more chances of your going bust with a 16 than any other hand (unless you're holding two 8s for that 16, which isn't a bad hand as it can—and should—be split). And there's the dealer sitting with a 10, which is one of the best cards he can hold. What's worse, you've got a good bit of money sitting on the table. Your heart drops. You figure you're going to lose that hand, and all that money, and there's no way around it. Your goose is cooked, right? Well, not necessarily.

FACT

In his book *How to Play Winning Blackjack*, Julian Braun explains that a player holding 16 against a dealer's 10 can expect to lose 76.6 percent of the time, or a loss of more than $53 for every $100 bet. A hand totaling 15 is almost as bad, carrying more than a 70 percent chance of losing.

If you're playing at a casino that offers surrender as an option, you can drop out of the game for a moment, ditch that hand, and preserve at least part of your bet. Yes, just part. For the privilege of not taking a chance on your poor hand, you will have to give up half of your bet. But in doing so, you also get to save half. If, for example, you had a $100 bet on the table, you'd get back $50.

Surrender can be a very powerful player option, especially in the long run. It can significantly affect the outcome in adverse situations by putting you less behind financially than you would be if you played out the hand. For many players, sacrificing half a bet is vastly preferable to losing everything, especially when the odds seem in favor of the latter. Of course, how things end up playing out might not be as awful as you thought, but that's the chance—the gamble—you take.

If this player option is something you haven't heard of before, or don't know very much about, you're in good company. Many blackjack players are unfamiliar with it, as it's not offered in too many places. Because of this, many players don't take advantage of surrender, or don't use it correctly when they're playing in casinos that do offer it. Learn when to use surrender and you'll have a solid strategy for losing less when you play.

Don't be surprised if you get some guff—or a quizzical look or two— from other players if you decide to surrender your hand. Many blackjack players ignore the surrender option because they aren't familiar with it and don't know how to use it. Others see it as something that only unskilled players use to bail themselves out of situations they don't like.

Surrender's Beginnings

The first casino to offer the surrender option was the Continental Casino in Manila, in 1958. At the Continental, the house rules allowed players the opportunity to give up their cards—and a part of their wagers—when the dealer showed an ace. But players could only do so after the dealer checked for blackjack. If the dealer did not have blackjack, players could drop out of play and surrender their cards to the dealer, no questions asked. If the dealer had blackjack, players lost their hands (and their bets) as usual.

Enter Early Surrender

When casino gaming became legal in the state of New Jersey in the late 1970s, surrender was used as a marketing ploy to lure gamblers to the new casinos opening there. Like Manila's Continental Hotel, players at Atlantic City's Resorts International could toss in their cards if they so chose. But unlike the Continental, house rules at Resorts International let players surrender *before* the dealer checked for a blackjack.

This new option, called early surrender, was great for players who knew basic strategy. In fact, this option gave them the ability to play at even or better odds with the house. For players who coupled basic strategy with card counting, the odds were even better.

FACT

Early surrender gives players close to a .60 percent advantage over the house. When you consider that six-deck blackjack games give the house a .54 percent advantage over players, you can see why early surrender was so popular with players: it allowed them to take on casinos head-to-head, and play at even or better odds than the casinos had.

On paper, the early surrender option looks amazingly favorable to players. In reality, it wasn't as great as it seems, or as some old-timers will tell you it was. Since surrender was (and is) an uncommon rule, many players didn't know how to use it properly. Some players surrendered every time they felt they held a weak hand and the odds were against them being able to win with it. Others would surrender every time they didn't have a blackjack. Kind of makes you wonder why they even bothered playing, doesn't it?

The End of Early Surrender

As it turned out, early surrender wasn't around for long. In fact, it lasted for only about four years before the Atlantic City casinos did away with it. The reason has much more to do with a lawsuit that involved the infamous Ken Uston than it does with any amounts they lost to savvy players who knew how to use this player option correctly.

You remember Ken Uston from Chapter 1 as being the king of card counters. In 1981, Uston, who was perpetually being thrown out of casinos for his beat-the-house skills, sued the Atlantic City casinos. He challenged their right to ban "knowledgeable" players—specifically, players who counted cards.

Uston won the battle, but in many respects, he lost the fight. In a 1982 ruling, the New Jersey Supreme Court determined that neither the state nor the casinos located there could ban players based on their abilities or playing strategies. This decision technically assured fair treatment at the tables for Uston and other skilled players. But the casinos, concerned over the potential effect the ruling would have on their revenues, asked the New Jersey Casino Control Commission for some protection against players like Uston. The Commission put into effect a rule called "shuffle at will," which let the casinos take decks out of play and reshuffle them at any time during a game. This is a big deterrent to card counters, as it renders useless the benefits of counting.

The casinos also put other measures in place that affected all players, not just the card counters. Two of the most significant were:

- **The dealer's ability to move the cut card.** If you remember, when a player cuts the cards, he inserts the cut card into the decks. If the dealer doesn't like where the player places the card, he or she can move it.
- **No more early surrender.** If card counters were going to be welcome at the tables, or at least not immediately forced to leave, the casinos weren't going to continue offering a player option that would put those who counted cards so far ahead of house odds.

ESSENTIAL

One of the theories why casinos continue to offer surrender is that it makes it easier for them to spot card counters, as there are certain surrender strategies card counters employ that players who don't count cards aren't as likely to follow.

Late surrender, on the other hand, doesn't give players of any skill level that much of an advantage. In fact, it only improves player expectation by .06 percent, and that's when it's used perfectly. But most players agree that .06 is better than nothing.

Check the rules at various casinos, both land-based and online, and you'll find surrender offered at a good number of them. It's becoming an extremely popular option in Las Vegas, and in other areas that follow Las Vegas rules. You'll also find it in Atlantic City and other casinos across the United States.

You'll still see the early surrender option on occasion, primarily as a promotional tool to attract gamblers. But it remains a rarity. The difference in the odds—somewhere in the neighborhood of 0.62 for early surrender and 0.065 for late surrender—simply gives players too much of an advantage over the house.

How to Surrender

Unlike other player options and moves in blackjack, there isn't a hand signal for surrender. You simply say, "Surrender" (there's no need to preface it with "I") and turn in your hand.

In some casinos, dealers are required to tell their pit bosses that a player is surrendering his or her cards. Don't worry if this happens to you when you're playing. You didn't do anything wrong. All the dealer is doing is telling management that he has a player at his table—you—who knows how to take advantage of this rule.

However, because surrender doesn't do as much for players who are simply following basic strategy as it does for card counters, announcing a surrender when it takes place can also alert the pit bosses to a potential card counter. Don't be surprised if your play is more closely scrutinized, if the cards are suddenly shuffled, or if a new dealer miraculously appears after you use the surrender option.

Arguments Against Surrender

Surrender is such a favorable player option that you won't hear too many people deride it. If you do, you might hear comments like, "If you're going to give up half your bet, why not just bet half as much to begin with?" Other people simply don't like the concept, and feel that surrender goes against the spirit of blackjack. "If you're going to play the game, play the game. Don't wimp out halfway through" is pretty much how their logic works. And that's fine—for them.

The only negative thing about surrender is the temptation it offers to overuse it. It is always to your advantage to lose only half of your bet, instead of the entire amount, should the cards take a turn for the worse. That said, it is almost always better to play out a hand than to surrender it and give up half your bet. But when strategy says you should surrender, you will, over time, cut your losses and increase your winnings. And no one can argue with that.

Knowing When to Use It

When should you surrender? The simple answer is any time when your cards don't favor a positive outcome—in other words, when conditions seem favorable for the dealer to take the hand over you. Using our 16-value hand again as an example, even if you stood on that 16 instead of hitting, the chances of your losing are still strong—about as strong as they are if you hit the hand. But let's say you decided to surrender your crummy hand. You'd cut your losses in half. No matter how you look at it, it's better to lose half than it is to lose everything.

You should surrender when your chances of winning are less than 25 percent, or when the casino's odds for beating you are greater than 50 percent. How can you tell when these conditions come up? Fortunately, you don't have to—not on your own, anyway. The thinking has already been done for you. There are basic strategy charts that will show you when to throw in the proverbial towel and call on this player option.

FACT

Some casinos offer a version of surrender that they call "five-card surrender." Here's how it works: Let's say you draw five low-value cards without going bust. Instead of prolonging the agony, you can throw in your hand and keep half of your bet.

Basic Surrender Strategy

Surrender is only an option on the first two cards that you're dealt—most of the time, anyway. Some casinos have some fancy rule variations in place that let you surrender on more cards. However, most of the time you're only allowed to surrender on the first two cards. If you take a third card, the surrender option is no longer available to you, and you're going to have to play out your hand. For this reason, be sure to clearly signal your intention to surrender if you've decided that's what you're going to do.

Again, since there are so many different variables that can affect how blackjack is played, there are different strategy charts for surrender.

Let's take a look at ones that take into account the most common conditions you're likely to encounter while playing. The first chart, **TABLE 5-1**, shows when to surrender in a multiple-deck game.

Dealer's Up Card	2	3	4	5	6	7	8	9	10	Ace
TABLE 5-1: The Late Surrender Option in a Multideck Game										
Player's Hand										
T-6	S	S	S	S	S	H	H	SU	SU	SU
9-7	S	S	S	S	S	H	H	SU	SU	SU
T-5	S	S	S	S	S	H	H	H	SU	H
9-6	S	S	S	S	S	H	H	H	SU	H

S = Stand, H = Hit, SU = Surrender

Pretty easy, right? One thing you might notice is that this is a pretty short chart. There's a good reason for it. There are only a few situations in which it's to your advantage to use the surrender option. Only a few hands offer odds so against you that you should consider surrendering. More often than not, you'll do better in the long run if you do play out your hands.

That said, there are a few additional rules you can add to this chart that reflect additional situations and rules:

- Unless you're holding two 8s, always surrender a hard 16 against a dealer's 10. Remember, 16 is the worst possible hand you can hold. The odds are somewhere in the neighborhood of 80 percent against winning with it, no matter how well you play or what rules are in effect. However, if you're holding two 8s, you should split them. You'll learn more about this in Chapter 7.
- If you're not a gutsy player and prefer to play it safe, surrender a hard 15 against the dealer's ace.
- If you know that there aren't many 10-value cards left, consider hitting 16 against a dealer's 9, and 15 against a 10.
- If there are a good number of 10-value cards left, surrender 15 against an ace.

- If you're playing in a casino where dealers stand on soft 17, surrender 15 against a 10, or a 16 against a 9, 10, or ace.
- If the dealer hits on soft 17, surrender against a dealer's ace if you have 15, 17, or a pair of 8s. This rule gives you worse than a 1 in 4 chance to win when you're holding these hands.

A casino rule that affects surrender is whether the dealer stands or hits on soft 17. In games where the dealer stands on soft 17, players will gain an edge of 0.07 percent by using surrender correctly. If the dealer hits soft 17, players gain an edge of 0.10 percent. The next table, **TABLE 5-2**, is for a single-deck game with a late surrender option.

TABLE 5-2: The Late Surrender Option in a Single-Deck Game										
Dealer's Up Card	**2**	**3**	**4**	**5**	**6**	**7**	**8**	**9**	**10**	**Ace**
Player's Hand										
T-6	S	S	S	S	S	H	H	H	SU	SU
9-7	S	S	S	S	S	H	H	H	SU	H
7-7	P	P	P	P	P	P	H	H	SU	H

S = Stand, H = Hit, P = Split, SU = Surrender

Again, this is a simple chart, and for the same reason: the conditions for surrender don't come up that often, even when you're playing single-deck games. Remember, it's best to surrender only when your player expectation is less than 50 percent. Try not to fall into the trap of using surrender simply because you're feeling a little insecure. Surrendering every time you think you might go bust is simply a bad strategy. Instead of saving you money, it will cost you money in the long run.

Finally, **TABLE 5-3** is a basic strategy chart for early surrender. There aren't many hands this applies to, so this table lists only the few situations in which you'd take advantage of this option. Why bother learning it if it's so rare? Because early surrender is still offered in some parts of the world, including

Korea, the Philippines, and Panama. Should you ever find yourself in any of these countries, why not be prepared?

TABLE 5-3: The Early Surrender Option in a Single-Deck Game			
Dealer's Up Card	9	10	A
Your Hand			
10-6	SU	—	—
5-7	—	—	SU
9-7	SU	—	—
any hand that totals 14-16	—	SU	—
any hand that totals 12-17	—	—	SU

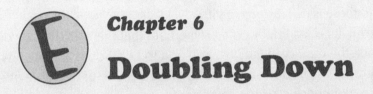

Chapter 6

Doubling Down

Suppose you have just been dealt a 7 and a 4, for a point total of 11. Pretty nice hand, right? And the dealer's up card isn't much—a 6. She's likely to bust with that card. You know that the odds are in your favor to win this hand. Wouldn't it be nice if you could put down more money at that point? Guess what? You can!

Double the Pleasure

One thing that is important to always keep in mind about blackjack is that the odds are against your being a big winner at the tables. More often than not, you will not have the edge, and the dealer will have cards that will beat yours. This simple fact has been mathematically proven time and time again, and there is no way around it.

However, it is also important to remember that there are things you can do to attack the casino's edge over you and to help you come out a winner more often. As you'll soon see, doubling down is one of the more effective weapons in your edge-slashing arsenal.

FACT

It bears repeating: when you are playing blackjack, you stand to win less than 50 percent of the hands dealt to you—47 percent, as a matter of fact. Over the long term, you'll lose more hands than you win. So betting wisely when you have a better chance of winning is crucial.

What is doubling down? It's exactly what it says it is—doubling your bet after you are dealt your first two cards. Doing so gives you the opportunity to increase your profit mid-hand if you feel you are in a good position to beat the dealer's hand.

Doubling down is simply a move designed to help you make more money—in other words, maximize your winnings and cut your losses— when you play blackjack. It does not improve bad hands, nor does it improve your chances of winning hands.

The Rationale

Like other player options, doubling down doesn't make you infallible. It will not guarantee a winning hand, as you will still lose hands when you employ it. In fact, there is a good chance that you will lose more hands doubling down than if you just hit them. Why? One simple reason: when you double down, you only get one more card.

If the card you are dealt is not the card you need to give you the edge you need over the dealer, you can't ask for another one. Instead, you have to stand on what you've got. This means there is a greater chance that you are going to lose the hand and everything you bet—both your original bet and the additional money you plunked down when you decided to double.

Bad scenario, right? So why would you want to double down at all? Because, even with these drawbacks, double down is still one of the most effective approaches to eliminating the house edge. Even if you do lose more hands when you use it. Because when you do win with it, you'll win more money.

QUESTION?

Why do casinos offer double down if it gives players an edge against them?
Make no mistake about it: casinos make a lot of money on this player option, mostly because many players don't know how to double down correctly. Some people say the casinos instituted double down for exactly this reason. Others suggest that the casinos simply wanted to attract more people to blackjack by giving them an opportunity to shave the house edge.

Double down is an offensive move. You don't find too many of these in blackjack. Usually you are defending yourself against the dealer because her hand has a greater probability of beating yours. But when you double down, you are attacking the dealer, as you typically double down when there is a good chance of the dealer busting—in other words, you've got the edge. Or, better put, based on what you know, you are pretty sure you have it, and you are willing to take the risk and see if you are right. This means that you are in a positive expectation situation. These situations don't happen that often—only in about 9.6 percent of all hands played. So when they do come up, you should take full advantage of them.

How to Double Down

It is easy to place a double down bet. To indicate you're doubling down, slide a second wager into the betting circle, next to your original bet. Do not put the additional bet on top of your original wager, as the dealer might think you're trying to increase your original bet, which is illegal.

If you're doubling down on a pair of 5s or 4s, which are hands that are better to split than double down on, the dealer will probably ask you to confirm your intentions verbally.

If you win, the dealer will pay you even money on both of your bets, which means that you receive double your original wager. If you lose, the dealer removes both bets. If you tie with the dealer, you get both of your bets back, but no additional money.

Analyzing Double Down

Let's take a closer look at why double down is such an effective player option. To do so, we are going to analyze just one possible hand—in this case, a player's 5 and 4 (point total 9) against a dealer's up card of 5.

If you were to put this hand to statistical analysis using blackjack simulation software, you would come up with the following:

- Hitting it would result in your winning 59 times out of 100.
- Doubling down would make you a winner 57 times out of 100.

In other words, you stand to lose two more hands by exercising the double down option than if you decided to just hit the hand. You might be thinking that 2 percent, or two hands, really doesn't make that much of a difference. Or does it? Actually, it does.

Let's say you're betting $10 a hand. In the first scenario, you would win $590 and lose $410, for a net profit of $180. Not bad, right? But you can do better! Now, suppose you doubled down and increased your bet to $20. You would win $20 fifty-seven times, for a total of $1,140, and you would lose $860, for a net profit of $280. That is an extra $100, even though you lost two more hands.

Now that 2 percent doesn't seem so insignificant, does it?

Doubling down will not improve your chances of winning a hand. For this reason, the frequency of winning a hand doesn't determine whether you should double down. In fact, you should expect to lose a bit more often when you double down. So don't let the fact that you'll lose more hands govern your double down decisions. Instead, consider how much you stand to gain if you do double down and win.

Double Down Rules

The rules on doubling down vary from one casino to another, and some casinos will have rules that are more favorable to the player than others. Many casinos restrict when you can double down. For this reason, it is always a good idea to find out what rules are in effect before you play. With some double down rules giving the house as much as a 7 percent edge over players, it's to your advantage to do a little research and to play at casinos with less onerous rules and as few restrictions as possible.

Here are some of the rules you will see and how they can affect player expectation:

- **Double down only on 10 and 11.** This option gives the house a 0.25 percent advantage.
- **Double down only on 11.** This option gives the house a 0.69 percent advantage.
- **No soft doubling (i.e., no doubling down on hands with aces).** The house gains a 0.13 percent edge with this one.
- **Double down only on 9, 10, or 11.** This restriction is the best of them (relatively speaking), and yields a 0.10 percent advantage for the house.
- **Double down is allowed after pair splitting.** A good rule, giving players a 0.13 percent advantage.
- **Double down on any two cards.** This is another good opportunity for players and should be sought out.

Most casinos will only let you double down after you look at your first two cards. In other words, you can't take a hit and then say, "Geez, this is looking good. I'd better double down." It's a nice idea, but it just doesn't happen, at least not in most gaming establishments.

However, casinos are always looking for ways to lure more players to blackjack tables, and they often jazz up the basic game of blackjack by tweaking certain rules to make conditions more favorable for players. For this reason, you will sometimes run across some interesting double down variations. In some casinos, for example, players can double down on three or more cards. In a blackjack variation game called Spanish 21, players can double on any number of cards, but the house retains its advantage by removing all 10s from the deck. Face cards, however, remain in. This simple condition change makes Spanish 21 a very good game—from the house's perspective, that is.

ALERT!

Allowing players to double down on more than two cards might give players a nice gain—in this case, somewhere around 0.2 percent and even a bit higher. However, this rule variation often comes at the cost of other gains, such as blackjack paying off 1 to 1. When you run across rules that have been changed to favor the player, be sure to check the other rules in place—they might be less favorable for players. As such, they can cancel the gains offered by the player-friendly rules.

With so many possible variations on double down, it can be difficult to memorize all the rules you need to know to employ this option to your best advantage. For this reason, it is a good idea to play at casinos that offer double down options that match the strategies you know. Save the more unusual offerings for later. Or consider avoiding them entirely, especially if they're decidedly adverse to players and if, when added to other rules, they give the house such a strong edge that it's barely worthwhile to go up against it.

Making the Double Down Decision

When should you double down? You need to consider two factors—your hand and the dealer's face card—when making this decision. Once again, however, you don't have to make the decision in a vacuum. Mathematicians have already studied the probabilities and come up with the strategy that gives you the best chances of winning. Basic strategy charts will show you when to double down. Often you will find them incorporated into basic strategy charts that reflect other player options. You'll find a chart like this in Chapter 4.

In general, though, double down rules are fairly simple. Instead of memorizing basic strategy charts for them, many players simply memorize the rules. If you don't want to memorize rules for various situations, such as multiple- versus single-deck play, you can stick to the following simple strategy. It's not perfect, but it will work in more situations than not. Double down on the following hands:

- Hard 9
- Hard 10 (including two 5s, which you should always treat as a 10 and never split)
- Hard 11
- Soft 13 through 18

One of the biggest mistakes new blackjack players make when doubling down is doubling down on hard 12. It is never a good idea to double down on any hand that you can bust on with one card, which is the case with a hard 12 (and, of course, all the hard totals above 12). You also never double down on a soft 12, which is two aces. Always split the aces.

Multiple-Deck Doubling

The strategies here assume multiple-deck games that don't allow doubling down after splitting. For multiple-deck games where you are holding a hard hand, go by the following rules:

- Double on 11 when dealer shows 10 or less.
- Double on 10 when dealer shows 9 or less.
- Double on 9 when dealer shows 3 through 6.

Some casinos will let you double down when you are holding a soft hand. This might seem to defy logic, but it can actually be a pretty powerful play. By doubling soft hands, it is possible to reduce the casino's edge by about 1.3 percent in multiple-deck games.

Doubling down on soft hands is the most complex aspect of basic strategy, and it can be tricky to master. In general, however, doubling down on soft hands is a good move when the dealer shows a 5 or a 6, which are the weakest up cards he can hold, and you are holding A-2 through A-7.

More specific rules call for doubling down on the following soft hands:

- Soft 13 (A-2) and 14 (A-3) when the dealer's up card is a 5 or 6.
- Soft 15 (A-4) and 16 (A-5) when the dealer's up card is a 4, 5, or 6.
- Soft 17 (A-6) when the dealer's up card is a 3, 4, 5, or 6.
- Soft 18 (A-7) when the dealer's up card is a 3, 4, 5, or 6.

It's pretty easy to see why doubling down on 9, 10, or 11 makes sense—if you draw a 10-value card, you end up with a very strong hand. But the logic behind doubling on soft hands isn't as obvious, which is the reason why it is the most complex aspect of basic strategy. Many players avoid soft doubling down because of this. If you're good at memorizing tables, though, this strategy is worth learning, as it further increases your chances to win more money.

Single-Deck Doubling

The rules for doubling down are a little different if you should happen to come across a single-deck blackjack game. For these rarities, go by the following rules:

- Always double on hard 11.
- Double hard 10 when the dealer's up card is 2 to 9.
- Double hard 9 when the dealer's up card is 2 to 6.
- Double hard 8 when the combination is 5-3 against a dealer's up card of 5 or 6.

For soft doubling in a single-deck game, use these rules:

- Double down on A-8 against the dealer's 6.
- Double down on A-7 against the dealer's 3 through 6.
- Double down on A-6 against the dealer's 2 through 6.
- Double down on A-5, A-4, A-3, or A-2 against the dealer's 4 through 6.

Your Double Down Bet

To maximize the effectiveness of doubling down and take full advantage of doubling, you should always match your original bet when you exercise this option. Many, if not most, casinos will let players double down for less than what they originally bet. If you're not sure about your chances, or you're worried about your bankroll, it's an option to consider, but it somewhat defeats the purpose of doubling down.

If the thought of doubling down puts you in a cold sweat because the amount you'd have to put up moves you out of your comfort zone, you're probably playing at a table with stakes higher than what you are comfortable with in general. Do yourself a favor and drop back to a table where you can take the best advantage of this powerful player option.

Chapter 7

Splitting

In blackjack, splitting up can be good to do. Like doubling down, splitting is a powerful tool for blackjack players who want to increase their winnings. And, like doubling down, splitting your cards gives you a chance to increase your bet in the middle of the hand that you are playing. You can only split two cards of the same value, and there are times when you shouldn't split. In this chapter, you'll learn what cards you can split and when you should split them.

Doubling the Fun

Splitting cards in blackjack is an option that many players look forward to. Not only does it increase their chances of making more money on certain hands, it's simply fun to be able to play two hands at once.

Unfortunately, you won't get the chance to use this player option very often if you are following basic strategy, which dictates splitting only a little over 2 percent—2.55 percent, to be exact—of dealt hands. Still, it's an option that, when paired with a strong hand, can further enhance the chances of winning that hand, and of winning more money when you play it.

As an example, let's say you are holding a 9-9 against a dealer's 6. That's 18 for you, which is a count you'd usually stand on without even thinking about it. If you were to do so when you're not holding a pair, you'd have an expected win of 20 cents for every dollar you bet. On a $10 bet, that's an additional $2. Not bad, right? But let's take a look at what could happen if you split those 9s.

You'd then have two hands to play, and two wagers to make. By splitting the 9s, you are now betting each 9 against the dealer's 6. Each hand now carries an expected win of around 24 cents for every dollar you bet. On a $10 bet, that's $2.40. Again, not bad, but not that much of a gain. So why bother taking the risk?

When you split pairs, you double your chances of winning, especially if you know basic strategy for splitting and you follow it correctly. Instead of winning just $2.40, you now are in a position to double your winnings for a total of $4.80. Yes, it's a little riskier, as you can win both hands, lose both hands, or win one and lose the other. However, most players don't mind the risk, because the increased odds and payoff are worth it.

FACT

Splitting pairs in blackjack is a player option that can further reduce the casino's edge over you. Using it correctly, which means learning basic strategy for splitting in various situations, and applying it correctly can shave another half percent or so off that edge.

How to Split Your Hand

If you are dealt a pair and you want to split them, you must make the dealer aware of your intentions when your turn to play comes up. If your cards were dealt face down, turn them over and place them a couple of inches apart. If they were dealt face up—remember, you never touch the cards if they are dealt this way—point to your cards and say "split" when the dealer asks you if you want a card. He will acknowledge your choice by separating your cards by a few inches. Your original bet will go next to one card. You place your new bet (the same value as the original bet) next to the other card. You then play each card separately, as two separate hands, as you would at the beginning of a new hand.

Breaking Up a Bad Hand

As you'll soon see, splitting pairs can also improve a poor hand. Let's say you're holding a pair of 8s against a dealer's 6. Those 8s total 16, which is one of the worst blackjack hands you can hold. When compared to the dealer's 6, it carries an anticipated loss of more than 15 cents for every dollar you put down on the table. Now let's say you decide to split those 8s. Doing so vastly improves what was previously a very bad hand. When split and played separately, each of those 8s now offers a projected win of more than 11 cents for every dollar you wager. Definitely a better deal, right?

As a further example of the power of splitting, let's take a look at a pair of 4s, which is another nightmare hand for players. Statistically, the dealer has the edge on this hand eight out of thirteen times, which is enough to make anyone groan. The following table shows the expected gain or loss on a pair of 4s against each possible dealer up card, with an initial bet of $10. This table is based on an eight-deck shoe, with doubling allowed after splitting.

Dealer Up card	Hit	Split
2	-$0.20	-$1.88
3	$0.11	-$0.98
4	$0.46	-$0.02

Dealer Up card	Hit	Split
5	$0.80	$1.04
6	$1.22	$1.64
7	$0.86	-$1.69
8	-$0.59	-$3.26
9	-$2.10	-$5.09
10	-$2.48	-$6.21
A	-$1.98	-$5.63

As you can see, there are definitely times when splitting certain cards makes a lot of sense under these specific conditions, such as against a 5 or a 6, which are prime bust cards for the dealer. And there are clearly times when it doesn't, such as when the dealer is holding anything higher or lower than a 5 or a 6. In fact, in most cases, you'll lose more money if you split those 4s than if you played them as an 8.

The same is true for other sets of rules and playing conditions. Sometimes it makes sense to split. Other times, it doesn't. Knowing what the rules and playing conditions are, and matching your play to them, will help you make the best splitting decisions at the tables.

The rules and conditions in place where you're playing are significant factors when deciding whether cards should be split. For this reason, it's always a good idea to know the rules before you start playing. If they're different from what you are accustomed to, plan on researching their effect on basic strategy before you hit the tables.

Splitting can also be a good way to lessen your losses in the long run. This approach is called defensive splitting. An example of defensive splitting is breaking up 8s when the dealer shows a 10 or ace. Over the long run, you'll still lose money playing against the dealer, but you'll lose less—about five cents less per dollar wagered—than if you hit or stood on your 16-count hand.

Offensive splitting is when you turn a hand with a negative expectation into one with a positive expectation through splitting. As an example, let's say you're holding 8s and the dealer is showing a 5. Split those 8s and play them separately, and you've gained a 31 percent edge over the house. If you stand on those 8s and play them as a 16-count hand, you not only lose that edge, you give the house a 17 percent advantage over you.

How House Rules Affect Splitting

The basic house rules for splitting are fairly standard regardless of where you play. You can split your first two cards if they have the same value, and you must make this decision before you decide to hit or stand. When you split your cards, you have to place a second bet equal to the first. You then play each card as the beginning of a new, separate hand.

The two new hands are subject to some restrictions. These restrictions are also fairly standard, but they can vary somewhat depending on where you play:

- Surrender, if offered, is typically restricted to the original hand, not split hands.
- Each split ace only receives one additional card.
- An ace-10 combo on a split hand scores 21, not blackjack.
- Doubling down on split hands might not be permitted.
- Resplitting to three or more spots might not be allowed. In other words, it you split two 9s and got another 9 on one of the split cards, you might not be allowed to resplit.
- Some casinos don't allow resplitting aces, even if they let you resplit other pairs.

Basic Strategy for Splitting

Regardless of house rules and other conditions in place, there are certain pairs that you should always split, no matter what. There aren't many of them, though, which makes this basic strategy rule easy to remember:

- Always split aces.
- Always split 8s.

Like sure splitters, there are some pairs that you never split up, no matter the circumstances. Doing so is simply never a good idea. Again, there aren't many of these pairs, which also makes this basic strategy rule a virtual no-brainer:

- Never split 5s.
- Never split 10s, even if you're holding a 10 and a face card. The values are the same. Keep them together.

You have a far better chance of winning with these pairs if you keep them together, regardless of conditions and what the dealer shows as an up card.

ALERT!

Study blackjack theory long enough, and you'll see that virtually every gaming writer advises against splitting 10s. However, there are times when splitting 10s isn't a bad idea. If the dealer is showing a 5 or a 6 as an up card, and you know there are lots of 10-count cards left to be played (because you're counting cards), splitting 10s can be a good play. However, in the long run, you'll make more money if you stand on those 10s as a 20-count hand, especially if you're not counting cards.

Splitting strategy on all other pairs depends on two factors: what the dealer holds as an up card and the house rules in effect. As an example, let's say you're playing in a casino that allows doubling down after splitting pairs. If you were to split a pair of 4s and get a 7 to make one hand a two-card 11, you'd want the option to double down on split hands. If you are playing in a casino with this option, you split this pair. If you aren't, you play the hand as an 8.

The following charts show basic strategy for splitting in several different situations. **TABLE 7-1** is a comprehensive table showing splits for all pairs when playing in a multiple-deck game.

TABLE 7-1: Splitting Pairs in a Multideck Game									
Dealer's Up Card	**2**	**3**	**4**	**5**	**6**	**7**	**8**	**9**	**10**	**A**
Player's Hand										
A-A	P	P	P	P	P	P	P	P	P	P
T-T	S	S	S	S	S	S	S	S	S	S
9-9	P	P	P	P	P	S	P	P	S	S
8-8	P	P	P	P	P	P	P	P	P	P
7-7	P	P	P	P	P	P	H	H	H	H
6-6	H	P	P	P	P	H	H	H	H	H
5-5	Always treat as a 10, never split									
4-4	H	H	H	H	H	H	H	H	H	H
3-3	H	H	P	P	P	P	H	H	H	H
2-2	H	H	P	P	P	P	H	H	H	H

H = Hit, S = Stand, P = Split

TABLE 7-2 shows strategy for splitting when playing multiple-deck black-jack in casinos that allow doubling after splitting:

TABLE 7-2: Splitting Pairs in a Multideck Game, Doubling after Splitting Allowed									
Dealer's Up Card	**2**	**3**	**4**	**5**	**6**	**7**	**8**	**9**	**10**	**A**
Player's Hand										
2-2	P	P	P	P	P	P	H	H	H	H
3-3	P	P	P	P	P	P	H	H	H	H
4-4	H	H	H	P	P	H	H	H	H	H
6-6	P	P	P	P	P	H	H	H	H	H

H = Hit, S = Stand, P = Split

Finally, **TABLE 7-3** shows the strategy for splitting when playing with a single deck in casinos that permit doubling after splitting.

TABLE 7-3: Splitting Pairs in a Single-Deck Game, Doubling after Splitting Allowed										
Dealer's Up Card	**2**	**3**	**4**	**5**	**6**	**7**	**8**	**9**	**10**	**A**
Player's Hand										
2-2	P	P	P	P	P	P	H	H	H	H
3-3	P	P	P	P	P	P	H	H	H	H
4-4	H	H	P	P	P	H	H	H	H	H
6-6	P	P	P	P	P	P	H	H	H	H

H = Hit, S = Stand, P = Split

Here is another way of looking at basic strategy for splitting pairs. This list is also based on multiple-deck play. It incorporates the information in the previous tables, and boils it down to seven rules that are fairly easy to remember:

- Always split aces and 8s.
- Never split 5s or 10s.
- For 2s and 3s, split if you can double down when the dealer's up card is 2 through 7. If doubling after splits isn't allowed, don't split 2s and 3s when the dealer is holding 2 or 3. In this case, only split when the dealer shows 4, 5, 6, or 7.
- For 4s, if you can't double after splits, don't split them. If you can double, you can maximize your winnings when the dealer shows 5 or 6.
- For 6s, split against 3, 4, 5, or 6 regardless of circumstances. Split against 2 if doubling after splits is permitted.
- For 7s, split when the dealer shows 2 through 7.
- Nines are the trickiest pair to split. You should separate them if the dealer shows 2 through 6, and 8 or 9. Keep them together if the dealer has a 7, 10, or ace as his up card.

I split 8s against the dealer's 10. Was this wrong?

Not at all. This is a tough split, though, as it can be a little scary to split high cards like 8s when the dealer is showing a 10. However, if you do it, you'll end up losing less money in the long run than if you held the two 8s for a 16-count hand. Hold the 8s and you'll lose around 54 cents for every dollar you bet. Split them and you'll cut your losses to 48 cents per dollar wagered.

As a reminder, you can ask for as many additional cards as you need if you have split anything other than aces. If you split aces, you only get one more card for each hand.

If you're playing in a casino that allows resplitting, and you're again dealt pairs, follow the procedure for cards that are dealt face up. If you split aces, and you're dealt another ace, you might be able to resplit, depending on where you are playing. If not, you'll have to live with a 12-count hand, and pray that the dealer busts.

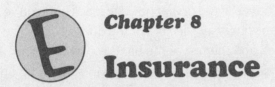

Chapter 8

Insurance

We like a little protection against the adversities in life, which is what insurance is all about. Doing something to keep your assets safe makes a lot of sense when it comes to things like your home, your car, your family, and your health. It may even seem like a smart move to add a little protection to certain hands when you are in a perilous situation during a black-jack game. But is it?

The Ins and Outs of Insurance

In blackjack, insurance is a separate bet, or a side bet, that "insures" your original bet in the event that the dealer has blackjack. The opportunity for insurance occurs every time the dealer gets an ace as her face-up card. Players have the chance to take an insurance bet before any other actions are taken on any players' hands. If the dealer has blackjack and you've taken insurance, you'll win 2:1 on your insurance bet. If she doesn't have blackjack, you lose the insurance bet, and the rest of the hand is played out as usual.

Taking insurance gives you the opportunity to win something and not lose everything should the dealer have blackjack. It has nothing to do with the value of the cards you are holding or whether you have a blackjack or not. In fact, the only thing you are doing when you take insurance is betting on whether the dealer's hold card is a 10-value card.

FACT

Most casinos offer insurance, and with good reason: it makes a lot of money for them, as many players think it is a good idea and opt to use it more often than not. If these players knew the math behind insurance, though, they might change their minds: for this one option alone, the house advantage can range from 5.8 percent to 14.3 percent, and even higher, depending on the rules and conditions in place.

How to Place Insurance

There is a good chance you'll rarely, if ever, place an insurance bet. Remember the standard layout of a blackjack table? It includes a semicircular area that reads "Insurance pays 2:1." When the dealer gets an ace face up, he'll ask the players if they want insurance. If you choose to take it, place a bet in the amount of half of your original bet in this area. Some casinos will let you make an insurance bet for less than half, but don't, even if you have the option. You might as well win as much as you can if you are going to use this player option.

Understanding the Insurance Bet

For the privilege of protecting your original bet, you are required to part with a little more of your bankroll. Not too much—typically, just half your original bet.

Insurance bets pay out at 2:1 odds, which, at a quick glance, might seem like a pretty good deal. But as you will soon see, it really isn't. Still, many players like to take advantage of this player option, and they do so often. If you were to ask them why, you would likely get answers along the lines of:

- "Insurance is a great way to protect a blackjack."
- "I always take insurance on strong starting hands."
- "I always insure weak hands so I won't lose my bet."
- "If I have a hunch that the dealer is going to come up with a black-jack, I take insurance."
- "Why not? It's only half of my original bet, and it's good protection."
- "I always take insurance, no matter what."
- "I take insurance when I think there are lots of 10s left in the deck, and it seems like it's time for the dealer to get one."
- "My father (mother, brother, aunt, uncle, etc.) always took insurance, and they did pretty well at the tables, so I figure why not."

FACT

Some land-based casinos will let you bet less than half of your original bet when you place an insurance bet. None of them, however, will let you wager more than half of your original bet. Virtually all online gaming sites require half of your original bet for insurance bets, and again, none will let you bet more than this.

The truth is, none of these reasons are based on solid logic or sound probability theories. But many blackjack players are not that familiar with either, and instead play more on superstition and gut feelings. As you now should know—and, even if you do, it bears repeating—neither is a good approach if you are serious about blackjack, and serious about making money at it in the long run.

Are you beginning to have second thoughts about insurance? Good. If you're a hard-core skeptic, and you're still not sure that insurance is that bad a bet (after all, why could it be when so many people like it so much?) let's take a closer look at how this particular bet plays out at the tables.

Insurance Options

To analyze insurance in greater depth, we're going to go right to the blackjack tables—figuratively, of course—and play some games in which the option to take insurance will come up. First, however, let's review how insurance works. Insurance is offered each time the dealer turns up an ace. This gives you two options: you can take insurance, or you can refuse it. Each option has two outcomes, with different consequences. Let's start by examining what happens if you chose *not* to insure. Two things could happen:

- **The dealer won't have blackjack.** You'll play out your cards as usual, and no money exchanges hands.
- **The dealer will have blackjack.** In this case, a natural blackjack beats all other hands. The dealer will pick up your money, then your cards, and deal a new hand.

Let's say you decide to take insurance. Again, there are two possible outcomes:

- **The dealer doesn't have blackjack.** He'll come around and pick up all the insurance bets. Since by placing an insurance bet you bet the dealer had a blackjack, you lose this bet. You'll then play out your hand against the dealer's ace.
- **The dealer does have blackjack.** This is where insurance gets tricky. The dealer's natural blackjack beats your hand, and the dealer will collect your original wager. Your insurance wager, however, is a winner. The dealer pays your insurance bet at 2:1. In the end, you come out even.

Insurance Scenarios

Each of the following examples reflects various scenarios that can happen when you take insurance. In all of them, your original bet is $10, and your insurance bet is half that, $5.

- **The dealer has blackjack, and you don't.** You lose your original bet of $10. But you win the insurance bet. You are paid $10, since the insurance bet pays off at 2:1. Total amount wagered: $15. Total amount paid: $10. You take back your $5 insurance bet, plus what you won on this bet, for a total of $15. You're even.
- **The dealer doesn't have blackjack.** You lose the insurance bet. You then play the hand out, and you win. You are paid $10—your original bet, paid at even odds. Total amount wagered: $15. Total amount paid: $10. You take back your original bet ($10), plus the amount you won on this bet—another $10, for a total of $20. You're up $5.
- **The dealer doesn't have blackjack.** You lose the insurance bet. You then play the hand out, and you bust. Total amount wagered: $15. Total amount paid: $0. You take back nothing. You're down $15.
- **You have blackjack, but the dealer doesn't.** You again lose your insurance bet—remember, insurance is a bet on whether or not the dealer has blackjack, not whether you do. You get a 3:2 payoff for getting blackjack—in this case, $15. Total amount wagered: $15. Total amount paid: $15. You take back your original bet of $10, plus your winnings of $15, for a total of $25. You're up $10.
- **You and the dealer both have blackjack.** Your insurance bet pays out at 2:1. Your blackjack bet is a push—neither you nor the dealer wins this hand. Total amount wagered: $15. Total amount paid: $10. You pull back your blackjack bet of $10 and your insurance bet for $5 for a total of $25. You're up $10.

As you can see, in three of these five scenarios—more than half—you will finish money ahead from where you started. You'll end up even in one, and lose in another. So the question now becomes: will the dealer get an ace up card often enough during the course of a blackjack session for you to want to play the odds? The answer to this question is "perhaps." Let's see why.

Of all the player options in blackjack, insurance is the one that probably draws the most controversy. Beginning players almost always fall into its allure, even though they shouldn't. Here's why: insurance is almost never a good bet. There are times when it can be, but you have to know how to recognize them. This calls for having some card-counting expertise, which rookie players typically don't possess. The truth is, the gaming world is full of what gamblers refer to as "sucker bets," which are bets that seem like a good idea to the uninformed, or to new players. In reality, though, they aren't.

Doing the Math

To answer the previous question, it is necessary to go back to the basics of blackjack probability for a moment. In a fifty-two-card deck, sixteen cards carry a value of 10. This means there are more 10-value cards than any others. Now, this might seem like there should be a greater chance of the dealer combining an ace with one of these 10-value cards for a natural, which would make insurance seem like a good bet. However, this simply isn't so. The chances of a dealer getting a 10 to match his ace are around 1 in 3. That's not good enough for insurance to be a good bet.

Not convinced yet? Let's take a look at the same scenario from a different perspective. This time, you are playing at a table with a multideck shoe. Do you think chances of the dealer getting blackjack will be greater? Think again.

The laws of probability for this situation state that for every thirteen times a dealer has an ace as the up card, he will have blackjack four times. The other nine times, he won't. Put another way, the dealer will have blackjack 31 percent of the time—almost identical odds to the single-deck scenario. Again, this is hardly sure bet territory, as it is far from the 50 percent mark that makes a bet worth taking. Are you beginning to see why insurance is such a poor bet for players, and why it is such a great deal for the house? If not, maybe a short money lesson will make you a believer.

Taking Insurance When You Have Blackjack

When in doubt, it is always a good idea to figure out how the odds affect your cold hard cash. Let's say you are playing a long, long game of blackjack at $10 a hand. And over the course of your game, there are thirteen hands in which you get blackjack when the dealer's up card is an ace. Should you hedge your bet and protect your hand by taking insurance? Let's do the math. Remember, statistics say you stand to win nine of these thirteen hands. The other four will be a push with the dealer. As a reminder, your total bet, with insurance, is $15. Blackjack pays 3:2. Insurance pays 2:1.

- **With insurance:** You will win $10, or even money, each of the thirteen times, for a total of $130.
- **Without insurance:** You will get push four times for $0. You will be paid $15 nine times for a total of $135.

In the end, you'll make an additional $5 if you don't take insurance.

QUESTION?

Does taking insurance make sense if you're playing in a casino where blackjack pays 6:5 instead of 3:2?
Probably. Let's use a previous example in which you're betting $10 per hand and $5 on insurance. With insurance, out of nineteen hands you'd get $10 on thirteen of them for a total of $130. Without insurance, you'd push four times for $0, and you'd make $12 on nine hands for $108.

The difference between taking insurance and not taking insurance might not seem like much, but it definitely adds up over time. And the difference in this example shows only the least amount you stand to lose. If you were to add in other factors that can affect probability, you would end up losing much more than $5. In fact, the real number comes closer to $25 for this example. Why this is so goes into some pretty involved computations that, frankly, are beyond the scope of this book, and beyond the scope of beginning players.

They're also not that necessary to know. But it is necessary to accept the theories behind them and what they tell you, which is that insurance typically is not a good bet. The only time it is worth taking is when you know there are lots of 10s left in the deck.

Taking Insurance When You Don't Have Blackjack

Do the odds get any better when you insure hands other than naturals? Let's take a look at the numbers. Again, you're playing for $10 a hand, blackjack pays 3:2, and insurance pays 2:1.

Let's say you're dealt a 9 and a 10 for a hand valued at 19. The dealer is showing ace up, and asks if anyone wants insurance. You figure there is a good chance that the dealer has blackjack, and you don't want to lose such a good hand, so you say yes.

The following scenarios reflect what could happen next, and what you stand to gain (or lose):

- **The dealer has blackjack.** You win your insurance bet of $5, which pays off at 2:1, so you make $10. You take back your $5 insurance bet for a total of $15. You lose your original bet of $10. You're even.
- **The dealer also has a hand valued at 19 points.** You lose your insurance bet of $5, and you push on your original bet. You take back your original bet of $10. This results in a net loss of $5.
- **The dealer has 18.** You lose your insurance bet of $5, but you win the hand, and are paid $10 for your win. You take back your original $10, for a total of $20. You're up $5.
- **The dealer has any other total than 17**, which means he has to hit. He does, and he busts. You win $10 on the hand, and lose your insurance bet. You're up $5.
- **The dealer has any other total than 17**, which means he has to draw. He draws to 21, beating your hand. You lose your insurance bet (remember, it only pays off if the dealer has a natural), plus your original wager, for a net loss of $15.

Now remember, in each situation where you won, you could have taken away $5 more if you hadn't taken insurance. In the second scenario, you would have finished even if you hadn't taken insurance. In the fifth scenario, you would have lost $10 instead of $15.

Even Money

Here is another scenario you might encounter when playing blackjack: You get a blackjack, and the dealer is showing an ace as her up card. You expect her to ask if you want insurance. Instead, she asks if you want even money. Even money? What is that all about?

Even money is a 1:1 instant payoff that the casino offers in situations when players have blackjack and the dealer is showing an ace. This is the only time it is ever offered. If you take even money when you are offered it, you'll get an amount equal to your original bet, regardless of what the dealer's hole card is. If you bet $10, you'll be paid $10. Even if the dealer ends up with a blackjack on her own, you still win. If you decide not to take even money and the dealer has blackjack, the hand would be a push, and you'd win nothing.

A good deal? It is just about the only sure payoff you'll ever get when you're playing blackjack. But being assured of winning something doesn't necessarily make even money a winning proposition. Is even money better than insurance? No. Even money is actually the same as insurance, and the odds aren't any more in your favor if you say yes when the dealer offers it.

FACT

Even money is simply a different way of taking insurance. Either way, you are basically betting that the dealer has blackjack. With even money, however, you know what you'll win no matter what, as you're settling for an even odds payout on your original bet.

Some people like even-money payouts, as they are assured of making something, regardless of what the dealer has as a hole card. If you bet $10, you get $10 back, for a net win of $10. How easy is that? And taking even money doesn't require making an additional bet. This has to be a good deal, right? Even money might seem like a good deal, but it simply isn't. All a casino is doing when it offers even money is cutting to the chase. To see how this works, let's put even money to the test. Again, we'll go back to our hypothetical blackjack game. In this case, there are three possible scenarios that can play out. Let's take a look at each of them. The following factors are at play in each situation: you have blackjack, the dealer is showing ace up, and your original bet is $10.

ALERT!

The next time you're tempted to take insurance when you're holding a 20 against an ace up, think again. Many people think it's a good idea to automatically make an insurance bet if they have blackjack or other very good hands. But it isn't. Here's why: it makes more sense to make an insurance bet if your hand does *not* contain a 10-value card, as this would mean there is a better chance of the dealer's hole card being a 10 or face card.

- **You take even money.** The dealer matches your $10 bet with another $10—an even-money payout. Your net gain: $10.
- **You decline even money, but take insurance.** Since your original bet was $10, you have to put down an additional $5 for the insurance bet. The dealer shows her hole card, and she does have blackjack. You win your insurance bet. It pays out at 2:1, so you get $15. Subtract what you put down—$5—and your net gain is $10. Since you pushed on your original bet, you neither win nor lose, so the bet just comes back to you. Your net gain for the entire hand? $10. Exactly the same as what you'd get if you took even money!
- **You decline even money, but take insurance.** The dealer doesn't have blackjack. You lose your insurance bet of $5, but you win $15 for your blackjack. Subtract all the bets you placed—your original $10, plus the $5 insurance bet—and your net is $10. Again, exactly the same as if you took even money.

Of course, there is an additional scenario that could play out. It is the best of all possible options. You could choose not to take insurance or even money, and win $15 on your hand instead of $10. Now that you know the ins and outs of insurance and even money, doesn't this option make the most sense?

Basic Strategy for Insurance

By now, you should have heard the gospel loud and clear: insurance is a lousy bet. Most of the time, that is. That said, there are times when taking insurance does make sense. But the only way you will know when those instances arise is if you are keeping track of the cards being played (for more on counting cards, see Chapter 9). If you are, it does make sense to make an insurance bet if you know that more than one-third of the cards remaining to be dealt are 10s or face cards. If you aren't keeping track, insurance is simply a poor player option, and one that you shouldn't use.

Of all the basic strategies in blackjack, the one for insurance is the easiest to learn, and the easiest to remember. In fact, it consists of only two rules:

1. Unless you're counting cards, never take insurance.
2. If you are counting cards, take insurance only when you know that more than one-third of the cards remaining to be played are 10-value cards, as this means the dealer is more likely to have one as his hole card.

Always keep in mind that, on average, the dealer will have a 10 under her ace only four times out of thirteen. This makes a strong argument for just toughing things out even when the dealer keeps on coming up with aces. Do so, and you will average more on your blackjack hands than if you took insurance.

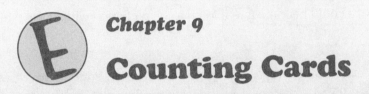

Chapter 9

Counting Cards

As a studious blackjack player, you should now know that certain cards (such as high cards) are of more help to players than they are to dealers when they come out of the deck. Now, let's say you were able to know how many of each type of card remained in the stack of cards left to be dealt. You could alter your betting to take advantage of the times the cards are in your favor. This is what card counting is all about.

Keeping Count

Card counting is a way of gaining an edge over the house by using what is known about the value of a deck of cards—specifically, the value of the cards remaining to be dealt during a game—to govern how much you should bet on your hands. Learn a card-counting system well and pair it with basic strategy, and you could become a real force to be reckoned with at the tables.

If you can master card counting, you can gain an edge of anywhere between 0.5 to 2 percent over the house, depending on the number of decks being played, the rules in effect, and how well you're able to employ the counting system you've learned. That said, if you have to choose between mastering basic strategy and learning how to count cards, you're better off learning basic strategy, which will serve you well in virtually every situation.

Card counting often seems kind of mysterious, or veiled in secrecy. Some card counters like to perpetuate the belief that it is mysterious, but it really isn't. While there is nothing all that mysterious about card counting, there are a number of myths surrounding it, including:

- **It's illegal.** It's true that casinos don't much like card counters, because they know these players can have a small yet measurable edge over the house. Therefore, they have come up with lots of ways to try to trip up or disarm the players who do it, but the technique itself isn't illegal. In a 1983 Nevada court case, the court ruled that card counters do not alter any of the basic features of the game and merely use their mental skills to take advantage of the same information that is available to the public.
- **Card counting is difficult to learn.** Wrong again. Yes, there are complex card-counting systems out there, but the basic premise behind card counting isn't all that difficult to understand. What's more, you don't have to be a rocket scientist to learn how to do it.

- **It requires memorizing the cards that are played.** Again, wrong. This is what Dustin Hoffman's character did in the movie "Rainman," and lots of people remember it so they think they have to do it too. But card counting isn't based on memorization.
- **Card counting is the only way to make serious money when playing blackjack.** And wrong again. As you'll learn more about later in this chapter, players who stick to basic strategy and don't count cards can also do very well at the tables.

How Counting Cards Works

Blackjack is what is known as a dependent variable game. This means that as each card is dealt from the deck or decks of cards, the odds constantly change regarding the next card that will come up. Knowing what the odds are for certain cards—especially 10-value cards, of which there are more than any other specific value cards in a deck—can help a player determine what his or her bet amount should be. When a deck has lots of high-value cards and is low in low-value cards (2, 3, 4, 5, 6, 7, and 8), players in standard blackjack games gain a slight advantage. When the reverse is true, and a deck has few high-value cards such as 9s, 10s, and aces, the house gets the edge.

A little confusing? Let's take a closer look at this theory. Let's say you are playing a single-deck game of blackjack. Before the dealer deals any cards, you know that the odds of any 10-value card leaving the dealer's hands are 16 out of 52—16 10-value cards (10s, jacks, queens, and kings) out of fifty-two cards—or a 4 in 13 chance.

Now, let's say you're playing at a table with one other player. He's at first base. You're playing a single-deck game. The dealer gives the guy at first base two 10s right away. This means the odds of the next card being a 10 drop to 14 out of 50, or a 7 in 25 chance. The odds suddenly got a little longer.

Think you'll get a 10? Well, let's say you do. What's more, you also get an ace. Blackjack! Now the odds of another 10 showing up have dropped to 13 out of 48. Still pretty long odds.

Think the dealer will get a 10? Let's say he deals himself an ace up. Now he asks if anyone wants insurance. Should you take it? You know there are still plenty of 10-value cards in that deck. But there are lots of lesser-value cards, too. Enough so you feel pretty confident about your blackjack. You decline.

FACT

Turning down insurance is the correct move in virtually every instance. The only time it isn't is when you know there is a greater percentage of 10-value cards than any other in the deck. Then insurance isn't a bad move.

Put a little more simply, the game of blackjack pretty much boils down to the relationship between high-value cards, which are good for players, and low-value cards, which are good for dealers. Why? Because dealers have fewer playing options than players do—specifically, they have to hit any hand that is less than 17. Because of this, they'd rather get low-value cards than high-value cards, which make them bust more often.

During a round of play, the advantage shifts from dealer to player depending on the cards that are played. If you pay attention to the concentration of high-value and low-value cards in the decks when you're playing, you'll be able to increase your bets when you know you have a bit of an advantage, and decrease your bets when the advantage swings to the house.

The Ten Count

Card counting is a technique born of the information age. When people like Ed Thorp and others, whom you read about in Chapter 1, began to apply computer-assisted analysis to the game, they learned some things they didn't know before. Specifically, they learned that high cards such as 10s are beneficial to players, while small cards are good for the dealer.

This knowledge led to the first true card-counting system, which was known as the Ten Count. This system called for keeping track of the ratio of 10s to non-10s left in a deck. If players raised their wagers when the ratio of 10s increased, they could gain the advantage over the house. The house would still win the majority of the hands played, but players could wager more, and come out ahead. In theory, anyway.

In reality, Thorp's Ten Count system was based on faulty mathematics and had some fatal flaws. One thing it didn't do was consider how each card, when removed, affected the remaining subset of cards. Depending on the card that was removed, this effect varied from a little to a lot, a point that author Peter Griffin drove home in *The Theory of Blackjack*. Griffin calculated the effects of removing various cards on the rest of the deck. These calculations, shown in **TABLE 9-1**, were computed by removing one card of each value and computing the house advantage on the remaining 51 cards.

TABLE 9-1: Effect of Removal (in Percentages) on House Advantage			
Card	**Effect of Removal**	**Card**	**Effect of Removal**
A	-.61	6	.46
2	.38	7	.28
3	.44	8	0
4	.55	9	-.18
5	.69	10	-.51

As you can see, the effect of removing just one card on the other cards in the deck can vary significantly. Today's card-counting systems take these factors into consideration. Some use many more. As such, they can get pretty complicated. But the basics behind the theory remain fairly simple.

Even though Thorp's Ten Count system has some flaws, it's a good system to use if all you want to do is decide whether or not to take insurance, as it uses the ratio of 10s to non-10s to determine betting and playing decisions.

Picking a Card-Counting System

If you play blackjack long enough, odds are you'll reach a stage where you'll want to learn how to count cards. Most people do. They get frustrated when they see players put big money on hands that basic strategy suggests aren't worth it, and walk away with big wads of cash when they do. Do these players know something the others don't know? Yes, and they've counted the cards to gain that understanding.

The Down Side

For many people, however, card counting is a phase they go through. They'll learn how to do it, and maybe use it for a while, but they won't stick with it, simply because it can be so distracting. Think about it. Playing properly by using basic strategy comes first. This can be hard enough to learn, so why lessen your chances of doing well by adding another thing to think about? Other players give up on card counting because it takes an activity they enjoy and turns it into a job. It requires work to stay focused at a table and continually run numbers in your head.

QUESTION?

My uncle just paid a bunch of money for a count system that he swears will make him rich. Should I learn this system?
If it's a simple system, you could consider it. If it's not, it's probably not worth your time. The difference in what you could possibly win when using a complex system versus a simple system usually isn't worth the headaches and aggravation that come with learning the system. When it comes to counting systems, simpler is better for most players.

Most players don't succeed at card counting. They don't possess the math and logic abilities that they need to really get good at it. This doesn't mean you have to be a genius to be a card counter. But the more complex programs do take some analytical skills as they employ more complicated formulas. If math and logic aren't your strong suit, it's tough to learn advanced card-counting systems. Many people don't succeed at card counting because they're scared of it. They've heard stories of players getting escorted out of casinos when they've been discovered counting. And they've heard stories of worse happening. It's no secret that casinos don't like card counters. And it's true that some casinos have made things pretty rough for individuals who use these skills when at their tables. Because big bet swings can quickly unmask a card counter, many counters get a little gun shy about taking advantage of favorable counts when they arise and betting big on them. This is understandable, but it pretty much negates the reason for learning how to count cards.

Lots of card counters simply have a hard time remembering the count. Now, the count doesn't have to be perfect. If you're close, it's better than nothing. However, if you're way off it won't do you any good at all.

ALERT!

Card counting doesn't work for playing blackjack at online casinos. Most of these establishments use gaming software that shuffles the cards after every hand. If you plan to play a lot online, don't even bother learning how to count cards. Learn basic strategy very well instead, and be sure to use the basic strategy rules that apply the game you're playing.

Finally, players often ditch card counting after they learn it because it's not as sure-fire a method as it once was. Back in the old days, blackjack was a single-deck game. Card counting was the method that blew these games away. When that happened, the casinos had to come up with ways to make the game more difficult so they could regain their edge over players. They did so in a variety of ways, including:

- **Using multiple decks.** It's tough to keep track of cards when there are 416 (the number of cards in an eight-deck shoe) to do it with.
- **Using continuous shuffling machines.** These machines immediately shuffle discards back into the shoe, making it virtually impossible for counters to come up with a true count.
- **Allowing dealers to shuffle up whenever they want.** Dealers no longer have to wait until the cut card to reshuffle the shoe. Instead, they can—and do—shuffle up at various points during a game. Sometimes they're not even halfway through the shoe when they do.

Again, none of this means that card counting has no value. Some systems do. Others are so tough to learn that it's hard to use them, which makes them fairly worthless. Sink big money into purchasing any of these systems, and you're doubly behind. The bottom line: it's best not to rely on card counting as a sure-fire way to make big money playing blackjack.

Considerations

We can't even tell you how many card-counting systems there are; it seems as if new systems and variations on old systems crop up with great frequency. With so many different card-counting systems available, how do you choose the one or ones you want to use? They all have their relative advantages and disadvantages, but there is a proven method for sorting through them all and selecting the ones you want to learn and use:

- Consider the kinds of games you play most often, or that you anticipate playing most often. If you're like most blackjack players, you'll be playing with multiple decks, so you'll want to pick a game that works well in these situations. If you're going to hunt down single-deck games, choose a system that takes this factor into consideration.
- Consider the amount of time you spend or plan to spend playing blackjack. If you're going to make a habit of it, a complex system that gives you more of an edge might be to your advantage. If you don't play very often, a simpler system will be easier to remember and less likely to distract you.
- Choose a count system that gives you the information you need in order to make three important playing decisions: when to bet more, when to deviate from basic strategy, and when to take insurance. If you plan on playing multiple-deck games, systems that indicate favorable betting situations should carry more weight in your decision process.
- Consider playing efficiency and betting efficiency factors. These figures, expressed as percentages, show the relative strengths or weaknesses of the various systems. Playing efficiency measures favorable playing conditions. Betting efficiency measures favorable betting conditions. The best system would have about a .98 percent betting

efficiency and a .70 percent playing efficiency. As betting efficiency goes up, playing efficiency goes down, which is why both figures are important. As previously mentioned, multiple-deck games typically call for high betting efficiency. In single-deck games, betting efficiency isn't as important.

Point Counting

The following approach is a good card-counting system to learn first. Called point count, or high-low, it's the granddaddy of them all, easy to learn, and pretty effective. As such, it is considered one of the better simple count methods you can use.

Point count assigns a point value to every card that is played out of the shoe, as follows:

- Plus one point for every 2, 3, 4, 5, or 6
- Zero points for every 7, 8, or 9
- Minus one point for every 10 and ace

You then keep a running total count of the cards played. You must count every card given to every player, as well as the dealer's cards. The total number gives you an idea of what's left in the shoe to be played still. The higher the number, the more favorable the deck is for you, because that means many low cards have already been played and there are more high cards remaining in the deck. And as you already learned, high cards in the deck are good for players, because they mean that the dealer is more likely to bust. Likewise, a low point total means there are more low cards left in the deck.

As an example, let's say the following cards come out of the shoe: A (-1), K (-1), 4 (1), 9 (0), 7 (0), 10 (-1), A (-1), J (-1), 6 (1). Starting from zero, your count at the end of this run is -3. This would be a very unfavorable position for you to be in, as lots of high cards have already left the deck.

Let's run through another scenario. This time more low cards than high cards are dealt: 2 (1), 4 (1), K (-1), 8 (0), 6 (1), 10 (-1), A (-1), K (-1), 5 (1), 5 (1). Starting from zero, your count at the end of this run is +1.

How do you use this information to determine what your bet should be? It's easy, just follow these guidelines.

- For a count of 1 or less, bet one unit.
- For a count of 2 or 3, bet two units.
- For a count of 4 or 5, bet three units.
- For a count of 6 or 7, bet four units.
- For a count of 8 or more, bet five units.

This system has a betting efficiency of .97 percent and a playing efficiency of .51 percent, which means it's good for betting purposes and fair for playing your hand properly.

The drawback to point count is that it was developed for playing a single-deck game. But you can also use it for multiple-deck games. To do so, you have to calculate what's known as the true count. Here's how to do it: Take your running count and divide it by the number of decks you think are left in the shoe.

To get good at point count, you have to practice it. The easiest way is to simply take a deck of cards and start doing a count. Once you've got this down, deal two cards at a time and start memorizing the total count on them. This makes counting a lot easier.

Want an even easier and simpler system? Watch the cards as they come up and pay attention to general trends. If you notice that small cards have dominated the first few hands coming out of the shoe, this indicates that 10s and aces are still to come. It might be a good idea to increase your bets. This system isn't as effective as point count systems are, but it will at least give you a rough idea of when you have the advantage and when the house does.

Casino Counting Tips

There is a big difference between practicing card counting at home and doing it in a casino. The noise is a huge distraction for some people, and there are lots of other distractions, too, such as servers asking for drink orders, other players who want to chat, and so on.

Here's an approach to learning how to deal with the noise and interruptions in a casino. Simply simulate casino settings at home. When you practice, turn on the radio and television. If you have kids, ask them to come in and bug you every few minutes. Answer the phone when it rings. Keep a running (and accurate!) count of the cards in a deck in the midst of all the distractions you can find.

Players learn various techniques for keeping track of the count amid the noise and confusion casinos are all about. To be an effective counter, you should learn these techniques. Look like you're spending too much time concentrating on the cards being played, and you run the risk of attracting the attention of casino management. Should there be anything else about your play that could make them suspicious, they could ask you to leave.

What about your play could arouse their suspicions? Any and all of the following:

- **Varying your bets by large amounts.** To avoid problems with management, it's best not to make a substantial change in bet amounts. Pit personnel keep an eye on any player who raises his bet three times the amount of the first bet he made on the shoe.
- **Placing bets that go against basic strategy.** You're going to do this when you count cards. Again, you can make it a little less obvious by betting judiciously.
- **Spending too much time scrutinizing the cards.** If you spend too much time doing this, it will look as though you are trying to count cards.

How can you learn to keep the count when you're trying to look like you're not doing it? One simple way is to use your fingers. You'll want to do this surreptitiously under the table. If you rest your fingers on your thigh, it looks better. Some people use their knuckles, others use chips. Try a few ways at home, and see what works for you.

The Shuffle Track

Counting cards isn't the only beat-the-house ploy out there. Shuffle tracking, which helps players identify where 10-value cards accumulate in multideck shoes, is another approach. However, these techniques are complex and difficult to learn.

Shuffle tracking, or cluster counting, is based on the observation that cards tend to clump together in certain parts of a multideck shoe. The premise is that by observing how the cards are shuffled when the shoe is over, a player might determine the parts of the next shoe where high cards could be hanging out.

Here's how it works: As a new shoe is being readied, mentally divide it into sections of roughly one deck each. As the cards come out, keep mental note of the number of high cards and low cards that are played. As you do, match your observations to the divisions you've established. This will give you an idea of the areas that are rich in high cards.

When the shoe is over, watch how the dealer shuffles the decks. Try to keep an eye on where your high card dense clusters end up, and where they surface in the new shoe. This part is tough, and it's where many players simply give up. When you play the next round, increase your bets when you think the deal has reached those high-value pockets, and decrease your bets on the low-value pockets. (This method only works if the dealer is shuffling by hand; many use an automated machine that does the shuffling for them.)

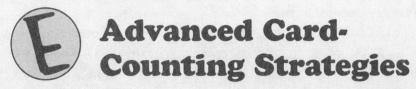

Chapter 10

Advanced Card-Counting Strategies

For many blackjack players, the card-counting strategies discussed in Chapter 9, paired with solid basic strategy play, will provide all the edge needed for doing well at the game. But some players want to take their skills to higher levels. For these players, more advanced card-counting strategies hold a great amount of appeal. There are lots of advanced card-counting strategies, ranging from fairly simple to amazingly complex. Are any of them worth your while? Let's take a look.

Going Beyond the Basics

As you now know, card counting allows players to gain an edge over the house by using what they know about the value of the cards remaining in the deck to maximize their betting strategies. This information allows players to increase their bets when cards are favorable and pull back bets when cards are against them.

All card-counting systems have the same basic premise at their heart. They're the same theories developed by Edward O. Thorp, whom you learned about in Chapter 1, and honed by others through the years. But one of the most intriguing things about blackjack, especially if you're mathematically inclined and you like to play around with numbers, is that it lends itself so well to analysis. Over the years, this aspect of the game has led many people to try to come up with better ways of playing it. Blackjack enthusiasts have thus developed a number of card-counting systems over the years.

FACT

One source estimates that more than 100 different card-counting systems have been published since Edward Thorp's *Beat the Dealer* came out in 1962. While mathematical analysis of the game has evolved over the years, all card-counting systems are based on one basic theory—that certain cards are more advantageous to players than others.

The Strategies Behind Card-Counting Systems

All card-counting systems are based on some sort of counting strategy. Some are trickier and/or more complex than others, but they all work pretty much the same way: they assign a positive, negative, or zero point value, or tag, to every card in the deck. Typically, low-value cards, such as 2 or 3, are assigned positive values. Tens get a negative value. But the specific values vary depending on how the system is put together.

All card-counting systems fall into one of two categories:

- **Balanced.** Balanced strategies start the count at zero. When all cards have been dealt, the count will end up at zero. This is the approach used in most card-counting systems, as it's easiest for most people to do. However, balanced counts work best with single- or two-deck games. If used for multiple-deck games, they must be adjusted (see the discussion of running count and true count methods below) in order to be accurate.
- **Unbalanced.** Unbalanced count strategies start or end on a number other than zero. Because of this, they can be harder to remember. However, unbalanced counts automatically factor in the number of undealt cards that are left, so they don't require an additional true count adjustment.

Counting systems also use one of the following counting methods:

- **Running count.** These systems rely on the sum of all cards dealt. They're known for being easy to use.
- **True count.** True count systems take running count up a notch by dividing the running count by a number representing the number of cards still to be dealt, usually based on the number of decks remaining to be played. True count strategies are typically more accurate than running count.

From here, a number of approaches can be used to further hone the counting system. They include:

- **Primary count.** A variation of the running count, primary count assigns a negative value to all 10-value cards. Primary count systems can be balanced or unbalanced.
- **Secondary count.** Another variation of the running count. It gives some numbers positive values and some numbers negative values. Tens are not factored. Secondary count approaches can be balanced or unbalanced.
- **Adjusted count.** Another running count variation. It adjusts for a surplus of certain cards, typically aces.

- **Ace-reckoned count.** These systems include aces as part of the main count by giving them a positive or negative number.
- **Ace-neutral count.** Ace-neutral counts do not assign a value to aces.
- **Compromise count.** Compromise counts split the difference between ace-reckoned and ace-neutral counts. They give aces a value somewhere between 0 and the value given to 10s.
- **Side counts.** Some strategies use one or more side counts. The most common is counting aces separately. Some strategies call for counting 5s.
- **Suit/color-aware counts.** Some counting systems, notably Red Seven and KISS, assign different tags to red and black cards.

Many counting systems are multiparameter, which means they use a combination of the above approaches.

Understanding the Levels

Card-counting systems are also ranked by levels, which refers to the highest value assigned to the cards:

- **Level 1 strategies.** These are the most popular and easiest to use. These strategies assign point values of -1, 0, or +1.
- **Level 2 strategies.** They're more efficient and more accurate, but efficiency and accuracy come with greater difficulty and a higher margin for error. These systems assign point values of -2, -1, 0, +1 and +2 to various cards.
- **Level 3 strategies.** These are even more efficient and more accurate than Level 2, which makes them harder to learn and easier for making errors.

Level 4 and 5 strategies also exist, but most experts feel they're not worth the time and effort to learn as they're extremely complex and carry a high margin of error.

FACT

Back in the days of single-deck blackjack, counting systems didn't have to be very sophisticated, as all they had to do was keep track of the cards remaining in one deck. Counting strategies were therefore geared toward single-deck games. As casinos implemented approaches to foil card counters, such as multiple-deck games, a number of other counting strategies were developed.

Exploring the Systems

With the hundreds of counting systems out there, it's impossible to discuss any of them in any kind of depth here. What you will find is a quick overview of some of the better-known systems. From this, you can get an idea of what they're about and where to go if you want to learn more.

How to choose the strategy that's right for you? First of all, if you're currently using a strategy that you like and that works for you, give some thought to why you want to change. Are you bored? Do you simply want to try something new? Have you heard someone else talk about a great system that works for him, and you're itching to try it? Did you see a Web site espousing a certain program, and it sounds too good to be true? These are valid reasons for doing a little exploring, but not necessarily good reasons for ditching your current strategy.

That said, there really isn't one "best" system. They all have their relative strengths and weaknesses. The system that works for your best friend might be one that doesn't fit your style of play or the rules where you typically play. For these reasons, it's always a good idea to follow your own path when selecting a counting program.

ESSENTIAL

Many people select card-counting systems that were developed by players they admire. Often these are the systems that resonate with them and make the most sense to them, as they feel a kinship with the player.

In general, it's a good idea to balance the following factors:

- **Your playing level and ability.** If you're just learning the game, an advanced card-counting strategy won't do you much good.
- **Your math and memorization skills.** If they're not the greatest, stick to Level 1 counting strategies.
- **The reliability of the counting system.** Highly reliable systems can be more difficult to learn.

You can also assess the various systems based on the following factors, which measure the effectiveness and accuracy of the system. They're taken from *The Theory of Blackjack* by Peter Griffin, a must-have book if you're serious about the game:

- **Betting efficiency, or betting correlation.** This is a measure of how well a card-counting system factors the player's advantage in various situations. It's an important factor in multideck games. The best betting efficiencies approach 100 percent.
- **Playing efficiency.** This reflects how well a particular strategy deals with all the various changes that can be made in playing strategy. This is an important factor in hand-held games.
- **Insurance correlation.** This is a measure of how well the system predicts when insurance bets should be placed.

Want an easy way to figure out a card-counting strategy that suits your skills and playing level? Go to *www.qfit.com/blackjack-strategy.htm*, where you'll find a blackjack strategy advisor. Plug in the answers to a few questions, and the advisor will return a list of possible strategies for you, ranked from best to worst, based on your playing skills, your mathematical skills, and other factors.

You'll need something called an efficiency calculator to determine these factors. There are gaming software programs specifically designed for blackjack that include these calculators. Or you can do an Internet search for Web sites that contain this information. We've also included a couple of sites in Appendix C.

Specific Counting Systems

The list of counting systems that follows is presented in a casual ranking from easiest to hardest. Many of them are proprietary, which necessitates reading the creator's book or buying software that presents the complete details of the system. We've also included betting and playing efficiencies and insurance correlations for a number of them. Keep in mind, however, that these figures can vary a bit depending on playing conditions and other factors. It's best to consider them a general indication of the system's strengths.

The inclusion or exclusion of a counting system in the following list is by no means meant as a reflection of the relative value of the system. Nor should inclusion be considered an endorsement of the system. Our goal here is merely to present a quick overview of some of the more popular systems.

K-O

The K-O (which stands for knock-out) system was devised by Olaf Vancura and Ken Fuchs and presented in their book *Knock-Out Blackjack*. An unbalanced strategy, it's easy to use and very popular.

A	2	3	4	5	6	7	8	9	10
-1	1	1	1	1	1	1	0	0	-1

Betting Efficiency 0.98   Playing Efficiency 0.55   Insurance Correlation 0.78

Red Seven

This method was developed by Arnold Snyder, the editor and publisher of *Blackjack Forum*, a quarterly publication (no longer published) that many serious card players considered an essential. Red Seven is another popular and easy-to-use counting system. It's based on the high-low system detailed in Chapter 9.

A	2	3	4	5	6	7	8	9	10
-1	1	1	1	1	1	.5	0	0	1

Betting Efficiency 0.98   Playing Efficiency 0.54   Insurance Correlation 0.78

Canfield Expert

From Richard Canfield's *Blackjack Your Way to Riches*, this is an easy, balanced Level 1 counting strategy.

A	2	3	4	5	6	7	8	9	10
0	0	1	1	1	1	1	0	-1	-1

Betting Efficiency 0.87   Playing Efficiency 0.63   Insurance Correlation 0.76

Uston Advanced Plus-Minus

By now, Ken Uston should need no introduction. Here's one of his easiest counting systems, from his book *Million Dollar Blackjack*.

A	2	3	4	5	6	7	8	9	10
-1	0	1	1	1	1	1	0	0	-1

Betting Efficiency 0.95   Playing Efficiency 0.55   Insurance Correlation 0.76

Revere Advanced Plus-Minus

This Level 1 strategy was developed by Lyle Revere and published in the book *Playing Blackjack as a Business*.

A	2	3	4	5	6	7	8	9	10
0	1	1	1	1	1	0	0	-1	-1

Betting Efficiency 0.89   Playing Efficiency 0.59   Insurance Correlation 0.76

Hi-Opt I

This is one of several strategies developed by Lance Humble and Carl Cooper and published in *The World's Greatest Blackjack Book*. It's a simple Level 1, balanced strategy.

A	2	3	4	5	6	7	8	9	10
0	0	1	1	1	1	0	0	0	-1

Betting Efficiency 0.949   Playing Efficiency 0.609   Insurance Correlation 0.867

QUESTION?

Will learning advanced card-counting strategies significantly impact my success at blackjack?

Unless you're a highly sophisticated player, probably not, as the advantages between systems are often amazingly slim. Because of this, they're typically only of interest to the most serious players, and mathematical whizzes who love to massage the numbers.

Silver Fox

This popular system comes from Ralph Stricker, author of *The Silver Fox Blackjack System—You Can Count on It.*

A	2	3	4	5	6	7	8	9	10
-1	1	1	1	1	1	1	0	-1	-1

Betting Efficiency 0.96   Playing Efficiency 0.54   Insurance Correlation 0.69

Zen

This is a Level 2 counting strategy developed by Arnold Snyder. For more on Arnold Snyder's philosophies on card counting, check out his book *The Blackjack Formula*. It analyzes eight popular counting systems based on the "blackjack formula," which factors each system's playing efficiencies and betting correlations.

A	2	3	4	5	6	7	8	9	10
-1	+1	+1	+2	+2	+2	+1	0	0	-2

Betting Efficiency 0.96   Playing Efficiency 0.63   Insurance Correlation 0.85

Omega II

This is a balanced, ace-neutral, Level 2 strategy from Bryce Carlson's *Blackjack for Blood*.

A	2	3	4	5	6	7	8	9	10
0	1	2	2	2	2	1	0	-1	-2

Betting Efficiency 0.98   Playing Efficiency 0.67   Insurance Correlation 0.87

Wong's Halves

This Level 3 strategy was developed by Stanford Wong, a mathematical whiz and professional card player known as the Godfather of Blackjack. It's considered one of the most reliable systems.

A	2	3	4	5	6	7	8	9	10
-1	.5	1	1	1.5	1	.5	0	-.5	-1

Betting Efficiency 0.99   Playing Efficiency 0.57   Insurance Correlation 0.73

Uston APC

Another Uston counting system, this one is a Level 3 balanced strategy and was published in *Million Dollar Blackjack*.

A	2	3	4	5	6	7	8	9	10
0	1	2	2	3	2	2	1	-1	-3

Betting Efficiency 0.98   Playing Efficiency 0.69   Insurance Correlation 0.91

Chapter 11

Managing Your Money

Abig part of winning big is being smart about how you handle your money. This goes beyond knowing how much to bet when. It also means understanding your limits, both emotionally and monetarily, and staying within your comfort zone on both fronts. There are as many ways to bet as there are gamblers. However, none of them is very effective unless you learn the basics of money management first. You must know your limits and know how to protect your bankroll.

Be Smart about Gambling Money

Gamblers like to be winners. It's simply not much fun to lose. But losing is inevitable. We might have short-term wins, but you now know that over the long run, the casino always wins.

You can, of course, minimize the amount of money that you're going to lose. Picking a game with a reasonable house edge is one way to do it. This is a big reason why people like blackjack, as it offers a relatively low house edge. Learning how to play games well is another way to keep losses to a minimum. Learning how to handle money responsibly is also key.

FACT

People lose at gambling for a number of reasons. Sometimes they choose games that are so stacked against them that the odds are simply not in their favor. Others aren't very good at the games they play. Even choosing a good game isn't going to help much if you don't play wisely.

Of all the factors that affect winning and losing, poor money management is at the top of the list. Some people simply don't handle their money well, or appropriately. They come to the tables with small bankrolls—not enough money to get into the game they want to play. Or they overbet because they're desperate to win the big bucks. But even gamblers with lots of money to spend often make mistakes in handling their money. Whether you're a high roller or a low roller, there are certain steps you can take to protect your personal bankroll and maximize your enjoyment of gambling.

Risky Business

The satisfaction of playing a game well, whether they win or lose, is enough for some gamblers. But let's be honest here. Most of us are attracted to gambling because of the money we might win when we play. While it's never a good idea to chase dreams and riches, they could be as close as the next hand you're dealt. Gambling typically attracts people who aren't afraid to risk something to make something. These individuals derive a certain amount of pleasure from taking risks. To them, the uncertainty involved is part of the thrill. People who are risk-averse usually aren't attracted to gambling. For these individuals, the uncertainty involved simply makes them uncomfortable. For the truly risk-averse, even betting small amounts moves them out of their comfort zone.

Know Your Comfort Zone

Chances are good that you're somewhere in the middle. You like to gamble, and you feel comfortable at a certain betting level. It could be $5 a hand. It could be $50. You're likely to seek out games that match your comfort level and play within it. Most of the time, anyway. Just about every gambler knows what it feels like to get in a little too deep. If you haven't gambled enough to determine your comfort level, there's an easy way to do it. Simply seek out tables with the lowest minimums. It's pretty easy to find tables with betting minimums of $5 a hand. Some even offer minimums as low as $2 a hand. You might have to wait your turn at these tables, as they're often packed with players. But the wait is worth it.

FACT

Even low-minimum tables are rarely packed at certain times of the day, such as midmorning or early afternoon, or certain days of the week. Time your play for these periods and you'll have a better chance of getting a seat.

It's never a good idea to play at a table where the minimum bet moves you out of your comfort zone. You might do okay when you're placing your opening bets, but what if you get a hand that you should split or double down on? The extra amount you'd need to wager might be enough to discourage you from making good choices. If it is, you're playing too high.

Ignore Peer Pressure

It's never a good idea to let others determine what you should bet. Hitting the casinos as part of a group is fine. Playing at the same table with your friends might not be. Casinos aren't a good place to play "mine is bigger than yours." Never try to prove something by placing a bet simply to match or top another person's bet. Ignore your friends' ribbing, especially if your bet levels are far below theirs. Don't run through your entire bankroll simply because you're trying to save face with your buddies.

Setting a Gambling Budget

Determining how much money you have to play with is one of the most important aspects of sound money management. This is an essential step no matter what kind of gambler you are or hope to be, how much you earn, or how much you're worth.

Knowing how you spend your money in general is necessary for determining how much you can spend on gambling. If you don't regularly track your expenses, you'll need to do so for at least one month before you set your gambling budget. There are software programs that will help you, or you can simply jot everything down in a small notebook. You'll also need a place to keep receipts. An envelope or file folder works well.

At the end of the month, total up your expenses. (Hopefully, they won't be more than what you take in!) The difference between expenses and income is what you can spend gambling. If your expenses are more than your income, you'll have to make some adjustments somewhere. Maybe you can cut out your daily lattes. Maybe your weekly dinner and a movie can turn into an evening at your favorite casino. What you don't want to do is gamble with money that you need to live on. Ever.

Regardless of what else you do, never play with mortgage money, car payment money, insurance money, or any other funds that are earmarked for other purposes. Gambling with borrowed money—even cash advances on credit cards—is never advisable. Always play with discretionary funds. Always.

There is no magic number when it comes to setting a gambling budget, but it is important to have enough to play with. Come to the tables underfunded, and you might not be able to play long enough to end up a winner.

For most people, having enough to play with means putting aside a certain amount of money over time—a week, a month, a few months. If you're hot to get to the tables, this might not be easy to do. You might be tempted to take money out of savings, hit the kids' college fund, or take a cash advance. Don't do it. Never put these funds at risk, and never borrow money to play. What you might win simply isn't worth the risk.

The money you budget for gambling is your bankroll. It is a finite amount of money that you can safely lose when you gamble (you don't want to do this, of course, but you need to be prepared for it). Once you start playing, you might be able to add your winnings to your bankroll. Or you might decide to start a new bankroll with your winnings, and put aside the original bankroll money for something else. Either way, you won't have to worry as much about pulling money out of your monthly budget. Should you get to this point, know that it's still important to set limits on what you spend when you play. When your bankroll is depleted, you quit playing.

Some players take into account nongambling expenses, such as meals, travel, lodging, and entertainment, when establishing their gambling budgets. To get the fullest picture of what you can afford to spend on gambling, this isn't a bad idea. If you want to do it, you'll need to determine what you think you'll spend for the following:

- Travel, including gas, parking, plane tickets, tolls, etc.
- Meals
- Lodging
- Nongambling entertainment
- Miscellaneous expenses, such as hiring a babysitter or boarding pets

Subtract these items from the amount you've budgeted for playing at the tables. What's left is your bankroll.

Establishing Session Limits

Money-conscious gamblers budget their money when they play. They go into each gaming session with a set amount—$50, $200, $500, whatever they think is an appropriate bankroll—and they stick to that amount. If they lose the entire amount, they simply quit. They don't take more money from the ATM or borrow some from a friend.

It's easy to establish a session limit. Simply multiply your minimum wager by the number of hands you expect to play in an hour. Then multiply this figure by the number of hours you want to play. As an example, let's say you're going to play blackjack for three hours at $10 a hand. You think you'll play about 12 hands an hour.

$$\$10 \times 12 = \$120$$
$$\$120 \times 3 = \$360$$

For this session, $360 would be an appropriate bankroll. This is all you should bring with you.

Let's say you're planning a Las Vegas weekend. You'll hit the tables more than once—hopefully, anyway. Blow your entire bankroll the first time you play, however, and you'll spend the rest of your trip away from the tables. You can improve your chances of making your money last by divvying up your bankroll before you play. Decide how many times a day you want to play, and how many hours you think you'll play per session. Take only enough money with you for that session.

Knowing When to Quit

Wise gamblers also know when it's time to quit, whether they're winning or losing. This is the best way to protect your bankroll—and your profits. To do so, you set win and loss limits. There is no magic formula for this, just what you're comfortable with. The main point to keep in mind here is stopping while you're ahead. This can be tough to do, as the next big win might be just around the corner. By now, however, you should know enough about probability and statistics to know that the odds vastly favor quitting when you're ahead, or when you're not too far behind.

Some players use a percentage of their beginning bankroll to set their win limits. Others simply determine a dollar amount that they're comfortable with. Some walk away when they've doubled their bankroll. Others take back their original bankroll when their winnings reach a certain point, and only play with that money. As an example, say you started with $200, and you won $200. You pocket your original $200, plus another $50 from your winnings. Your new bankroll is $150. And you're guaranteed a profit of at least $50, even if you lose the rest of your bankroll now.

An old casino saying says, "Anybody can get ahead; nobody leaves ahead." Never try to make up for your losses by continuing to play when you know you should quit. There is always another day, and always another game to play. If your money is gone, you won't be able to take advantage of a new day and a new game.

Loss limits can also be whatever you want them to be. A typical loss limit might be half your bankroll. Once you've lost half your bankroll, call it quits for the day. Period.

Sticking to Your Budget

Staying within your limits when gambling is a little like going on a diet. You know it's a good idea, and you want to comply, but it's your willpower against the thrill of the deal. Here are some tips for keeping you on the straight and narrow when it comes to sticking to your casino "diet":

- Only bring your session bankroll to the table. Keep the rest of your money stashed elsewhere.
- Don't hit your credit cards if you're on a losing streak. Walk away instead.
- Leave your ATM card at home. Do not tap into credit lines.

Like forbidden foods, some players find it too tempting to have cash around. If you're one of them, consider opening a credit line at the casinos where you play. Credit lines are basically short-term loans that casinos offer as a convenience to gamblers. Like other forms of credit, you'll have to fill out an application to get one. The casino will use this information to check your bank references, balances, and credit history.

FACT

Casino deposits, also called "front money," are similar to credit lines as they eliminate the need to bring money to the table. Here, you deposit funds with the casino, and draw against them when you play.

When your casino credit line is established, instead of taking money to the tables, you borrow against your account by using a marker, which is basically a check written against your credit line. After you're done playing, you can settle the marker with your winnings, by check, or credit card. If your credit is good enough, the casino might bill you.

Rendering to Caesar

Knowing how to budget your money is a big part of being a responsible gambler. Protecting your bankroll in every respect is equally important. This includes paying taxes on your winnings. Failing to do so is one of the best ways of destroying your assets, and not just the ones you win at the gaming tables.

Does it come as a surprise to learn that your gambling winnings are taxable? It shouldn't, as the money you win when you play is income, and the IRS expects U.S. citizens to pay taxes on almost all the money they receive, regardless of the source. To comply with the law, you are required to report your winnings as miscellaneous income, and to pay taxes on them. This is the case whether you're playing in land-based casinos or online. There aren't specific tax laws on Internet gaming (at least, not yet), and the operators of online gaming sites typically don't file winnings reports on players. However, this doesn't mean you're off the hook if you gamble online and win. You are still responsible for reporting these winnings when you file your tax return.

All About the W2-G

The IRS uses a form called the W2-G, or Statement of Gambling Winnings, to track some gambling income. Land-based gaming establishments must issue WG-2 forms in the following situations:

- If your winnings are $600 on things like dog races, horse races, jai alai, and state lotteries, and other wagering transactions in which the winnings are at least the amount of the wager.
- If your winnings are in excess of $1,200 for bingo or slot machines.
- If your net proceeds from a keno game are greater than $1,500.

The IRS recently added wagering pools to this list, but didn't provide a detailed description of what constitutes a pool. For this reason, the regulation isn't evenly applied at this time. In some parts of the United States, the IRS requires casinos to treat tournaments as wagering pools, and requires them to withhold taxes from winnings of more than $5,000 in addition to filing W-2Gs. Most casinos simply issue W2-Gs for tournament winnings of $600 or more.

ALERT!

Failing to report gaming wins is illegal. At a minimum, you'll pay penalties and back taxes on your winnings if the IRS catches you. But that's just the beginning. You also run the risk of being prosecuted for criminal tax evasion.

The rules for table games are a little different, as it's not unusual for high rollers to bet and win in the thousands of dollars. Here, the IRS's money laundering rules require casinos to report aggregate cash transactions of $10,000 or more in a day. However, casinos aren't limited to reporting only when cash transactions are that high. They can, and do, start reporting when gamblers win an aggregate of $2,000. What's more, if they know who you are and they have your social security number, they don't have to tell you when they do.

What if your winnings fall under $2,000 in a day? Are you still required to report them? Absolutely. The fact that casinos don't have to report table games winnings of lesser amounts doesn't mean you're off the hook.

While today's IRS is kinder and gentler than it once was, make no mistake about it: the agency's business is to collect taxes when taxes are due. Agents will work with taxpayers who are willing to work with them. Avoid or evade them, though, and you're setting yourself up for serious trouble.

Wins and Losses

It's best to be safe and report your gaming wins even if they aren't reported to the IRS. But here's some good news: you can reduce the amount you claim by keeping track of your losses and deducting them from your winnings. This is good news, but only to a certain extent. You can only deduct losses equal to winnings. If you lose more than you win during the course of a year, that money is gone forever. You can't take it as a deduction, nor can you carry it over or back to offset gambling income in other tax years.

You can only deduct your gambling losses if you itemize. For tax purposes, gambling losses are considered a miscellaneous deduction, and are entered into the appropriate area on Form 1040, Schedule A. However, if your standard deduction is greater than your total deductions from Schedule A, you can't deduct any Schedule A losses, including your gambling losses.

As an example, let's say you kept track of your winnings for a year, and you ended up with $5,000. You also tracked how much you bet during that year. As it turns out, you lost $8,500. When you file your taxes for the year, you can only deduct losses totaling $5,000. If the reverse were true, and you ended up in the black to the tune of $3,500, you would owe taxes on this amount.

Keeping Track

Since you are required by law to report your gambling winnings as income, it's to your advantage to deduct as many losses from your winnings as possible. To do so, you have to keep good records. In fact, the IRS requires it.

This might seem like an onerous task, but it doesn't have to be. Nor is there any reason to make it more complicated than it needs to be. You don't need a computer or a PDA (personal digital assistant), although you can use either or both if you want. Nor do you need a special software program, although, again, you can use one if you want. You can even write your own spreadsheet program to keep track if you like.

However, when it comes to keeping track of wins and losses, the KISS principle (keep it short and simple) is perfectly fine with the IRS. For this system, all you need is some discipline, a small spiral notebook, and a place to put receipts and other information. And you need to know what to keep track of.

Guidelines for Record Keeping

In 1997, the IRS issued Revenue Procedure 77-29, which details the agency's record-keeping requirements for gambling activities. It requires gamblers to maintain "an accurate diary or similar record" that contains "at least" the following information:

- Date and type of wager made
- Name of gaming establishment
- Address or location of gaming establishment
- Names of other people, if any, who were with you when you played
- Amounts you won or lost

That's not so bad, is it?

In addition to a diary or other written record, the IRS also requires that you keep supplemental records, which it defines as "W-2Gs, wagering tickets or receipts, canceled checks, credit records, bank withdrawals, and any receipts provided by the gambling establishment." This can include information the casino gathers on your play through player's club cards and at some tables that are equipped with smart card technology. All you have to do is ask casino management about getting it.

Keeping good records is the best way to avoid problems with the IRS. The best approach is to set up a record-keeping system *before* you start playing, and enter wins and losses as you incur them. If you didn't do this when you started playing, it's never too late. Backtracking is hard, and it's never 100 percent accurate, but having some records is better than none at all.

Organizing Your Info

Everyone has different record-keeping styles. The IRS really doesn't care how you do it as long as you follow their guidelines for what to include. You can keep information diary style. Here's an example of what such entries look like:

April 12. Blackjack at the Bellagio in Las Vegas. Buy in was $300. Cash out was $500. Net gain: $200. Total for day: $200

April 30: Blackjack at Caesar's. Buy in was $200. Cash out was $50. Net loss: $150.

Video poker at Caesar's. Buy in was $100. Cash out was $150. Net gain: $50. Total for day: -$100.

Total for year: $100.

Or you can set up a simple chart. Here's an example:

Date	Place	Who With?	Buy In	Cash Out	Day Total	Year Total
3/12	Caesar's	Bill	500	700	+200	+200
3/20	Bellagio	alone	250	50	-200	0
4/2	Gold Dust	Steve	700	1,000	+300	+300

In addition to your diary or log, you need to keep all your receipts and other written information in one place. The easiest way to do this is to put an envelope where you typically empty your pockets, purse, or wallet. Stick all your gambling receipts in the envelope. If the information on the receipts is a little sketchy, take a moment and jot down a few notes before you put them in the envelope. Don't figure you'll come back and do this later—you won't, and even if you do, memories fade pretty quickly.

How long do I need to keep my diaries and receipts?
Tax professionals recommend keeping all records for at least four years. If you think there's a chance that you could be audited, keep them longer.

Reporting Your Winnings

For tax purposes, the IRS lumps gamblers into two categories: recreational players and professionals. Each category reports income and deductions differently.

- **Recreational players:** Report winnings on Form 1040, page 1, line 21 (other income). Report losses on Form 1040, Schedule A, line 27 (miscellaneous deductions). Spouses who file joint returns can combine wins and losses.
- **Professional players:** The Supreme Court defines professional gamblers as individuals who "gamble with regularity, continuity and with an expectation of profit." If this describes you, you'll need to file a Form 1040 Schedule C, which details wins, losses, and expenses related to your gambling activities. You'll also have to file a Schedule SE and pay self-employment taxes. Depending on your situation, you may be required to file other schedules as well.

Self-employed individuals, regardless of occupation, can deduct such expenses as professional training, professional advice, office expenses, transportation, meals, and others. Regulations in this area frequently change; consulting a tax advisor or planner is highly recommended should you want to make a business of gambling.

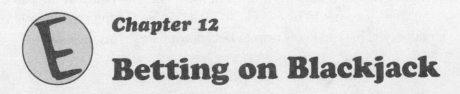

Chapter 12

Betting on Blackjack

Winning at blackjack calls for knowing basic strategy and employing it correctly. However, basic strategy knowledge and prowess are just part of the equation. Knowing how to bet, and how and when to vary the size of your bets, can mean the difference between merely winning at blackjack and winning big. Betting on blackjack well isn't all that easy. There are many different strategies—and not much agreement on the ones that work the best.

Betting on Bets

Knowing how to bet can be one of the most mystifying aspects of blackjack for new players. The intricacies of basic strategy pale in comparison. Most newbies know enough about the game to realize that sticking with minimum bets will simply keep them in the game. But being in the game isn't all when it comes to blackjack. To really derive the full pleasure out of the game, you have to know how to bet appropriately. This includes:

- Knowing when to stick to minimum bets
- Knowing when to increase minimum bets, and by how much
- Knowing when to decrease bets, and by how much

It can be extremely frustrating to watch other players vary the size of their bets on various hands when you don't know the rationales they follow for making such moves. That's right, rationales. The truth is, there isn't one single approach or method when it comes to betting on blackjack.

Why Betting Is Complex

We can predict with certainty the kinds of plays to make based on basic strategy. The formulas for these plays have been tested millions, if not billions, of times. Therefore, we're assured of them working as they should if we use them correctly. Even card counting is based on a specific set of proven, tested approaches that, when applied correctly, can result in increased returns from our bets. However, there is really no one perfect approach, no black and white, no sure thing when it comes to betting on blackjack. Because of this, a lot of betting approaches are simply that—approaches, not theories that can be subjected to scientific scrutiny.

Due to their structure, some betting systems will move players out of their comfort zone. If you're worried about betting outside your limits, you'll want to avoid the betting systems that require large variations in betting.

Betting on the Count

Many blackjack players believe that the only way you can know for sure how to bet on blackjack is by knowing when the cards are in your favor. In other words, you have to be a card counter to be a big winner.

There's some truth to this, as knowing when you're more likely to win a hand is definitely a factor in feeling confident about increasing your bet amount. But what if you don't want to learn how to count cards? Can you still come away a winner? Absolutely. There are tons of blackjack players who do just fine at the tables and don't count cards. They do use basic strategy, though, and they follow betting patterns that work for them, including:

- Never betting on hunches or gut feelings
- Using basic strategy to guide betting decisions
- Never betting more than they can afford to lose
- Setting a limit on the amount of money they will lose that day

The third and fourth points were discussed in some detail in Chapter 11, but they are both good points to review here as they are tough for many people to stick to. Setting a betting limit is one of the best betting strategies you could ask for. People who fail to set a limit on how much they'll lose during a gaming session simply pile up more losses than those who have developed this discipline and follow it.

Why do people have such a tough time with this? There are plenty of reasons. Ask your fellow players, and you're likely to hear things like this:

- "It's only money." Sure, but why lose more of it than you need to?
- "I just know the big win is right around the corner. I can feel it in my bones." Bone (or gut) feelings usually don't pan out, although they sometimes do.
- "I gotta go for the big win." Why? Many smaller wins are better than one big loss.
- "It's found money since I won it. Why not keep going?" Money is money. Regardless of how it comes to you, it has the same value.
- "Aw, I would have blown it on something else anyway." Probably so, if this is your attitude.

As you learned in Chapter 11, money management is essential to gambling success. You need to know how much money to keep in your bankroll, how much to bet, when to increase bets, and when to decrease bets. The bottom line: never bet what you can't afford to lose. The aftermath simply isn't worth it.

Demystifying Blackjack Systems

The fact that so many people have such a hard time betting on blackjack has led to the development of what are known as "blackjack systems." Sometimes you'll see them called money management systems.

About the best thing that can be said about these systems is that they make good money for the experts who develop them. Not at the tables, although they probably make money there, too, but from the people who pony up money in the hopes that the next great system will be the one that will unlock the keys to the kingdom and make them rich.

This isn't to say that these systems aren't valid. However, if they're any good, they'll be based on a set of common, basic betting theories that are free and accessible to anyone interested in them. Once you understand the logic behind them, you can decide which of the "systems," if any, you want to use. Or you can simply learn the theories that they're based on, and save your money for the tables.

ALERT!

Blackjack betting schemes do make money—for the people who sell them. While it seems as if they offer foolproof, proven approaches to maximizing your bet decisions, many of these methods don't stand up to statistical analysis. Bottom line: don't waste your money on them.

Basic Betting Strategies

When all is said and done, betting on blackjack boils down to two basic strategies:

- **Increasing your bet amounts when you are on a winning streak.** Many people take this approach on the premise (or perhaps, the hope) that the winning streak will continue.
- **Increasing your bet amounts when you are on a losing streak.** This is a favorite approach when people think, for whatever reason, that they're due for a win. It's also a favorite bet of people trying to recapture their losses in a hurry, as the payoff, when it comes, is typically very large.

Increasing bets when you're winning is known as positive progression. It's positive because you're betting more when you win. Betting systems based on positive progression require less capital and are typically used to take advantage of winning streaks. The opposite of positive progression—increasing bets on a losing streak—is called negative progression. This approach requires more money and is typically used by gamblers who are chasing their losses during a losing streak.

There are also insurance betting systems, which are designed to maximize the amount won while preserving the greatest amount of a player's bankroll as possible. As such, they are compromise, play-it-safe systems that don't require as much money as negative progression systems do, but are more expensive for your bankroll than positive progression systems.

Negative Progression Betting Systems

Negative progression betting systems call for increasing bet amounts when you're on a losing streak. This approach may seem illogical. It isn't, but the fact that it's not doesn't necessarily make these systems good choices. Played out to the bitter end, negative progression systems will pay off. However, unless the bet amounts are very small, say $1, very few people have the nerve, or the bankroll, to ride them out until the wins come.

The Martingale Betting System

Martingale betting is one of gambling's oldest known betting systems, if not the oldest. It's an extremely simple approach, developed more than 200 years ago by a man named Henry Martindale (somewhere along the line, the "d" turned into a "g," but no one knows why) for betting on even-money games such as roulette. The logic behind martingale betting goes like this: You will lose a finite number of times in a row. But you'll eventually win. Pretty simple, right?

But simplicity doesn't make the martingale system a winner. Here's why: martingale betting requires doubling your bet every time you lose. When you eventually win, the amount you win will cover everything you've lost, plus an amount equal to your original bet. It can take a lot of money to ride out those losing hands before you come up a winner. And when you do, you don't win very much.

FACT

A martingale is also a piece of riding equipment that is used to keep a horse's head in proper position. Some riders call it a tie-down, which is also how some blackjack players feel about martingale betting systems, seeing them as encumbrances more than anything else.

Here's how martingale betting works. You start with one betting unit. If you win, you put up the same bet amount. If you lose, you double your bet. Each time you lose, you double the amount of your last bet. As an example, let's say you bet $10 and you win. You are paid $10, and you get your $10 bet back, for a total of $20. Under the martingale system, you would take back your original $10 bet, and use the winnings from it to place your next bet. You win that one, too, so you follow the same procedure—take back the $10 you won, place a $10 bet on your next hand. Easy, right?

Now, let's say you lost this hand, so you're down $10. You would double your bet to $20 on the next hand. You lose this one, too. Your next bet is $40. And so on. Until you win, and you're eventually bound to win. When you do, you recover all your lost bet amounts, plus one betting unit equal to your initial wager. In other words, a profit of one betting unit.

How does the martingale put money back into your pocket? Let's look at the numbers. Say you start with a bet of $10, and you lose. What's more, you lose three more hands before you win.

First hand: Bet $10, lost.
Second hand: Bet $20, lost.
Third hand: Bet $40, lost.
Fourth hand: Bet $80, lost.

Now, at this point you've bet $150 and you haven't won a thing. Here comes the fifth hand: Bet $160, win. Yay, you've covered all your bets, and you're up $10. That's right. $10.

If this seems like a lot to go through for a measly ten bucks, you're exactly right. But let's say you didn't win that fifth hand. Instead, your losing streak continued. What's worse, it continued for another five hands. Here's what things might look like:

Fifth hand: Bet $160, lost.
Sixth hand: Bet $320, lost.
Seventh hand: Bet $640, lost.

Now you're in stratosphere land when it comes to the size of the bets you're placing. What's worse, this scenario couldn't really take place in a casino. If you were playing at a $10 minimum bet table, the maximum bet would be $1,000 (or even less). You would have to stop with your seventh hand, as your bet amount would have exceeded the table limit on the eighth hand. You'd be down a total of $1,120, with no way to recoup your losses. Ugly, right?

For the purposes of this example, pretend that this table has a limit of $10,000. So you keep going.

Eighth hand: Bet $1,280, lost.
Ninth hand: Bet $2,560, lost.
Tenth hand: Bet $5,120. Yay! You finally win.

The total amount of your bets: $5,110. You're up $10 again.

If you are set on using a negative progression system, the best way to approach it would be to set a limit for doubling your bets. If you don't go beyond $50 or $100, you're still betting more than most other players.

ALERT!

There are lots of variations on the martingale system. They all require large bankrolls, have low returns, and are very high risk due to maximum bet limits. If you run out of money or reach the house limit, you can lose a lot with no chance to recover your losses. No matter how good any of them look, or how excited a friend might be about one of them, avoid negative progression systems like the plague.

The LaBouchere System

The LaBouchere system is another negative progression system. It's sometimes called a cancellation system, but don't let that term fool you. It's just a kinder, gentler term for negative progression.

Like martingale systems, there are lots of variations on the basic LaBouchere system. In its simplest form, you write down a series of numbers. The numbers you choose don't have to be sequential, and the series can be as long or short as you want to make it. Each number represents the units you're going to bet. When you place your bet, you use the first and last of the numbers to determine what your bet size will be. If you win, you cross out these numbers. Your next bet will be the total of the next two first and last numbers in the sequence, and so on. If you lose, you add this bet amount to the end of the series, and you'd use it to determine the amount of your next bet. Kind of confusing, isn't it? Let's see how it works.

For this example, you've chosen a simple sequential series from one through six.

1   2   3   4   5   6

Your first bet will be one plus six, or seven units. You win the bet, so you cross one and six off your series. Your next bet will be a total of two and five, which is again seven units. You win that one. Cross the two and five off your list. Your third and final bet will be the total of three and four—seven again! But you lose this one, so you add seven to the remaining numbers. Your series now looks like this:

3   4   7

Your next bet would be ten units, the total of three and seven. Just for fun, let's say you lost it again. Add ten to the series, which will now look like this:

3   4   7   10

Your next bet will be thirteen units. You win this one, so you cross off the three and the ten. Your next bet, which will be your last bet since you're out of numbers after it, will be eleven units.

If you do the math, you'll see that the amount of the winning bets is greater than the losers when you eventually wipe out all the numbers in the sequence (called a coup by those who use it). This is why this system is sometimes called a cancellation system. As such, it's just like the martingale system.

Let's run the numbers, based on the previous example:

First hand: Bet seven units, won. The sequence is   2   3   4   5
Second hand: Bet seven units, won. The sequence is   3   4
Third hand: Bet seven units, lost. The sequence is   3   4   7
Fourth hand: Bet ten units, lost. The sequence is   3   4   7   10
Fifth hand: Bet thirteen units, won. The sequence is   4   7
Sixth hand: Bet eleven units, won. You're done with this series of numbers.

You've made a total of six bets for fifty-five units. Of these, you won four bets for a total of thirty-eight units. You lost two bets for a total of seventeen units. You're up twenty-one units. (Which is $21 if we assume your betting units are $1.) Let's compare this to playing six hands of blackjack where you simply bet $10 a hand. You win four hands for $40. You lose two hands for $20. Your net winnings are $20, $1 less than if you used the LaBouchere system.

Let's take another look at this system, using a different series.

1   1   1   2   2   3

Let's say you lost your first bet. You would then add four to the end of the series, which now looks like this:

1   1   1   2   2   3   4

Your next bet will be five units. You lose this one, too. Add five to the end of the series.

1   1   1   2   2   3   4   5

Your next bet will be six units. Dang, you lose this one, too. Add six to the end of the series.

1   1   1   2   2   3   4   5   6

Your next bet will be seven units. You win this one. Subtract one and six from the series. From here, let's suppose you win every following hand. Here's what the progression will look like:

1	1	2	2	3	4	5	= six units bet
1	2	2	3	4	= five units bet		
2	2	3	= five units bet				
2	= two units bet.						

Total units bet: forty. Total units won: twenty-five. Total units lost: fifteen. Net win: ten units.

ALERT!

Unless you're very good at keeping track of number sequences in your head, the LaBouchere system calls for writing down these sequences. Many casinos will not allow players to watch the cards, bet, and write things down at the table. Try it, and you may be asked to leave in a very unceremonious manner.

Again, let's compare this sequence to simply betting $10 a hand for eight hands. The won/lost ratio of 5:3 is the same. You win five hands for a total of $50. You lose three hands for a total of $30. Your net win: $20. The bottom line with this system: when you complete a series, you'll see a profit. However, like the martingale system, you could end up betting large sums of money before you do.

The D'Alembert System

This system is a hybrid of two betting systems—negative progression and insurance—that was invented by Jean le Rond d'Alembert. He theorized (wrongly, it turned out) that if a fairly tossed coin landed heads-up time after time, tails was increasingly more probable.

Following the d'Alembert system calls for raising bet amounts by one unit after each losing bet, and lowering them one unit after each winning bet. As an example, let's say you placed an opening bet of one unit and you lost. Your next bet is two units. You win that one, so you drop the units bet back to one. You bet one, and lose this hand, so you double your bet for the next hand. And so on.

Positive Progression Betting Systems

Had enough of the negative progression systems? Let's take a walk on the positive side instead. But take the term "positive" with a grain of salt. Some of these betting systems aren't any better than what you've just learned about.

The Paroli System

This betting system is the opposite of the martingale system. You start with one bet and increase the amount of the bet when you win instead of when you lose. To make this system effective, you have to decide how big you'll let the bet build before you take it down to the initial starting point, and how much you'll raise after each win. This will depend on the game you're playing and the odds of the bet.

This system doesn't require a large bankroll. It is a "let it ride" system, as it lets profits run and cuts short losses. Let's see how it works. You bet

$10. You win, and you let the win ride, so your next bet is $20. You win this hand. You let this win ride, too, so your next bet is $40. Whoohoo! Another winner. Let it ride again, and your next bet is $80. Whoops. You lost. You go back to your original starting point of $10 to minimize your losses. You lose this hand, too, so you put up another $10. You win this hand, and you let your winnings ride for the next hand. You win this one too. This time you get blackjack. Let's see how the money looks:

Hand 1: Bet $10, won. Let $20 ride to next hand.
Hand 2: Bet $20, won. Let $40 ride to next hand.
Hand 3: Bet $40, won. Let $80 ride to the next hand.
Hand 4: Bet $80, lose. Take bet amount back to $10.
Hand 5: Bet $10, lose. Keep bet amount at $10.
Hand 6: Bet $10, win. Let $20 ride to next hand.
Hand 7: Bet $20, blackjack. Pays off at 3:2.

Now for the math on this example:

Hand 1: You win $10, you are up $10.
Hand 2: You win $20, you are up $30 ($10 + $20).
Hand 3: You win $40, you are up $70 ($10 + $20 + $40).
Hand 4: You lose $80, you are down $10 ($70 - $80).
Hand 5: You lose $10, you are down $20 (-$10 + -$10).
Hand 6: You win $10, you are down $10 (-$20 + $10).
Hand 7: You win $30 on a $20 blackjack, you are up $20 (-$10 + $30).

Total win: $20. How would things compare if you simply bet $10 on each of these hands? Let's see:

Hand 1: Win. Up $10.
Hand 2: Win. Up $20.
Hand 3: Win. Up $30.
Hand 4: Lose. Up $20.
Hand 5: Lose. Up $10.
Hand 6: Win. Up $20.
Hand 7: BJ Win. Up $35.

Total win: $35. This demonstrates that systems are not always the best bet.

The Parlay System

Parlay betting is similar to paroli systems, as it pyramids your wins. Here's how it works: You make a bet of the amount of your choice. If you win, you reinvest the winnings on your next bet. If you lose, you drop back to your original bet level.

The 1-3-2-6 System

The name of this positive progression system describes its betting pattern. It's based on the premise that you can win four times in a row. Here's how it works: Your initial bet is one unit. If you win, you let your winnings ride, and you add another unit to what you have for a total of three units bet. If you win again, you decrease the units bet to two. If this bet wins, you add four units to the bet. If this bet wins, you take everything off the table and start all over again.

Let's do a real-money analysis of this system. For the purposes of this analysis, and to keep things easy to understand, we're going to suppose that you win four hands in a row (the chances of this happening, by the way, even in a best-case scenario, are 1:16):

Hand 1: You win a $10 hand, you're up $10.
Hand 2: You win a $30 hand, you're up $40 ($10 + $30).
Hand 3: You win a $20 hand, you're up $60 ($10 + $30 + $20).
Hand 4: You win a $60 hand, you're up $120 ($10 + $30 + $20 + $60).

At this point, you take everything down and start over again. Now, let's compare the 1-3-2-6 system to simply letting your wins ride.

Hand 1: $10 bet, win. Up $10.
Hand 2: $20 bet, win. Up $30 ($10 + $20).
Hand 3: $40 bet, win. Up $70 ($10 + $20 + $40).
Hand 4: $80 bet, win. Up $150 ($10 + $20 + $40 + $80).

Your investment is the original $10. Your profit is $150.

Two-Level Progressive Betting

This is a simple system, yet very effective. All you have to do is decide what you want your minimum and maximum bets to be. You'll bet the smaller amount after you lose and larger amount after you win. As an example, let's say your minimum bet is $10 and your maximum bet is $20. You win your first bet, so your next bet will be $20. You'll keep on betting $20 a hand until you lose. When you lose a hand, you go back to your minimum bet of $10.

The Tom Hagen Betting System

Finally, we present the Tom Hagen Betting System. This is a combination negative/positive progression system that calls for decreasing wagers on a losing streak and increasing bets on a winning streak. It also sets a bet limit, so you know in advance how much you're going to spend. Ready? Let's go.

Start with a set buy-in. For the purposes of this example, we'll start with $100. Place a wager equal to 20 percent of your stack. In this case, that would be $20. On winning hands, press your bet by one-half the bet amount. In this case, your next bet would be $30. On losing hands, reevaluate your stack and place a bet of 20 percent of the stack. In this case, let's say you lost the first hand. You would have $80 left. Twenty percent of that is $16; round this amount and place a $15 bet. Continue on, following the basic formula: After a winning bet, up your wager by 50 percent. After a losing bet, wager 20 percent of your stack.

The advantage to the Tom Hagen system is that your wager gets smaller and smaller on a losing streak, making it hard for you to get beat out. If you're on a winning streak, your bets continually increase so you can take advantage of your luck. The disadvantage is obvious. It takes a lot of practice and math skill at the tables. However, if you have basic strategy down cold and you don't have to think about how you're going to play your hand, it can be fun to figure out what your bet should be. The other disadvantage: your bets will often go over the limit at which you'll be watched and evaluated as a possible counter. This can be upsetting or make you uncomfortable if you aren't accustomed to it.

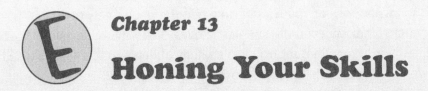

Chapter 13

Honing Your Skills

With anything you learn that tests your skills, you get better at it the more you do it. The same is true for blackjack. People who get to be experts at gaming spend lots of time at it, both in casinos and away from them. This one factor can make a big difference between being a so-so player and getting really good. Plus, it can help you get better fast.

Why Practice Is Important

There are lots of ways to hone your skills and get better at blackjack, and one very good reason for doing so: it's the best way to insure your success at the tables! When you're new to the game, you don't know enough about it, nor have you played it enough, for moves to come naturally to you. You'll often wonder what you should do when the dealer gets to you. Your mind can go blank on even the simplest moves. You'll make decisions based on what you remember about basic strategy, then second-guess yourself and wonder if you made the right moves.

This is all fine, and to be expected, especially when you're just starting out. But many players never get beyond this level. They either don't play the game often enough for it to become familiar to them, or they do play it but they don't think it's necessary to hone their skills at it. As a result, they never get very good at the game, they never get as good at it as they could, and they probably don't derive as much enjoyment from playing it as they could.

FACT

People might disagree on lots of points when it comes to playing blackjack, but good players never disagree on the importance of practice. Of all the things you do as a player, it is the one strategy that is guaranteed to make you a better player. What's more, it's the easiest thing you can do.

Practice is important for more skilled players, too. After you've played for a while, it's easy to become complacent about basic strategy, and to think you have it mastered. You might. Then again, you might not. Many players do very well with the aspects of basic strategy that they encounter most often, but they get tripped up by some of the more obscure situations. Because of this, they make simple mistakes that they could easily avoid if they only spent some time practicing the game.

Some people simply find it hard to memorize basic strategy charts, grids, or lists. It's a lot of information to process, and they'll only take it so far before they decide they know enough to not make complete idiots of themselves when they play. They might bring basic strategy charts to the tables with them. Many are too embarrassed to do so and will instead rely on what they were able to commit to memory.

Have you ever watched a really good blackjack player, someone who awes you with his knowledge and playing ability? If so, know that this individual might be a little smarter than you, maybe a little better able to memorize charts and plays. Then again, he might be less capable in both areas. But it's a good bet—in fact, a sure bet—that he has spent hours practicing his plays, drilling himself on hands that don't come easily to him, making sure he knows the correct strategy play for every possible situation. What's more, he'll keep doing it for as long as he wants to maintain his winning edge.

Are you convinced that practice is important? Good. Now let's look at where you are as a player, and the areas in which you could improve your game.

QUESTION?

How often should I do blackjack drills or practices?
It's a very good idea to do daily drills if you're serious about getting good at blackjack. At a minimum, set some time aside one day a week for blackjack practice. Don't let too much time go by between practice sessions. Doing so increases the chances of your forgetting many of the more finite aspects of the game.

Basic Skills Assessment

To get a better idea of where you are as a player, let's start with a quiz. Your answers will help you get a better idea of what you need to practice or better memorize. Try to answer the following questions without looking at other chapters, using a basic strategy card, or checking the answers, which come after the quiz. Ready? Let's go.

1. You should always stand on 15s and 16s when the dealer shows a 7.
   a. True
   b. False

2. When you have a 16, you should surrender against a face card.
   a. True
   b. False

3. Basic strategy calls for doubling down on a 10 against a dealer's 10.
   a. True
   b. False

4. You should never double on a hard 12.
   a. True
   b. False

5. A smart player always takes even money.
   a. True
   b. False

6. You hold a hard 12 into the dealer's 3. Do you:
   a. Stand
   b. Hit
   c. Surrender

7. You hold an 11 into the dealer's ace. Do you:
   a. Stand
   b. Hit
   c. Double Down

8. You hold a pair of 8s into the dealer's face card. Do you:
   a. Stand
   b. Hit
   c. Split

9. You hold a soft 18 into a dealer's 9. Do you:
   a. Stand
   b. Hit
   c. Double Down

10. You hold a hard 9 into the dealer's 7. Do you:
    a. Stand
    b. Hit
    c. Double Down

11. It is best to split 5s:
    a. Against the dealer's 3 through 6
    b. Never
    c. Always

12. It is best to double down on a soft 17:
    a. Against the dealer's 3 through 6
    b. Against the dealer's 2 through 7
    c. Always
    d. Never

13. You are playing a six-deck shoe. It is best to split 9s:
    a. Against the dealer's 3 through 6
    b. Against the dealer's 2 through 9, except for 7
    c. Never

14. You are allowed to double after a split. You have a pair of 6s and the dealer is showing a 2. Do you:
    a. Stand
    b. Hit
    c. Split

15. You are playing on a shoe that allows doubling after a split. You have a pair of 4s and the dealer is showing a 4. Do you:
    a. Hit
    b. Double Down
    c. Split

Quiz answers:

1. (b) False. You hit both.
2. (a) True
3. (b) False
4. (a) True
5. (b) False
6. (b) Hit
7. (b) Hit
8. (c) Split
9. (b) Hit
10. (b) Hit
11. (b) Never
12. (a) Against the dealer's 3 through 6
13. (b) Against the dealer's 2 through 9, except for 7
14. (c) Split
15. (a) Hit

If you answered any of these questions wrong, you definitely need to practice, practice, practice!

Now that you've got a better idea of where you are when it comes to your knowledge of basic strategy, it's time to look at ways to make your play better. The most popular approaches fall into four basic categories:

- Writing drills
- Playing drills
- Flash card drills
- Computer or hand-held game drills

Which approach is the right one for you? It depends on how you learn the best. Some people retain information better when they write it down, others are more visual and do well with flash card drills. For some players, seeing and touching the cards is the key. Many players use a combination of approaches, which is a good idea as it doesn't tie you into any one of them. You might not always have a computer or hand-held device with you, but you can almost always pack a deck of cards or write up a simple chart.

Putting It in Writing

One of the easiest ways to improve your basic strategy knowledge is simply to copy every basic strategy chart over and over again. Repetition is the key to this approach. However, it doesn't work to just *read* the charts. You have to take the time to write them down.

When you first start doing this drill, you'll probably find that you need to refer to the basic strategy charts in order to get through it. You'll find them, and a blank chart for this exercise, in Appendix B. After you write them down a few times, try to do this drill from memory. Just use the charts to check your answers.

Basic Strategy Test

This is a test you can do just about anywhere you are as long as you have a piece of paper and something to write with. Simply write down the basic strategy rules. You can do them in any order you wish. Here's one you might like to follow:

- Hit or stand hard hands
- Hit or stand soft hands
- Rules for splitting pairs
- Rules for doubling down
- Rules for surrender

When you're done, check your answers against the basic strategy charts in Appendix B.

Build Your Own Quiz

You can use the same quiz format used earlier in the chapter to design your own tests, based on various conditions and variables. This is a great way to proof your game if you are planning to play under a different set of rules than you're accustomed to, such as at Atlantic City when you're used to playing on the Las Vegas strip.

As an example, let's say you're planning to play single-deck blackjack in a casino in downtown Las Vegas. You've researched the rules, which are as follows: dealer hits on soft 17, dealer checks for blackjack when dealt 10 or ace, splits are allowed three times per game for a total of four hands, aces only split once, each ace only gets one additional card, double down permitted on first two cards, can double down after splitting, late surrender is offered.

FACT

Practicing and drills may sound tedious, but they are the best way to hone your skills at anything you do. Professional card players spend hours doing these drills on the way up, and they don't stop when they reach professional level.

You then formulate a set of questions based on these variables, such as:

- You're dealt 7, 7. The dealer is showing a 10. What would you do? (Surrender.)
- You get an ace, 3 against a dealer's 3. What would you do? (Hit.)
- You get a 4, 4 against the dealer's 6. What do you do? (Split, since casino offers it. If it didn't, you'd double.)
- You have a soft 17 into the dealer's 7. What do you do? (Hit.)
- You have a hard 10 in the dealer's ace. What do you do? (Hit.)
- You have a soft 18 into the dealer's 3. What do you do? (Double.)
- You have a pair of 9s into the dealer's 9. What do you do? (Split).
- You have a pair of kings into the dealer's 5. What do you do? (Stand.)

And so on.

When you build your own quiz, be sure to use the rules that are going to govern play at the casino where you plan to play, and apply the appropriate strategies for the situation.

Deal Yourself In

Playing lots of real blackjack hands is another extremely effective basic strategy drill, and another very easy one to do. All you have to do is deal yourself hands of cards and make a decision about what to do in each case. Compare your plays to a basic strategy chart to make sure you're right. This also helps you get used to looking at the cards as you're making decisions, which is a little more concrete than just recalling numbers from memory.

Basic Strategy Deck Drill

This drill calls for a single deck of cards. First, choose a card from the deck as the dealer's up card. It can be any card. Put it face up in front of you. Next, start dealing yourself two-card hands from the deck. Decide what to do for each hand (use your basic strategy charts for this if you have to), based on the dealer's up card. The only cards that change are yours—the dealer's card remains the same throughout this drill. Do not play out the dealer's hand—just play yours.

Deal yourself new hands until you reach the end of the deck. Then shuffle the deck, pick a new up card, and do the drill over again. To maximize the effectiveness of this drill, pick dealer up cards that you have problems making decisions against.

Need to practice soft hands? Deal yourself an A-2. Give the dealer an up card, and play out the hand. When you're done with that hand, give the dealer a new up card, and do it over again. When you're done with the A-2, give yourself an A-3. Keep going until you've run through every soft hand.

Another Basic Strategy Drill

There can't ever be enough basic strategy drills. This drill is a little more complex than the previous one. You're again using a single deck. However, with this drill you're playing against a different up card for each player hand. Deal three cards at a time—the dealer's up card and your two-card hand. Proceed as before, again making your decisions based on basic strategy.

This is a great drill for working on various aspects of basic strategy, as it can be modified for practicing such player options as splitting and double down. As an example, let's say you're having trouble with certain pair splits, such as 4s, 6s, and 7s. Take those cards out of another deck, and load your drill deck with them. Or let's say you're shaky on doubling on certain dealer up cards. Load the deck with those cards.

Flash Cards

Flash cards might remind you of learning multiplication tables when you were in grade school, and may seem incredibly dorky because of that. However, they're an excellent way to learn basic skills, and an excellent way to learn basic strategy.

Flash cards can be used for any and every playing situation. Some people use them for learning every aspect of basic strategy. Others limit them to player options or drilling on less common moves or borderline hands. You can buy ready-made flash cards, but they're very easy to make yourself, so why not save your money for gaming instead?

All you need is some lightweight cardboard or poster board. Office supply stores usually carry these. So do hobby stores and some drug stores. A deck of index cards works fine. Use something that can stand up to some abuse, as you should use your flash cards regularly. Write down each hand on one side of a card (include both the dealer's up card and the cards in your hand). On the back of each card, write down the correct play for that hand. Then run through your cards, reciting the correct basic strategy for each hand.

Putting every possible hand on flash cards will result in more than 300 cards. If you don't want to make that many, simply write in a possible hand on the front of each card (not including the dealer's up card), and write the basic strategy for it on the reverse. As an example:

On the front of the card: 10-4
On the back of the card: Stand on 2 through 6, hit on 7 through ace.

Another option would be to just make cards for the plays that cause you the most problems. Flash cards are a great portable training aid. Make them small enough, and you can slip them into your pocket or wallet for an impromptu drill session when you're waiting in line at the bank, or at the drive-up window at a fast-food joint.

Computer-Based or Hand-Held Game Drills

Surf the Internet a bit and you'll see tons of blackjack training and drill programs that you can play online or download to your computer or hand-held device. Some are free or available for a slight fee; many others aren't. Some are game simulation drills, others are flash card drills. There are so many game simulations, drills, and game programs available that it's impossible to recap them all here. The following list is just a sample of what's out there and, in our opinion, worth checking out:

- *www.hitorstand.net*. This program is geared toward teaching players to make moves based on the highest probability of success, and shows correct moves when you make wrong ones. Scores are determined by the number of correct moves made, not on the amount of money won. You can choose between two levels of difficulty.

- *www.blackjackinfo.com*. There's a super blackjack strategy trainer at this site that lets you choose the parameters of the game. Enter the number of decks and the playing rules, and you're good to go. You can also choose to use the strategy coach if you wish. If you do, a pop-up screen will display the correct strategy when you make a wrong move. The trainer also keeps track of hand values for both player and dealer, money won and lost, cards dealt, and hands played. And the site contains a blackjack basic strategy engine that will calculate basic strategy charts tailored to any set of blackjack rules.

- *www.bju21.com*. This is a bare-bones site, but don't let the lack of bells and whistles mislead you—there is some great stuff here, including free basic strategy and counting drills, a basic strategy engine for generating charts, and casino reports, which recap rules of play at casinos in the United States and abroad.

- *www.qfit.com*. This site offers for purchase the highly rated Casino Verite blackjack game simulation software and trainers for card counters and shuffle trackers. Free demo downloads, which aren't fully functional, are available. Also free at this site are calculators that compare counting strategies, a basic strategy advantage calculator, and an outcome calculator.

- *www.deepnettech.com.* This site offers blackjack training and counting shareware developed by DeepNet Technologies for several platforms—Windows, Palm OS, and PocketPC. All programs can be downloaded to your computer or handheld device and are fully functional. You'll be reminded to register (and pay the shareware fee) until you purchase a registration code, and the program or programs you download will occasionally reset to default mode until you ante up some dough.

ALERT!

Be sure to test drive any blackjack game simulation or training software before you buy it. Some of it is definitely better than others. Many Web sites that offer this software will let you download demo versions. They might not be fully functional, but you'll be able to do enough with them to get a general idea of how they work.

You can also use your computer to hone your skills by playing for free at online gaming sites. Just about all of the top sites offer free play. Some of the game setups are better than others, but they'll all let you practice your skills in conditions that are pretty close to what you'll encounter in casinos.

Chapter 14

Welcome to the Casino

With their bright lights, whoops of excitement, and seemingly non-stop ka-chings of silver coins and tokens hitting pay drawers, there's virtually nothing that comes anywhere near close to the excitement of live casino gambling. In this chapter, we will tell you what you need to know so you can play blackjack—or any other game—in a casino, and feel comfortable as you do.

The Lay of the Land

Casinos are, first and foremost, places for gamblers to gamble. While casinos come in all shapes and sizes and offer all sorts of things to delight and dazzle the senses, none of them varies one bit from a casino's basic purpose, which is making money for its owners through gaming. Yes, you will find entertainment at many of them. Most serve drinks and food. But anything a casino offers in addition to gambling is secondary to its main function.

There are thousands of casinos around the world, and it would take much more room than we have here to cover all of them. For this reason, the information you'll find in this chapter primarily applies to casinos in the United States.

If you're thinking about playing at casinos outside of the United States, know that many of the basics, such as what casinos look like, their personnel, how they're laid out, and the games they offer, are very much the same the world over. However, it is always a good idea to check the local rules and regulations regarding the games you want to play. This way you'll know what to anticipate, and know whether the local rules are favorable for blackjack.

While specific layouts will vary somewhat, all casinos are designed to tantalize and tempt gamblers by leading them past as many gambling opportunities as possible. For this reason, no casino is laid out in a strictly linear fashion. Stay in one of Las Vegas's billion-dollar megasized gaming complexes, for example, and you'll typically have to traverse the casino to get anywhere you want to go—your room, the pool, restaurants, show rooms, etc.

In fact, casino floor plans can seem a bit mazelike, with no obvious exits. It's easy to go around in circles in almost all of them. Sometimes it's just easier to stop for a moment, take a break, and drop a few coins into the nearest slot machine. That's exactly what the people who run casinos want you to do. They'd rather you didn't leave. They want you to stay and play.

FACT

Two things you generally won't see in casinos are clocks and windows. Both can distract players from doing what casino owners want them to do, and what players come to casinos to do—gamble. Most casinos minimize distractions around gaming tables by locating noisier games, such as slot machines, a certain distance away from them.

Unless local or state laws prohibit it, casinos typically offer three forms of gaming:

- **Slot machines.** They're the biggest moneymakers in the casino industry, as it takes no skill whatsoever to play them, and you can play them at your own speed. All you're doing is betting that a computer inside the machine will spit out a winning combination at the exact moment you hit the spin button or pull the lever.
- **A variety of table games.** The most popular casino games are blackjack, craps, roulette, and baccarat. Other table games include pai gow, pai gow poker, Caribbean Stud Poker, and blackjack variation games.
- **Race and sports books**, where gamblers can place bets on their favorite sporting events and races.

The Blackjack Pit

Most casinos set aside a specific area for table games. You'll find that many of the tables in this area are blackjack tables, which reflects the game's popularity.

The area in which blackjack tables are organized is called a blackjack pit. Each pit typically consists of at least four tables grouped in a circle. The dealers and other pit personnel stand in the center of the circle. In big casinos, blackjack pits can be quite large, and look more like two rows of tables than a circle, or even an oval. If you look closely, however, they'll still approximate a circle, albeit a long, skinny one. You won't ever see just a single row of blackjack tables. This arrangement leaves the backs of the tables exposed and creates security risks for casino personnel and players. Grouping gaming tables together makes it easier for casino management to keep an eye on the action at those tables—both the dealers' and the players'.

In the Pit

Blackjack tables are staffed by a group of employees who know the ins and outs of the game. Some are hourly employees, others are salaried managers, but they all work together for a common purpose: to keep play going as it should at the blackjack tables. The table games manager is the highest pit employee. He or she is ultimately responsible for everything, from games selection to gaming numbers to overall pit operations.

Shift bosses, assistant shift bosses, and pit bosses are also stationed inside each cluster of tables. They typically wear suits and ties instead of uniforms, which makes them fairly easy to identify as management. Shift bosses are in charge of everything that goes on in the pit during their shifts. They supervise play and attend to tasks that dealers aren't authorized to handle, such as rating players and determining comps. Depending on the size of the pit, there might be several assistant shift bosses or none at all.

ALERT!

Casino personnel follow a well-defined chain of command and fairly rigid procedures. The casino sets them, and they aren't often apparent or known to players. For this reason, it's a good idea to focus your interactions on the dealer and ignore the other personnel who might be in the pit. Even if you think a situation merits a pit boss's attention, it is exceedingly bad form to call one to the table yourself, and you'll probably be ignored should you try to do so. Always talk to the dealer first.

Pit bosses handle the action in individual pits. Depending on the size of the casino, they could be responsible for a few tables up to a couple of dozen. This group of individuals bears no hands-on responsibility for your play at the tables. For this reason, they typically keep to the background, although they'll sometimes come over to the tables to chat with players, or to monitor or discourage suspicious or inappropriate behavior. The following are just a few of the situations that merit a pit boss's attention:

- Cash or credit transactions over a certain amount
- Irregularities such as dropped or bent cards or a dropped chip
- Player complaints
- Player unruliness

You'll find a dealer behind every blackjack table. They're easily identified, as they are required to wear uniforms and name badges. These casino employees serve as the host and conductor of the game. They exchange all money, handle all equipment (cards, chips, shoes, etc.), ensure fair play according to local rules and procedures, and help customers feel welcome and comfortable.

You may notice that dealers clap their hands and turn them palms up when they leave the table. Why is this? It's a casino tradition, done to show management that dealers aren't concealing chips when they leave their tables. Watch dealers at work, and you'll notice that they refrain from doing seemingly innocent things like tucking in their shirts, straightening their ties, tying their shoes, or adjusting their collars, all of which could disguise a quick chip drop.

Dealers also provide a certain level of assistance to players, depending on what the casino feels is appropriate. They help set the table's ambiance (or lack thereof), and are on the front line in case of a confrontation.

FACT

In gambling's early days, dealers almost always wore short-sleeved or half-sleeve shirts. This kept their forearms bare so players and management could see that they had "nothing up their sleeves." In today's casinos, advanced security systems replace short-sleeve shirts as a theft deterrent.

You'll also see other individuals working away in the pits. Floormen are the soldiers of pit management, and do most of the work at the tables. There are also boxmen, who supervise the action at craps tables, and pit clerks, who assist pit personnel on things like entering customer ratings, customer credit, table fills and so on into the casino's computers. Depending on the size of the casino, you can find people working any or all of these positions at any time, day or night.

More senior members of casino management, such as floor managers or even the casino's general manager, occasionally stop by blackjack pits. Most often, they're simply observing play. Sometimes they want to welcome a special guest at a table. Other times they just like to gauge the atmosphere in the casino. As they do, they might engage in a little informal fact-finding by chatting with players.

Outside the Pit

There are hoards of casino personnel whose jobs are corollary to the blackjack pits. Some you'll come into contact with on a fairly regular basis. Others you'll just see if you play certain games, or as they go about performing their normal duties. Many of them, like slot machine attendants and runners, work the casino floor. Others, like shift bosses and credit managers, are behind-the-scenes players.

The wait staff serve players' needs outside of the pit. Most often, they're women, and they go about offering complimentary beverages to players who are actively playing. If you're not one of them, it goes against casino etiquette to cadge a free drink. Go to the bar and buy one instead.

Security people are responsible for keeping casinos safe for players and personnel. It's best to let them go about their jobs undisturbed. It's okay to ask casino security people for directions to a restaurant, but avoid prolonged conversations that could keep security personnel away from their duties.

Cashiers usually can be found in an area somewhat aside from the main action behind caged areas. They handle transactions such as making change for playing slots and cashing in chips won at gaming tables.

Most of the time, the security staff keeps an eye on the casino's general security by roaming the casino's playing areas. They don't spend much time at the tables, but you will see them if a large amount of money is coming to or exiting a table. They'll also appear if there is suspicious activity at a table.

One time when you'll often see security people at gaming tables is when they're being set up to open. Opening a table involves a procedure that is about as involved as a Japanese tea ceremony, and almost as deeply steeped in tradition. As such, it's virtually the same in every casino. It takes two to four people to open a blackjack table. At a minimum, a dealer and a pit boss must be present. Depending on the casino, the procedure might also be monitored by a supervisor and a security person.

There is no real reason for the rituals surrounding table openings beyond the fact that casinos have well-established rules and procedures for virtually everything that happens within their confines. Having set procedures for setting up and opening tables ensures that they're done the same way every time. In the swirl of activity that is a casino, it is easiest to pick out that which does not belong. If everyone handles things the same way all the time, pit bosses and other personnel know that everything is all right. If it is different, something's wrong.

QUESTION?

How do I meet a casino host?
There are two good ways to do this: by phone prior to arriving at the casino, or when you check in. Just introduce yourself and tell the host something about yourself—the kinds of games you like to play, what your betting levels are, and so on. If you're booking a room at a casino hotel, ask about the qualifications for casino rate, which can knock anywhere from 25 to 50 percent off the hotel's standard room rate.

Of all the people who compose a casino's management team, casino hosts are the ones you're most likely to interact with on a regular basis. Aside from dealers, they're the most visible and accessible casino employees. Casino hosts work to keep players happy. While you'll most often hear about the special privileges they bestow on high rollers, the reality is that casino hosts are responsible for cultivating relationships with all players, regardless of playing level. The high roller of tomorrow could very well be the nickel slot player of today, and casino hosts are well aware of it. It is a very good idea to get to know the casino hosts where you play. Establishing relationships with these individuals is the pathway to comps, which can save you money on things like meals, show tickets, and accommodations.

Types of Casinos

While all casinos share certain common aspects, they vary significantly in many ways. They can be big or little, located in major metropolitan cities or on Indian reservations far off the beaten path. You'll find them on riverboats in some parts of the country. Take a cruise and there's a good chance you'll find a casino on board.

Some casinos have gaming rules and regulations that give players a pretty decent chance. Others might not offer such favorable conditions. Blackjack rules, in particular, can vary enormously from place to place. You'll find more detail on this in Chapter 15.

Different Casinos, Different Personalities

Like people, casinos have different personalities. Even casinos owned by the same company will vary somewhat in their look and feel. They will offer different payouts, promotions, and comps. Certain amenities will vary by location and will often reflect the part of the country in which the casino is located.

Why do casinos vary so much? Part of it has to do with the casino's ownership. The gaming industry is extremely competitive, and the companies that own and run casinos are always looking for ways to entice players to their establishments. They also work extremely hard to develop loyal patrons who will come back again and again. The other reason why casinos vary so much has very little to do with casino ownership and everything to do with where they are located. Many of the day-to-day aspects of casino operations are dictated by the laws in place where the casino is located. For this reason, playing blackjack on a riverboat in Louisiana can be a very different experience than sitting down at a table on the Las Vegas strip.

The States and Casinos

Gaming is one of the most highly regulated industries in the United States, and it is the states themselves that hold the cards (pardon the pun). Each state that allows gambling—which is just about every state in the United States—has laws in place that govern what can happen in gaming establishments. Casinos must follow these laws. If they don't, they can lose their gaming licenses.

The desire to stay in compliance with state laws governs virtually every aspect of casino operations. Casinos must comply with state-legislated accounting procedures and other requirements as dictated by voters and politicians. Some states restrict casinos to specific geographic locations—in Mississippi, for example, gaming is only allowed in counties bordering the Gulf Coast, or that have navigable waters of the Mississippi River or its tributaries running through them. South Dakota voters approved limited casino gambling in Deadwood in 1989. Apart from Indian casinos, it's the only place in the state that permits gambling. Deadwood casinos must offer a second business, such as restaurants, taverns, or gift and craft stores. Other states prohibit certain games. California, for example, doesn't allow roulette wheels in its casinos.

FACT

It's no secret that the "Mob" played a big role in Las Vegas's history, but it no longer does. As gaming became big business, laws were passed that gradually squeezed out the crime families and put organized gambling into the hands of major corporations. This isn't to say that crime doesn't still happen, but it's by no means as widespread as it was in the early days of legalized gambling, and it's typically not well organized.

Comparing the Casinos

With casinos in forty-eight states, and many different types of casinos to choose from, there will be a place somewhere to match your needs and expectations. However, it can take some time to sort through them all. You want to choose venues that offer the best value for your money, and, hopefully, have rules and regulations that are player friendly.

It's also a good idea to gamble at establishments that suit your personality and gambling style. Some players love the glitz and glamour of places like Las Vegas and can't imagine playing anywhere else. Others prefer more intimate, homey places. For some gamblers, convenience is a big factor. Other players save up for gambling vacations and choose exotic destinations that offer much more than gaming.

What's right for you? While we obviously can't make specific suggestions, we can help you decide by running down the kinds of casinos you'll find in the United States.

Big-Time Casinos

Two cities in the United States—Las Vegas and Atlantic City—are home to the kind of gaming establishments that most people picture when they think of gambling. Both cities are legendary gaming destinations, and they have lots to offer to all gamblers, regardless of playing level or ability.

Gaming Las Vegas Style

For a long time—since 1931, in fact—Nevada was the only place in the United States where you could legally gamble. Gaming here began on Fremont Street in Las Vegas and was initially limited to a three-block section of the street. In the early 1940s, California hotelier Thomas Hull decided to build a hotel in Las Vegas. His vision required more room than he could get on Fremont Street, so he built his hotel on the Las Vegas Strip, just outside city limits. Hull's El Rancho Vegas was the first resort hotel in Las Vegas, and served as the anchor for the city's resort hotel industry.

Today, there is nothing to match what awaits gamblers in Las Vegas. No other gaming destination can even come close. Resort hotels are now entertainment mega-resorts that offer fun and excitement for the entire family. While gambling is still the city's major draw, there is a lot to do when you're away from the tables. You can eat at fine restaurants or expansive buffets. You can shop at stores that rival the best that Beverly Hills has to offer. If you want to keep in shape, there are swimming pools, tennis courts, golf courses, and gyms. Want to see a live show? Some of the entertainment industry's most illustrious names regularly play Las Vegas. Some call it home.

One of the biggest mistakes you can make in gaming is playing a game you don't know. Doing so not only puts your bankroll in jeopardy, it also gives you a bad first taste of a game that you might enjoy if you knew how to play it. You can avoid both by taking advantage of the free lessons that many casinos offer. Some resort casinos even broadcast gaming lessons over closed-circuit television, so you can learn how to play from the comfort of your room.

The sheer size of Las Vegas's gaming industry has its benefits and drawbacks. If you like variety, Las Vegas is definitely the place for you. While the city is noted for its huge gaming complexes, there are smaller places to play as well. You can stay on the Strip, or venture downtown where some of the city's oldest gaming establishments are still in business. With so much competition, if you don't like one casino, it's an easy matter to find one that you do. But competition can also work against you. There are lots of great deals to be had in Las Vegas, though some of them aren't so great when you read the fine print.

Atlantic City Style

Casinos in Atlantic City are very similar to what you'll find in Las Vegas. Compare the two areas, however, and Atlantic City looks a little wimpy. That's the way legislators and voters want it.

Voters in New Jersey approved casino gambling in 1976 as a measure to improve the economies in Atlantic and Cape May counties—at the time, the two poorest counties in the state. A previous attempt at passing legislation on a statewide basis failed. But when supporters of the measure limited the referendum to Atlantic City only, it passed. Resorts International opened the first casino after the new laws passed. The company bought the Chalfonte-Haddon Hall Hotel, located on the historic Atlantic City Boardwalk, and mounted a $77-million renovation project. When it opened in 1978, it was a resounding success. Other well-known casino companies, such as Caesars, Bally's, Sands, and Harrah's followed. Hugh Hefner's Playboy empire owned and operated an Atlantic City casino for a while, but lost its casino license. Today, Donald Trump, who bought the former Playboy casino, is a key player in the Atlantic City casino scene.

Atlantic City is the second-largest gaming market in the United States. It has much of the glitz and glamour of Las Vegas, but not at anywhere near as high a level, mostly because it is so heavily regulated. It's a top-destination resort for people on the East Coast, largely due to its being within striking distance of big cities. Because there isn't much land that can be developed, Atlantic City doesn't come close to Las Vegas's hotel count. You also won't see the kind of mega-complexes that dominate Las Vegas's gaming industry. While you will see gamblers of all ages in Atlantic City, a large percentage of players here are retired and come to the city for a day of gambling, either by themselves or on tour buses.

Cozy Casinos

If glitz and glimmer isn't your style, there are lots of casinos that offer good gaming at a more sedate level. Some of them are legendary facilities in old gambling towns such as Reno and Lake Tahoe. But many others have also sprung up over the years, often in small towns that are either near or on the way to tourist destinations. You'll find them in places like Mesquite in Arizona, Cripple Creek and Central City in Colorado, and Deadwood in South Dakota. Some are owned by big casino corporations. Others are mom-and-pop operations.

Depending on state laws and your personal gambling style, these facilities can be lots of fun or not fun at all to play in. Most have fairly low table maximums, which means you can't win very much at them. On the plus side, to make up for these restrictions, they often have favorable odds, decent comps, and other incentives to get people to come and play. If you want to gamble in a relaxed, friendly atmosphere where people might even get to know your name, cozy casinos can't be beat.

Riverboat Casinos

Riverboats were popular gaming spots after the Civil War. Many states have revived this gambling tradition on modern-day riverboats. You'll find riverboat gambling in states in the Midwest and the South, including Iowa, Illinois, Louisiana, Mississippi, Missouri, and Indiana. Some riverboats actually cruise the waterways. Others are noncruising, and anchored to dockside platforms.

Riverboats can be a lot of fun to play on, but not especially player friendly. Because there's usually not much competition where they are located, they attract a captive audience that has to deal with whatever house rules the operators wish to set. The table limits on riverboats are typically low, which means they don't attract high rollers. Comps are fairly nonexistent unless the riverboat is part of a casino complex. Some riverboats can only be on the water for a certain period of time, after which players must disembark. Others restrict the amount of money players can lose per session.

Native American Gaming Establishments

If you're like most people who live in the United States, chances are very good that you live near a Native American casino. If not, there's probably at least one in your state.

FACT

In 2002, there were more than 300 gaming operations run by more than 200 of the nation's federally recognized tribes. Since there are no publicly collected and released statistics, there's no way to say how big Native American gaming is. In the mid-1990s, estimates ranged from $2.3 billion to $8 billion. In 2000, revenues from Native American-owned gaming facilities were about $10 billion, accounting for about one-sixth of all gaming revenues in the United States.

Native American gaming has become a huge industry over the past twenty years or so. It started with a couple of large bingo halls opened on tribal land to spur economic development during the late 1970s and early 1980s. Back then, state laws severely restricted what the tribes could offer in their gaming establishments. This changed in the late 1980s with the passage of the Indian Gaming Regulatory Act of 1988, which legalized gaming operations on a number of reservations. Other favorable legal rulings further expanded what tribal casinos could do.

Types of Native American Casinos

Today, Native American casinos run the gamut from out-of-the-way bingo halls to multimillion-dollar gambling complexes. Some, such as Foxwoods and the Mohegan Sun in Connecticut and Mystic Lake in Minnesota, rival those found in Las Vegas and Atlantic City.

The Indian Gaming Regulatory Act governs the games that Native American casinos can offer. This act established three gaming classes:

- Class I, which consists of games traditionally played by tribes in ceremonies or celebrations.
- Class II, which consists of bingo, pull-tab cards, punch board, and tip jars. Card games such as poker can be offered if they're non-banking—that is, if bets are made between players, not between players and the establishment. In certain states where banked card games were played before the act passed, they are also regulated as Class II games.
- Class III, which covers all forms of gaming not covered by the other classes, including all casino-banked games, roulette, and all slot machines.

Tribes that want to offer Class III gaming must enter into compacts with the states in which the casinos are located. These compacts can vary quite a bit. Most states restrict the kinds of games that can be offered. Some restrict the size and number of casinos that tribes can operate. In Minnesota, for example, video machines in Native American casinos can offer video poker, craps, slots, and keno. Blackjack is the only table game permitted.

In Wisconsin, Native American casinos can offer slot machines and video poker. And as in Minnesota, blackjack is the only table game permitted.

Sovereign Lands

Most, but not all, Native American casinos are located on reservations. The United States recognizes these areas as sovereign lands. As such, they are self-governing, which means that they're governed by a different set of laws than the rest of the United States. The fact that you're on sovereign land when you play in Native American casinos is really no big deal. You won't feel any different, or notice anything different. However, it's important to remember that any legal disputes that erupt on reservation land are settled in the courts of the tribe that operates the casino, not in state or federal courts.

Cruise Ship Casinos

Back when gaming was restricted to Las Vegas and Atlantic City, cruises were popular gaming destinations. As soon as the big ships hit international waters—three miles offshore—shipboard casinos could open for action. Since the ships were in international waters, which do not fall under state or federal government regulations, gaming on these vessels was perfectly legal. The operators of the cruise ships were the only authorities, and they could set whatever rules and payouts they wanted. Playing on cruise ships was fun. However, it was rarely player friendly. As you can imagine, lack of competition and a captive audience weren't incentives to offer games with a low house edge.

FACT

Some states now allow "cruises to nowhere," that take passengers into international waters for an evening or weekend of gambling. Table odds on these cruises might be better than on ships where gambling is just one small piece of your trip. Still, it's a good idea to check the ship's rules and regulations before booking passage.

While there are vastly more gaming opportunities now in the United States, cruise ships still tend to operate much as they did when there weren't. Audiences are still captive, and gaming is often secondary to other shipboard activities. As such, games in cruise casinos typically carry odds that are extremely friendly to the house. This doesn't mean that you shouldn't play them when you're blithely cruising about the high seas. It does mean that you want to play your best game when you do. Picking games with the best rules will minimize your losses. However, of all the gambling options available, it's probably good to stick this one at the bottom of the list.

Chapter 15

Playing Blackjack in a Casino

Now that you know more about what casinos are like, it's time to take a closer look at what it's like to play blackjack in them. In this chapter, you'll get the inside skinny on how to pick a casino and what you can do to make the time you spend inside it the most enjoyable it can be.

Picking a Place to Play

As you now know, blackjack is one of the most player-friendly games you'll find in a casino. The basic game has a small house percentage. You can shave that percentage down even further by learning and using basic strategy. You can also use the principles of basic strategy to pick a casino to play in.

Lots of factors can come into play during the selection process. For some players, convenience is key. They'd rather play in a small casino where they live than in a glitzy Las Vegas gaming palace. For others, ambiance—how the casino is laid out, its décor, what the dealers are like, etc.—swings their decision. Other factors you might want to consider include:

- **Comps.** As detailed in Chapter 16, these programs vary from casino to casino. Good comp programs can make up for deficits in other areas, such as dated décor or locations that are a little (or a lot) off the beaten track.
- **Player's club offerings.** Like comps, these programs vary quite a bit. If you have your choice, all other things being equal, it makes sense to play at casinos that offer prizes and promotions of interest to you.
- **Lessons and tournaments.** If you're a new player, taking lessons at a casino is a great way to learn the games you want to play. If you're an experienced player, tournaments offer the chance to pit your skills against other players.

These are all important things to consider, but to a certain extent they're only icing on the cake. What's most important? Playing in a casino that offers games with favorable rules and regulations. Even the best comp program won't cancel out rules that heavily favor the house.

Different Rules, Different Expectations

While the basic way that blackjack is played is pretty much the same wherever you go, specific rules of play can vary enormously from place to place. How they affect player expectation can vary from a lot to a little.

How much of a difference can rule variations make? A big one, depending on what they are. Here are some of the variations and rules you're mostly likely to encounter, and how they can affect your game. These figures are averages, so they're not engraved in stone. The exact rules in effect where you play will move them up or down a little bit, but not by enough to be statistically significant.

First, let's take a look at how much the number of decks in a game can affect your game. **TABLE 14-1** shows the effect on player expectation that playing with different numbers of decks has.

TABLE 14-1: Effect of Number of Decks on Player Expectation	
Variation/Rule	**Effect**
Single deck	No advantage
Two decks	-0.32%
Four decks	-0.48%
Six decks	-0.54%
Eight decks	-0.58%
Infinite decks	-0.60%

Clearly, the more decks you play with, the greater the house edge. Knowing this, you now know that it's a good idea to choose a casino that uses the fewest decks in its blackjack games. Next, let's take a look at how slight differences in payoffs can net big results for your wallet (see **TABLE 14-2**).

TABLE 14-2: Effect of Different Payoffs on Player Expectation	
Variation/Rule	**Effect**
Blackjack pays 1 to 1 (even money)	-2.10%
Blackjack pays 2 to 1	+2.30%
Blackjack pays 6 to 5	-1.20%

TABLE 14-3 shows how changes in dealer actions can affect the bottom line.

TABLE 14-3: Effect of Dealer Actions on Player Expectation	
Variation/Rule	Effect
Dealer hits soft 17	-0.20%
Dealer wins ties	-9.34%

Finally, **TABLE 14-4** takes a look at how variations in rules regarding player options can affect your game.

TABLE 14-4: Effect of Limits on Players' Options on Player Expectation	
Variation/Rule	Effect
Double down after splitting pairs	+0.14%
No soft doubling	-0.13%
No re-splitting any pairs	-0.03%
Re-splitting aces allowed	+0.04%
No splitting of aces allowed	-0.18%
Double down only on 11	-0.69%
Double down only on 10 or 11	-0.25%
Double down only on 9, 10, or 11	-0.10%
Double down on any cards	+0.20%
Double after splitting pairs	+0.14%
Late surrender	+0.05%
Early surrender	+0.62%

How do you use this information? Easy. Just find the rule variations that apply to where you're playing, and total them up. Let's say, for example, that you're going to play in a casino that uses a six-deck shoe. That's a negative player expectation of 0.54 percent. Next, total up the effect of the other rules in place. Subtract the positives from the negatives (or the negatives from the positives). The final figure is your player expectation.

To make things easier, group negative expectations and positive expectations together. Here's what things could look like:

Negatives

Six-deck shoe	-.54%
Double on 10 and 11 only	-.25%
Total	-.79%

Positives

Re-split aces	+.04%
Double down after split	+.14%
Total	+.18%

-.79% + +.18% = -.61%

This set of rule variations would give the house a .61 percent advantage over players. In real money, it would mean that for every $10 you bet, you should expect to lose an average of just over 60 cents. Not exactly great.

Now, let's look at the difference made by a couple of player-favorable rule changes:

Beginning expectation (from previous example)	-.61%
Late surrender	+.62%
Total	+.01%

This one rule change shifts the advantage from the house to the player. Not by much, but in blackjack you take what you can get. Here's another example:

Beginning expectation (from previous example)	-.61%
Double on more than two cards	+.21%
Five-card automatic winner	+1.40%
Total	+1.00%

Now the player has a huge edge over the house. For every $10 bet, you could expect to win $1.00. That's excellent, right? Before you get too excited, keep in mind that casinos that offer highly player-favorable rules like these typically offset them with a few that aren't as friendly. So be sure to read the fine print. A 1 percent advantage looks wonderful until you see something like naturals paying off at even money, a rule change with a -2.29 percent player expectation.

The bottom line? Always look for a table with rules most advantageous to the player, regardless of the number of decks in play. Remember that the same rules might not be in place for all the tables in the casino. Some casinos might offer a blend of games dealt by hand and from a shoe, both with their own set of rules. The best rules to look for:

- Late surrender.
- Early surrender.
- Doubling on any two cards.
- Doubling after split. Also known as DAS, this is a fairly common rule variation and is often found in multiple-deck games.
- Hitting split aces.
- Natural pays 2:1. (Not a common rule, as it reduces the casino's edge by 2.3 percent. But you will see it occasionally, mostly as a limited-time promotion.)

All casinos must make their rules available to players. Finding out which rules are in effect at the casino you want to play at can be as easy as doing an Internet search. If you can't find them online, you can call and ask. There are also basic strategy calculators online that will do the work for you. Some, such as ✍www.blackjackinfo.com, are free. Others, such as ✍www.trackjack.com, charge a subscription fee. If you're looking for analysis on blackjack variation games, check out ✍www.thewizardofodds.com.

The rules you should try to avoid:

- Dealer hits on soft 17.
- Double only on 10 or 11.
- No splitting aces.
- Natural pays 1:1.
- Natural pays 6:5.

Quick Guide to Blackjack Rules

As mentioned, the rules governing how blackjack is played can vary from place to place, and there might even be several different versions played in the same place. That said, there are sets of standard rules that you'll typically find in place in the big gaming centers—Las Vegas and Atlantic City.

The following lists will give you an idea of what to expect in these cities. We've also included a list of rules that you might find if you play blackjack in Europe.

Las Vegas Strip Blackjack Rules
- Uses anywhere from one to eight standard decks of fifty-two cards.
- Cards shuffled at end of each game.
- Blackjack beats other 21-value hands.
- Splitting rules: Maximum of three times per game, totaling four hands.
- Aces only split once.
- If aces are split, each ace receives one card. Hand automatically stands.
- Double down allowed after receiving first two cards.
- Double down allowed after a split.
- Double down bet is equal to the original bet.
- Insurance rules: Insurance offered if dealer's first card is an ace.
- Insurance costs half of original bet.
- If dealer has blackjack, insurance pays at 2:1.

Las Vegas Downtown Rules
- Uses two standard decks of fifty-two cards each.
- Cards shuffled at end of each game.
- Blackjack beats other 21-value hands.
- Dealer hits on soft 17.
- Splitting rules: Allowed three times per game for four hands total.
- Aces only split once.
- When aces are split, each dealt one card. Hand automatically stands.
- Double down allowed on first two cards.
- Can double down after splitting.
- Double down bet is equal to original bet.

- Insurance rules: Offered if dealer's up card is an ace.
- Insurance costs half original bet.
- Insurance pays out at 2:1 when dealer has blackjack.

Atlantic City Blackjack Rules

- Played with eight standard decks of fifty-two cards.
- Cards shuffled at end of each game.
- Blackjack beats other 21-value hands.
- Dealer stands on soft 17.
- Players can surrender cards and forfeit half original bet amount.
- 21-value hands do not equal blackjack.
- Splitting rules: Allowed maximum of three times per game for four hands.
- Aces only split once.
- If aces are split, each ace dealt only one card. Hand automatically stands.
- Double down allowed on first two cards.
- Double down bet is equal to original bet.
- Double down allowed after a split.
- No double down if blackjack.
- Insurance rules: Insurance offered if dealer's first card is ace.
- Insurance bet is half of original bet.

European Blackjack Rules

- Two standard decks of fifty-two cards.
- Cards shuffled at end of each game.
- Blackjack beats other 21-value hands.
- Dealer stands on 17, draws to 16 value of 17.
- Splitting rules: Allowed on two cards of the same denomination.
- 10-value draw card on a split ace is valued at 21, not blackjack. Rule also applies to 10-value splits.
- Double down allowed on 9-, 10-, or 11-value hands.
- No doubling after splits.
- Double down bet equal to original bet.
- Insurance rules: Insurance offered if dealer's first card is an ace.
- Insurance bet costs half the original bet.

Choosing a Table

This might seem like a no-brainer, but finding the right blackjack table to play at is an important aspect of the game for everyone, beginner and expert alike. Most casinos will have a number of blackjack tables available to choose from. At big casinos, there could be two dozen or more. While some players are superstitious about choosing the right table, as they think it could increase their odds of winning, a table is a table is a table when it comes to location. If the rules are the same, it doesn't much matter where you sit as long as the betting limits are comfortable for you. If you're counting cards, table choice can make a difference, especially if you join a table mid-game.

Be sure to check the betting limits before you sit down. It can be embarrassing to sit down at a table before you notice the betting limits and then realize they're too rich for your blood.

Bet Signs-Table Limits

If you're a newcomer, choosing the right table is especially important for one specific reason: betting limits. How much and how little you can bet will vary from table to table, and it's important to know what they are when you sit down. Doing so will save you the possible embarrassment of having to bet beyond your limits, or moving to another table mid-game.

Casinos post minimum and maximum allowable bets on tabletop signs. Many casinos color code these signs as an easy visual reference for experienced gamblers:

- Red = $5 minimum bet
- Green = $25 minimum bet
- Black = $100 minimum bet

Signs typically correspond to chip color. So any table that requires you to bet with $5 chips for the minimum (such as a $10 or $15 minimum bet table) will have a red sign. A green sign corresponds to the green chips, which have a $25 value. Generally, casinos set table minimums at $5, $10, $25, and $100 limits, with the maximum being 1,000 times the minimum. So if you're playing at a $5 table, the maximum bet is $5,000.

How do you know what an affordable betting minimum is? One way to figure it is to divide the amount you're willing to wager for the entire session by 20. This should be your maximum beginning bet per hand. For example, let's say you planned to bring a $400 bankroll to a playing session. Divide that by 20, and you're at $20 a hand. If you're counting cards, you might want to choose a table with a lower limit than what this formula suggests so you can decrease your bets when the deck goes against you.

Your Playing Partners

What about the other people at your table? Regardless of what some people believe, what your fellow players do has no effect on the game you play. However, if you're easily distracted, you might want to avoid a boisterous table, where the antics of the other players can cause you to lose your count or make mistakes in your playing or wagering strategies.

Should you pick a table where no one else is sitting? That's up to you. Some players prefer heads-up games with dealers. Others like the bantering and camaraderie that comes with having other players at the table. Some high rollers like to play the dealer one on one, so if you come up to a table with just one person at it, you might want to ask if it's okay for you to join the action before you sit down. This isn't as necessary at a low-limit table, but it's still a gracious move and one that marks you as a courteous player.

If you are very new to the game, it can be a good idea to pick a table that's less than full. You'll feel less intimidated about asking the dealer for help if there aren't bunches of other people around to hear you.

Deciding Where to Sit

As previously mentioned, since it's you against the dealer, you really don't have to be concerned about the other players at the table. That said, there are many superstitions about table position, and it's probably one of the most highly debated aspects of the game.

Many players believe that the mistakes made by other players at their table will decrease their playing advantage. However, statistics don't bear this out. Still, it's a good idea to avoid third base if you're new to the game. Doing so will protect you from glares and comments from players who do think that table position is important should you make a move they don't agree with.

The Dealer

If you have a choice between tables, take a few minutes and watch the dealers at them. Every dealer does things a little differently. Some deal faster than others, some call out hand totals as cards are dealt, some will provide more help to newbie players than others.

In general, you want a dealer who looks friendly and seems to enjoy what she's doing. Dealers who distribute cards at a moderate pace are a good choice for newcomers, as it gives players a little more time to ponder their moves.

Dealers work in twenty-minute shifts, which means that the dealer you start your game with might not be at your table for very long. It might seem like a good idea to follow a dealer you like to his or her new table; to casino management, however, it looks like you're trying to cheat and the dealer is in on the action. Don't do it, for any reason.

Buying Chips

Virtually all casinos require players to use chips at gaming tables. While it's technically okay to play with cold hard cash, casinos prefer it when players exchange their money for chips. This is for your protection as well as the casino's, as it's easier to see the value of a bunch of chips than it is a stack of bills.

You can purchase chips from the dealer or from a cashier, but most people buy them at the table they want to play at. All you have to do is present your money (if you've established casino credit, you'll ask for a marker) when there's a break in the action, typically after a hand is played. Some casinos prefer you wait until the dealer shuffles. The dealer will tell you what's appropriate.

When the break comes, put your cash on the table in front of you and wait for the dealer to pick it up. The dealer will lay your bills out on the table, in a specific pattern separated by denomination if you gave him more than one, so the security cameras can see what you're putting down. If you're exchanging more than a certain amount of money—typically $100—for chips, a pit boss must approve the transaction. This is a security measure, and they do it with everyone, so don't take it personally when the dealer calls the pit boss over. It has nothing to do with the color of your money or whether it's real or not—just casino procedure.

As the dealer takes your money, he'll make a quick announcement, typically something along the lines of "Cashing one hundred," which the pit boss will acknowledge. He'll then remove the correct amount of chips from the tray, place them in five-high stacks, push them to you, and drop your cash into a slot on the tabletop. When you get your chips, take a quick look to make sure you got the correct amount, and to make sure you know the values.

ALERT!

Never try to hand the money to the dealer. For security reasons, dealers can't take anything directly out of your hands. Always put your money directly down on the felt top of the table, and wait for the dealer to take the next step.

Determining Your Buy-In

How many chips should you buy? A typical buy-in amount is ten to twenty times your average bet. As an example, if you're comfortable placing $5 bets, buy $50 to $100 in chips. You can, of course, buy more than this. And you can buy more chips, if you need them, while you're playing. The same procedure applies: lay your cash on the table, and wait for the dealer to pick it up.

Chip colors are fairly standard across casinos, which makes it easy to know how much you're betting. Typically, casinos follow a system that matches the signs that indicate minimum and maximum table bets:

- Red = $5
- Green = $25
- Black = $100

If you're playing at a table with betting limits below $5, you'll also see white chips, which indicate $1, and silver tokens, which also are worth $1. Some casinos use $2.50 chips, which are often colored pink.

Once you get above the $100 level, chip colors do vary somewhat, depending on the casino. Purple is a common color for $500 chips.

Making a Bet

Each position at a blackjack table has a circle or box in front of it, printed on the felt. This is where players place their bets. Before each hand is dealt, you're expected to put your bet in this area to be part of the hand.

If you're betting chips of multiple denominations, say $5 and $2.50, place the smaller value chips on top of the larger denomination, in one stack.

Your bet must be placed before the hand is dealt. Once the hand is dealt, you can't touch your bet. If you need to refresh your memory about how much you've bet, such as in doubling or splitting situations, you can ask the dealer to count the chips for you. When the hand is over, the dealer will move around the table to each position. Winners will be paid, losers will have their chips collected.

If you've played a winning hand, the dealer will place your winnings in a stack next to your original bet. At this point, you can either remove all of your chips from the circle and place a new bet, or let your winnings ride by keeping all of your chips in the circle. If you do this, consolidate your previous bet and your winnings into a single stack.

Again, never touch your bet once cards are dealt. The only time you should ever go near it is when you're putting more money down on a double or a split. Even then, be careful not to touch your original bet. It looks suspicious to security, because players have been known to slip an extra chip or two under their stacks when they're in a good position to win.

Signaling Your Intentions

There are two ways to let the dealer know what you want to do with your cards: verbally or with hand signals. In noisy casinos, the latter is a good way to go, as you don't want to chance the dealer not hearing you correctly. Plus, surveillance cameras can pick up hand signals. They can't hear you speak. Many dealers will ask you to use a hand motion so the security cameras can pick up your move.

Here's what to do if you're playing a face-down game:

- Lightly scratch the table with your cards to indicate a hit.
- If you don't want another card, indicate a stand by placing your cards under the original bet.

It can take a while for players to master basic strategy well enough to play by memory. If this is you, don't hesitate to bring a basic strategy card to the table with you. Casinos won't discourage you from using them. However, it's a good idea to be judicious about their use. Try to not refer to your card on every hand—if you're playing with others, they'll get frustrated pretty quickly. Don't wait until it's your hand to consult the card. When it's your turn to play, you should be ready to go. The dealer and/or pit boss will let you know what the house is comfortable with—commonly, the card is kept either in the player's lap or on the table.

With face-down games, use only one hand to touch your cards. Don't bend them, and don't let your hand dip below the edge of the table. Your cards must always be where the dealer, and the surveillance cameras, can see them.

If you're playing a face-up game, you never touch your cards. Here's what you do instead:

- Indicate a hit by scratching the spot in front of your cards with your finger.
- Indicate a stay by waving one hand over your cards.

Tipping the Dealer

If you've had a good day at the table, it's appropriate to tip your dealer. It's also appropriate to tip a dealer who has been helpful in answering your questions.

There are three common ways to tip:

- When you're playing. This is typically done when a player has had a particularly good run of cards.
- During play, by placing a bet for the dealer. If you win your hand, the dealer wins, too.
- After the dealer's session, or at the end of your playing session.

It's tradition to tip a dealer after a premium hand, such as a blackjack, a winning double down, or a winning split. You'll find more information on tipping, including suggested tip amounts, in Chapter 22.

FACT

In the casino industry, a generous tipper is called a "george." People who are exceptionally generous tippers are "super georges." You might overhear an incoming dealer ask the outgoing dealer if he has seen a george. Players who don't tip well, or refuse to tip, are called stiffs or strokers.

Cashing In

When you're finished playing, it's time to exchange your chips for cash. To do this, wait until the end of a hand. Then push your chips out in front of you, between the betting boxes so they're not mistaken for a bet. You can say you're "cashing in" if you like. If you have a bunch of chips in various denominations, the dealer might do something known as "coloring up" your chips. All this means is exchanging smaller denomination chips for larger-value chips. He will sort the chips, count them out, and exchange them for a smaller stack of chips of equal value. Dealers color up for a couple of reasons. Sometimes they need lower denomination chips. Or they might want to show how much you won or lost. You then take your chips to the cashier's cage, where they'll be sorted and exchanged for bills and silver.

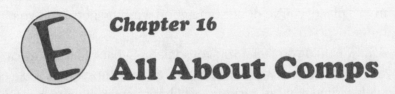

Chapter 16

All About Comps

You'll see all different types of gamblers in a casino. There are high rollers and low rollers, slot fanatics and table game aficionados. Some play for a few minutes at a time. Others settle in for the duration and play for hours on end. While casinos appreciate the people who come through their doors and spend money on their machines and their tables, they have a special affection for a certain type of gambler. What's more, they reward these gamblers for being the way they are.

Fringe Benefits in the Gaming World

Let's say you find a casino you really like playing in. You like the layout and the atmosphere. The dealers are friendly and helpful, the rules are player friendly. The wait staff is good about coming around with free drinks, and there's an afternoon snack buffet that can't be beat. You're happy in this place, you've done some good winning here, and you come back often.

Now, how would you feel if you got something back for your enjoyment and loyalty (besides your winnings)? Maybe a casino host offers you a certificate for a free dinner at the casino's restaurant, or hands you a book full of coupons for things like free premium drinks, a free $5 hand of blackjack, a lunch buffet, and so on. After a particularly good day at the blackjack tables, maybe you're offered a free room at the casino's hotel, or presented with a nifty club jacket emblazoned with the casino's logo. Would it make you feel even better about this casino? Possibly make you want to gamble here over anywhere else? Maybe make you want to play a little more often, perhaps even spend a little more money when you do?

That's exactly what casinos are after when they hand out comps to their players.

Comprehending Comps

Casinos are legendary for their marketing programs, and comps—the special spiffs that casinos bestow on favored players—are a legendary part of these programs. Play your cards right (pun intended), and all sorts of freebies can come your way, ranging from free meals to special room rates to all-expenses-paid trips to your favorite gaming spot.

FACT

"Comp" is short for complimentary or complimentary rewards. They date back to the 1960s, when casinos regularly organized all-expenses-paid gambling junkets to bring high rollers and other VIPs to Las Vegas.

Comps are designed to build customer loyalty, to keep players happy, and to keep them coming back. Without a loyal customer base, the casino business can get a little dicey. They can always count on walk-in traffic, but they make book on the customers they can count on. The gambling industry is competitive, and casinos can get pretty aggressive and very creative with their comp programs. That competition and creativity can be very good things for players.

The most common comp—so common, in fact, that many people don't think of them as such—are free drinks. They're readily available in virtually every casino, and available to all players. Depending on where you're playing and the rules and regulations casinos must follow, beverage choices will range from nonalcoholic sodas and juices to all kinds of mixed drinks. Another popular comp, although not as common, are snack buffets.

ALERT!

The best way to look at comps is to consider them part of the overall gaming experience. They're there, so you might as well learn more about them and use them to your best advantage. But don't let them become the reason for playing. And never use comps as an excuse to gamble recklessly. The freebie you're chasing—whether it's a room upgrade or a free trip to some exotic location—simply isn't worth playing foolishly.

For the most part, you have to know how to get the perks casinos are willing to dole out. Some, like free drinks, you'll get without asking. But you can get a lot more than this if you know what's behind casino comp programs, and what's in them for you.

Unfortunately, many people don't take the time to learn about comps. Some players aren't even aware that comp programs exist. Or they think these programs are for big-time players, and they don't even try to qualify for them or find out more about them. As such, lots of comps go unrewarded, and lots of players miss the opportunity for a little special treatment (or a lot), which is always a nice thing.

On the flip side are players who are comp obsessed. For them, getting things free is as important as what they do to get them, if not more so.

They comp shop casinos, and ask for comps every time they see a host or a pit person. It's not uncommon to see them get a little indignant or belligerent if their requests aren't honored. This attitude can be as counterproductive as not taking advantage of comp programs at all, as it can lead to disappointment and hard feelings. Chasing comps can also result in spending too much time in casinos, and betting beyond your means.

Becoming a Comps Customer

What do you have to do to be on the receiving end of casino comps? There really isn't much to it beyond spending money in casinos, and doing it on a regular basis. Asking nicely, which you'll learn more about later in this chapter, is also important. Casinos like courteous customers. Casinos put a lot of stock in players who visit them consistently and who spend decent amounts when they do, and these two factors weigh heavily in the formulas casinos use for computing comps. The more you play, and the more you spend, the more you're likely to receive in comps. It's as simple as that.

Casinos use another key piece of information to figure out how they comp players. They also take into consideration the house edge—what the house stands to win. The result is the magic number that unlocks the key to comp kingdom.

Understanding Comp Calculations

The following equation will give you an idea of what a comp formula looks like. This is a simple one; actual formulas for computing comps vary from casino to casino and are closely held secrets. They also take in other factors that, again, aren't public knowledge.

- The first part of the equation is average bet. No secret to this; it's the amount of money you bet, on average, when you play.
- Next comes hours played. Again, pretty self-explanatory: it's the time you spend gaming.
- Now comes bets per hour. This is how fast you play.

This information—average bet, hours played, and bets per hour, is multiplied together. The resulting aggregate figure is the total amount wagered. This figure is then multiplied by the house edge. The result of this calculation is the expected house win. This figure is what casinos use as a basis for factoring comps. However, comp levels are only factored on a percentage of expected house win, and this percentage goes down as the other numbers go up. At the low end, it's typically around 30 percent. At the high end, it could be much lower.

To put all of this into real money terms, let's say you visit your favorite casino and end up playing blackjack for three hours. You choose a table with a $10 minimum. You'll bet more than this at times, of course, but we're keeping things simple here, so we'll just stick with this number.

Casinos can and do consider other factors when factoring comps. A $5 comp level one evening might not be typical for you. Maybe you won more the last time you played. Maybe you've consistently bet more in the past. These are all factors that casinos look at. But there's no denying that spending more, and playing more, will put you in better stead for more and better comps. Casinos spend more on players who spend more on them.

The house edge is player friendly, right around 2 percent, not taking into consideration your skillful play. You're seated at a table with five other players, so the rate of play isn't too fast, and you sit out a few hands every so often, so you're actually completing about forty hands per hour. Here's what the comp formula above comes out to in this situation:

$10 (your average bet) × 3 (hours played) × 40 (bets per hour) = $1,200
$1,200 × .02 (the house edge) = $24

The final figure—$24—is what the casino expects to make from you during the three hours you're at that table. Multiply $24 by 30 percent for the final comp figure, and you end up with $7.20. Hardly a figure to write home about, and probably not enough to qualify you for even the cheapest comp. If you were to repeat this scenario a couple hundred times, however, you'd end up with a tidy sum that will put you in comp territory.

The basic factors that casinos use to calculate comps also characterize the types of players they comp. Gamblers come in all shapes and sizes. But there are several specific types that casinos concentrate their efforts on more than others.

Rolling in the Dough

Big bettors—high rollers—might not gamble that often, but when they do, they make it very worthwhile for casinos to treat them to such monster comps as VIP suites, tickets to the best shows in town, private gaming tables, private transportation, jewelry, and other gifts. How much do you have to bet to become a big roller? There is no set figure, but these folks typically spend at least a few thousand dollars per trip or visit. Really high rollers, often referred to as "whales," spend hundreds of thousands and even millions when they play.

If you ever see someone playing with a funny-colored stack of chips, chances are you're watching a high roller. They often play with chip denominations—$500, $1,000, and even higher—that are far beyond those used by ordinary gamblers.

Nailed to the Table

Betting big isn't the only ticket to comp land. You can also get there if you're a frequent player. For some people, this means hitting their favorite casinos virtually every day. Doing so is hardly a burden to them. The casino, and the people they meet there, is their social network, and it's an important part of their lives. Frequent players typically don't bet very much per visit, and they usually play low-limit games. Slots—especially nickel and quarter slots—are a particular favorite, as it doesn't take much of a bankroll to have hours of fun at them. But the money these players spend adds up over time, and it qualifies them for relatively decent comps such as room upgrades, free meals, show tickets, promotional items such as mugs, shirts, and jackets, and so on.

Conscientious Comp-ers

This group of gamblers fall somewhere in the middle. They don't play as often as frequent players, and they don't bet as big as the high rollers do. But they play consistently, maybe every month, a couple of times a month, or one day a week, and they spend a decent amount of money when they do—typically anywhere from $250 on up. Conscientious comp-ers take the time to research comp programs. They understand what they have to do to qualify for comps, and they use this knowledge to get the best comps they can for their level of play.

Getting Comps

Now that you know more about comps and why casinos hand them out, it's time to learn how you can get them, and how to get the best ones you can. There isn't a single approach, nor does the same approach work for everyone. But there are some basic strategies that you need to know to be successful at it.

Get the Card

Just about every casino has what's known as a player's club. Join the club, and you get a card. Some places call them players' cards. Others call them club cards. They are comp trackers. Casinos use them to keep tabs on you. One of the first things you should do when you walk into a new casino to play is head over to the casino's courtesy counter and ask about their player's club. The staff will give you a form to fill out, detailing such information as your name, address, phone number, and e-mail address. It might also ask questions about the games you like to play, what your other leisure time activities are, how often you travel, your birth date and anniversary date, and so on.

This is all critical demographic information for the casino's marketing department. They'll use it to develop a player profile for you, and they'll match their promotional offerings to it. As an example, if you indicate that you like to play blackjack, you'll get mailings about tournaments and special blackjack promotions. Tell the casino when your anniversary is, and you might get a special coupon for a free dinner during the month of your anniversary.

Don't be surprised if you get a comp or two, such as a dinner discount or a free premium drink, the moment you get your card. It's the casino's way of giving you a taste of what's to come. As you play, you'll accrue points for every dollar you wager. As they mount up, you'll start getting your comps.

Be sure to get the club's brochure and any other materials explaining how it works when you apply for your card. Every club operates a little differently when it comes to how dollars played translate into points earned, and what players get for their points. Typical benefits include comp meals, comp rooms, and promotional items like shirts, jackets, and so on. Some programs also offer special promotions and discounts to club members.

Use the Card

Getting a comp card is just the beginning. You have to use it. If you don't, the casino won't be able to track your vital statistics—how much you gamble and how long you gamble—and you won't qualify for your comps. Show the card every time you sit down at table. If you play slots or other machine games, such as video poker, always slip the card into the player's club slot on the machine.

Table Play Rating

Casinos originally designed comp cards to track the action of slot machine players. If you also played table games, your time at these tables was tracked separately and computed for comps separately. Many casinos continue to keep the two apart; some combine them. For this reason, it's always a good idea to ask to have your play rated when you sit down to play. To rate play, pit personnel keep track of the following: name, date, player's card number, table number, seat number, time in, average bet (determined by the floorman who asks for your card—this is very important to the amount of your comps so be nice to this person), amount of buy ins, amount of credit used and available credit limit, if the player brings chips to the table or buys in, the amount a player cashes out, total win/loss and quick determination of the player's skill level. This is done for each table the customer plays at. On a bigger scale, the number of trips the player makes, the total buy-ins, average bets, and win/loss are also kept on each player. The house keeps a lot of information that is used to figure theoretical win (or how much a player will statistically lose based on his or her play) and the player's comp value. Put your card on the table, too. Pit personnel will need this information.

Don't be embarrassed to ask to have your play rated. Pit personnel are used to players making this request. What's more, they expect good and savvy players to ask for it. They might even ask you if you want your play rated if you don't make the request yourself. If they do, say yes, even if you think it's not worth their time or yours. You never know. It doesn't cost you anything to have your play rated, so you have nothing to lose. And you might have lots to gain.

ALERT!

Be sure to ask for your play to be rated when you sit down, not after you've been playing for a while. It doesn't do you any good to ask for a comp halfway through a playing session that no one is keeping track of.

Asking for Comps

While belonging to a player's club is the easiest way to get comps, you can also get them simply by asking for them. It can be a good idea to do this even if you are a player's club member. Many people don't know this, and casinos definitely don't sing it from their rooftops, but casino personnel can spiff players at higher levels than what player's clubs offer. That is, if they want to. They don't have to. They can do it if your play warrants it. You can vastly improve your bargaining position, and make casino personnel more interested in comping you if:

- You're a courteous player.
- You ask nicely.
- You make reasonable requests.

If you're a high roller, chances are pretty good that you won't have to take the lead negotiating spot. Your betting level will quickly flag you as someone the casino would like to court, and someone will keep an eye on your play. When the time is right, a host or another casino representative will let you know they want to have a chat.

You don't have to be a high roller to ask for comps. You just have to know how to ask, and what's appropriate to ask for. A nice meal or a break on room rates are appropriate requests that just about anyone can make. Anything more than this is cause for treading a bit more lightly, especially if you're new to the casino or not sure that your play warrants higher consideration. You also have to be prepared to take the lead. If you aren't a high roller, you'll be flying under the casino's radar. The casino staff in charge of handing out comps probably won't come to you, so you have to go to them.

Asking for comps can be a little awkward at first, but rest assured that you're not doing anything out of the ordinary. Casino personnel field these requests all the time, and they are well versed in handling them. Remember, there are formulas and parameters in place for virtually every move a casino employee makes while at work. While they have the authority to grant comps, they also follow a fairly strict set of guidelines for doing so. Keep this in mind when you make your request, and you'll have a better chance of getting what you want.

How do you ask for a comp? Don't make a big deal out of it. Just throw out a casual query, maybe something like, "My girlfriend and I would like dinner at your restaurant tonight. Could you help arrange it?" Typically, you won't get a no. You might, however, be offered an alternative, such as a buffet-style dinner instead of table service, if your level of play isn't quite high enough to warrant your request. Or you might be told what you have to do to earn the comp you want.

If the alternative is to your liking, simply accept it. If it isn't, you can always ask if something else is available. It might be, it might not. But you'll never know if you don't ask.

If you are offered a premium comp, let's say a free room for the weekend, be aware that it is not necessarily a no-strings attached deal. When you accept a comp like this, casino management expects a little something in return—in this case, that you'll feel so rewarded that you'll spend the majority of your time at their casino, playing the casino's games. They won't be thrilled if your rate of play suddenly drops off, as it indicates you're spending your money elsewhere at their expense. Thanks to modern technology, casinos have long, long memories. The next time you're up for a comp, your chances of getting it will be substantially less.

You don't have to feel like you've sold your soul, but it is a good idea to do the right thing when you get a comp. Show your appreciation by spending the majority of your money at the casino that comped you. Don't get greedy and go casino hopping to see what other goodies you can score.

Keeping Comps in Perspective

Getting comps can be lots of fun, and they should definitely factor into your overall approach to gambling. They can make good days even better. When you're losing, knowing your losses aren't for naught—you accumulate points whether you win or lose—can make your losses sting a bit less. These are all good things, and if you remember to keep them in mind, you'll be able to keep comps in perspective. It's important to do so, as it can be a little too easy to get comp crazy.

ALERT!

If you ever find that your pursuit of comps is dictating your betting levels, or that you're playing longer just so you can get a comp, stop. Comps aren't free if you bet a lot more, or play longer, than you normally would to get them.

The comps you earn are always more expensive—sometimes, a lot more expensive—than they would be if you just paid out of pocket for them. As an example, let's say you're getting hungry after a nice afternoon of blackjack. You ask the pit boss about comping you to dinner in the casino's top restaurant. He counteroffers with a dinner in the café. Nice, but you had your heart set on the restaurant. You ask what it would take to eat there, and are told it would take a few more hours of play, and that you might want to think about raising your minimum bet.

Never for a minute think that you're not paying for that fine meal even after the casino comps you. You'll be far better off, and money ahead, if you pay for it yourself.

Comps may appear to be freebies or giveaways, but make no mistake about it: there is no such thing as a free lunch, even in the gaming world. Gamblers earn their comps, and they pay for them with their loyalty and the money they wager when they play.

Getting Good at Comps

Want to know how to get more and better comps? Here are some tips from the pros:

- Play at a table with low limits. If you're playing $25 a hand at a $5 minimum table, pit personnel are more likely to notice you.
- Start with a big buy-in. If your session limit is $500, buy all your chips at once instead of spreading them out.
- Don't give the impression that you're comp shopping. Remember, casinos want loyal customers. It's okay to play at other casinos—you'd miss out on a lot of fun if you didn't—and it's always a good idea to join the player's club wherever you are. But you'll put yourself into comp territory faster, and better your chances of getting good comps, if you concentrate on one or two places that you like the best.
- Play when casino activity is slow. You'll have better luck getting comps when things are slow, such as during the week or in off-season months.
- Don't ask for a comp from every pit boss or host you see. It looks greedy, and it is greedy.
- If the casino offers you a comp that you can't use right away, ask to have it credited to your comp account.

- Don't expect a comp just because you lose. They aren't consolation prizes. Remember, you're gambling, right? Losing is part of the risk you take when you play.

- Make it easy for casino personnel to say yes when you ask for a comp. Do your research; know how many points you need to qualify for player's club prizes.

- Treat casino personnel the way you'd like to be treated. Tip your dealer every once in a while. If someone has gone out of his way to be helpful, let management know. If you get to know some casino folks well, it doesn't hurt to do something nice for them once in a while. Something as simple as sending a Christmas card in care of the casino is a classy gesture, and it will be remembered.

- Accept comps gracefully. A simple thanks with a smile will do. Doing an air spike or jumping up and down in place with glee isn't necessary. Along these lines, be graceful about accepting denials, too.

- If you're staying at a casino hotel, charge your meals and incidentals to your room. At the end of your stay, talk to your casino host (you should have already gotten to know this person), and ask to see if any of these charges can be comped if they haven't already been.

Knowing how to take advantage of comps can make playing blackjack that much more fun. Be aware of your play and you may be able to take advantage of more comps than you think.

Chapter 17

Team Play

Blackjack can be kind of a solitary sport. While there might be other people at the playing table when you're there, it's still a game between you and the dealer. What other people do doesn't enter in. You're not winning one for the Gipper, you're playing for yourself. But blackjack can also be a team sport. What's more, it can be lots of fun to play it as part of a team.

Teaming Up

While the thought of playing blackjack on a team might be new to you, it's actually been part of the game for some time. When the subject of playing blackjack as a team comes up, it's usually as part of a discussion on card counting. This is certainly the team approach that has received the most attention over the years. When Ed Thorp tested his blackjack theories at the tables, he did so as part of a two-couple team in Las Vegas. The guys operated the tiny computers that showed them when to alter their bets. The gals were on the lookout for members of casino management, and were prepared to give the high sign to the guys in case it looked like trouble was brewing. When Ken Uston won his millions beating the casinos, he did it as part of an elaborately structured team composed of many players who played over a number of years.

Bringing Down the House

Receiving less attention, at least until fairly recently, is a group of math students at the Massachusetts Institute of Technology. These brainiacs regularly hit the blackjack tables to exercise their considerable brain power—specifically, their super card-counting skills, which they honed through advanced computer programs of their own devising. And they won big money as they did so. One team won more than $400,000 in just one weekend playing in the casinos in Las Vegas.

FACT

The 2002 book *Bringing Down the House: The Inside Story of Six M.I.T. Students Who Took Vegas for Millions*, detailed the story of these students and their escapades at the gaming tables. Author Ben Mezrich exposed the inside skinny on card-counting teams to millions of Americans in a compelling read that almost seems more like fiction than truth.

How did they do it? Pretty much the same way all card-counting teams do it:

- Training team members on team play
- Assigning team members to certain key positions
- Sharing information on card counts
- Pooling financial resources to enable betting big

The key slots on the M.I.T. card-counting team were the back spotter, who counted cards without playing and signaled teammates when high cards were imminent; the spotter, who consistently placed small bets at the table while secretly counting cards and relaying the information to team-mates; the "gorilla," who moved from table to table, always making large bets based on cues from spotters; and the "big player." The big player was the individual who placed big bets as the card counts at tables got more and more favorable.

When the team entered a casino, members would send card counters to a table that looked favorable for play. When it appeared that high cards were on their way, the counters signaled the "big player"—the designated heavy hitter—to the table. They used code words to tell the big player exactly how hot the cards were. The big player then wagered large sums of money until the shoe went cold.

The M.I.T. team operated for about a decade before casino manage-ment was able to break up their act. During that time, various team mem-bers came and went, and the team earned millions of dollars. Finally, fraud investigators skilled at recognizing card counters started tracking the play-ers. Soon, every member of the team was persona non grata in the casinos.

Card-Counting Teams Today

Card-counting teams are still very much in operation today. Typically, they're not as elaborate as the team that Uston cut his teeth on, nor as skilled as the M.I.T. players were. It's safe to say that they also play it a little safer than Uston's team or the M.I.T. team did, as there hasn't been a headline story on a card-counting team for the past few years. Either that, or they're better at disguising their play than the other teams were.

Why Play on a Team?

Most blackjack teams do consist of people who are skilled at counting cards. However, just as it's true that you don't have to be a card counter to play blackjack well, you also don't have to be a card counter to play blackjack on a team. You can still band together as a group and hit the tables en masse. There are certain aspects to team play that can benefit players even without counting cards, although it's most effective for those who do.

Advantages to Team Play

Why would you want to ditch the solo act and go it as a team? There are several good reasons:

- **Bigger bankroll.** You might not be able to afford to play the kind of game you want to, but there's strength in numbers when you pool your money with your friends. When you do, every player on the team can use the combined bankroll as his or her own.
- **Bigger bets.** When you're playing with a combined bankroll, you can bet larger sums of money.
- **Bigger wins.** The more money you can get on the table, the more you stand to win.

Beyond the possibility of greater monetary returns, playing on a team can simply be fun. Instead of going it alone, you've got a team behind you and with you. Together, you can toast your wins and cry in your beers. You can have a good chuckle, or cry a good cry. When you play as a team, you can play off of each others' strengths and minimize each others' weaknesses. You can learn from each other, and learn what not to do from each other.

Disadvantages to Team Play

There are, of course, some disadvantages to team play as well. If you're playing with a group of friends, you run the risk of ending up less than friendly should things not go well for your team. A team member could go on tilt—bet irrationally to recoup his or her losses—and bring the team's profits down.

Money does strange things to people, and you may find out that you don't know your friends as well as you thought you did. Team members could mysteriously disappear. A solid player could have one "losing" day after another. This doesn't mean you shouldn't give team play a try. It can be a fun way to add some spice to your gaming experiences, and if you set things up right, you can minimize the risks.

QUESTION?

How many people make a good team?
There is no magic number for team play, especially if you're not counting cards. So start with a number that feels good and seems to be manageable. Four is a good starting point.

Casinos are always on the lookout for team play, so you have to be careful to stay under their radar, or you risk getting barred from that casino, and possibly from other casinos that share information among each other. Team play is not illegal, but casinos don't like it.

Qualities of a Good Team Player

One of the best ways to minimize the risk of team play is to know what it takes to be good team player.

First and foremost is a big dose of honesty. Team players simply have to be on the straight and narrow. You never want to get the feeling that you're not getting the whole story when it comes to seeing how everyone did at the end of the day. Second, you need players who bring the same set of skills and similar playing abilities to the table. People aren't going to play the game the same way, but they should know basic strategy, and they should play it well.

Finally, players should have a similar philosophy about what they expect to get out of team play. Without this, you run the risk of bad feelings and disappointment should the end result not be what some players thought it would be.

Qualities of a Good Team

Without question, the best blackjack teams are composed of people who are:

- Like-minded
- Able to get along well together
- Trustworthy
- Realistic about their playing abilities
- Realistic about their expectations
- Aiming for similar goals

A team needs someone who is willing to be the leader or manager of the team. This person makes sure rules are followed and makes decisions that reflect the group's goals and objectives. You also need a bookkeeper to keep track of monies in and monies out. The manager can do this, but it's nice to share the burden if there are other team players who are willing to take on some responsibility.

Players need to be able to fund the communal bankroll. The money used in team play is pooled together and shared among all players. It's best if everyone can come in at the same level, or fairly close to it, but it's fairly common for teams to include a few players whose money and playing skills don't exactly match. Their advanced playing prowess makes up for the short-falls in their funding abilities. And likewise, winnings (or losses) are shared by the group as well.

Doing the Team Thing

Once you've decided to play blackjack on a team, you have two choices. You can assemble the team yourself or find a team to play on. If you take the latter approach, make sure you know what you're getting into and how the team works. If they count cards and you know nothing about counting, you're only wasting their (and your) time.

Once you've assembled your team, it's time to figure out your game plan. This should include:

- How often you plan to play. Weekly, monthly, semiannually?
- Where you're going to play. Do you live near a casino with favorable rules? Do you want to save up for gaming vacations to Las Vegas, the Caribbean, Europe?
- How often you plan to practice. This isn't as necessary as it is for teams that count cards, but you want to make sure that everyone's skills are up to snuff.
- How much money you plan to play with.
- Setting win and loss limits. This should be done for each player as well as the team.

If you've been the main impetus behind the team, you'll probably serve as the team's manager. If it's not a position you want, see if someone else is willing to take it over.

ALERT!

If you're not much of a team player in most situations, there is no reason to think you'll have a sudden personality shift and become one when you play team blackjack. It's not for everyone, so if you don't think it's for you, keep going it alone at the tables.

How to Play as a Team

In team play that includes card counting, several "small" players sit at various tables in a casino and bet only the minimum, playing straight basic strategy. This will put them at a very slight disadvantage, but with minimum bets their losses will be minimal. Their job is to count into the deck without giving any signs that they are a counter. When the deck becomes rich in 10s—advantageous to players—they will discreetly signal one of a few "big" players. These players will come to the table and immediately start placing large bets. Since they have not seen a portion of the shoe, the house does not suspect they could be counting. Since the "big" players are always making large bets (and not varying their bets wildly), their bets don't look suspicious. In this way the team gets to make large wagers when the odds are in their favor.

The purpose of a noncounting team is to put several players at different tables each using strict basic strategy and each using a betting system. The hope is that at least one of the players on the team will get hot, make money, and more than cover the losses of the other team members. This practice is not going to draw the attention of, or a penalty from, the casino the way a counting team might. While this approach may seem like a good idea, each member is still playing at a disadvantage, and since the cumulative team bet is higher than an individual's bet, the house gets a slight percentage more money. In other words, team play may be fun but in the long run it will not be profitable.

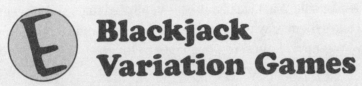

Chapter 18

Blackjack Variation Games

I n the never-ending quest to keep people interested in gambling and make it fun for them to play, casinos are always coming up with variations on basic themes. Of the various table games that casinos offer, blackjack is one that gets tweaked on a regular basis. What are these blackjack variation games all about? Are they worth playing? Are some better than others? We'll give you the skinny in this chapter.

A Little Variety

Even though blackjack is an old game—it's been around for centuries—it is still far and away the most popular casino table game. Aside from a few rule alterations, the basic game hasn't changed much over the years, which has both benefits and drawbacks.

On the plus side, blackjack has well-established rules and strategies that, once you learn them, stay with you. It's kind of like riding a bike—once you learn how, you never forget. You might get a little rusty at it if you don't ride all that often, but you always remember how to do it.

FACT

Casinos don't tweak blackjack games just to make them more fun for players. Doing so can also make a lot more money for the house, especially when players don't pay attention to rule changes and play game variations that give the house a big edge.

On the downside, blackjack is a very simple game. For many people, it simply isn't very exciting. It isn't a flashy game like baccarat, nor does it offer the kind of breathtaking thrills that games like no-limit poker can. Blackjack is a thinking person's game. As such, the thrills lie in making correct moves based on how well you know the strategies behind each play. Blackjack also moves fairly quickly. Unless there is a lot of money on the felt, it simply doesn't have the kind of suspense that other thinking person's games, such as poker, can and do create.

Casinos are very aware of blackjack's limitations, which is why they're constantly coming up with "new and improved" versions of the game. Many of these variation games simply offer ways for players to win more through side bets and bonus payoffs. Others use various twists and turns on game rules to lure gamblers to their tables. As gaming continues to grow in popularity, more and more casinos are offering various types of blackjack variation games. You'll find them in land-based casinos and on Internet gaming sites.

Should you play blackjack variation games? It depends on the kind of gambler you are, and what you want to get out of gambling. If you play for entertainment more than anything else, and you like a little variety, these games can be a lot of fun as they definitely can spice things up a bit. However, none of them offer what the original game does—favorable rules and odds that give players a sporting chance against the house. Blackjack variation games are, for the most part, a great way for casinos to part players from more of their money.

Strategies for Variation Games

Blackjack variation games are all based on the original game. However, the rules for some of these games are so complex that it can be hard to follow them. The people who deal these games have to know the rules, and they'll explain them to you if you get confused. Some casinos have brochures that explain the rules of the games they offer.

Every blackjack variation game requires learning a different set of basic strategies. If you play using the ones you learned for standard blackjack rules, you'll lose even more money than you otherwise would. If you're going to play blackjack variation games, don't let the house have a greater edge over you simply because you didn't know the correct plays. Get a copy of the rules before you play and calculate the correct basic strategy by plugging the variables into a blackjack rules calculator or game simulator.

To make it easy on yourself when calculating house odds or basic strategy on blackjack variation games, pay a visit to ✍ *wwww.wizardofodds. com.* This is an information-packed Web site, developed by a former Social Security actuary, that, among other things, details the rules and strategies for a number of variation games.

Side-Bet Variation Games

As previously mentioned, some casinos offer blackjack games that they've enhanced by adding side-bet gimmicks or bonus payoffs. For example, you might be allowed to place an additional bet on the following:

- Getting a blackjack with two cards of the same suit
- Your first two cards being the same suit
- Drawing multiples of certain cards, such as 7s
- Whether your two-card hand will be over or under 13
- Your first two cards being the same rank

The good news is that you can simply say no to these side bets if they aren't part of the basic game being played. When they are—and many casinos are offering games that do include such bets in their rules—you can't exactly say no. (Unless you just choose not to play at all.)

Side-bet games are far and away the most prevalent blackjack variation games out there, as they're only limited by the imagination of those who dream them up. For this reason, you'll see new side-bet variation games cropping up all the time. All of these games are variations on a theme, but some of them are pretty darned creative variations. That's exactly what the casinos are going for. The more creative the game, the more distracting it is to the player. Players who pay more attention to a game's bells and whistles are less likely to notice that they're not winning very often or as much as they would if they played good old basic blackjack.

Side-bet variation games can be lucrative when they pay off. However, the problem is that they rarely do, as the odds are so strong against many of these card combinations coming up. Because of this, players quickly catch on that they're losing money faster with these side-bet games, and they quit playing them. This doesn't mean that the games go away, though. Casinos are very good at coming up with new variation games to replace them.

21 Madness

This is a fairly common side-bet variation game. It calls for making a $1 wager in addition to your regular blackjack bet. If you are dealt a two-card 21, you get to push a button that activates the 21 Madness wheel. This is a lighted display that contains a random number generator just like those in slot machines. When the wheel comes to a rest, it displays a bonus payoff that typically ranges from $5 to $1,000.

Bonus Blackjack

In this variation game, players bet that they, the dealer, or both will get a blackjack on the first deal after a new shuffle. Wager amounts vary from $1 to $25 and can only be made on the first hand after the new shuffle. Wins pay off at 15:1.

A variation of this game offers a progressive jackpot. Players can qualify for it if they place bets on their hands and the dealer's hand. To win the progressive, a player has to get a blackjack consisting of an ace and jack of spades on the first deal after the new shuffle.

Royal Match 21

This variation game requires a side bet of $1 or more. If the first two cards the player gets are the same suit, he or she wins a bonus payoff at 3:1. A royal match, which is a queen and king in the same suit, pays off at 10:1. If the player wants to keep going, he or she can place an additional side bet in anticipation of being dealt another suited card.

Over-Under 13

This is another common side-bet game. Here, you wager that your initial hand will be over 13. Or you can bet that your first two cards will be under 13. Aces count as one for the side bet only. The house wins all 13-value hands.

Over-Under 13 pays off at even money; however, the house's advantage on this game—more than 8 percent—makes it a bad choice for players. If you're going to play Over-Under 13 (and you really shouldn't), take the over bet instead of the under bet. The odds are a little better on the former than the latter.

Red/Black

This is basically a variation of Over-Under 13. Here, players bet on whether the dealer's up card will be red or black. The rest of the rules are basically the same between the two games, with one exception: hands are a push if the dealer's up card is a 2 of the color you bet on. In other words, if the dealer has a 2 of hearts, and you bet that he'd have a red up card, your hands push. This game has a favorable house edge of 3.8 percent. Unless you're really desperate to play something—anything—do yourself a favor and stay far away from it.

More Side-Bet Games

We told you that casinos love to come up with new variations of these games, didn't we? These are just a few more that you might encounter.

QUESTION?

Are there any side-bet games worth playing?
For the most part, no. You're always going to be better off playing good old-fashioned blackjack. Another good reason to stick to basic blackjack: you won't have to learn lots of other basic strategy charts, which you should do if you're going to play games with uncommon sets of rules.

Dealer-Player Blackjack

In dealer-player blackjack, you simply bet on whether you or the dealer (or both) will have a blackjack in the next hand dealt. If you guess right, the payoff is at 7:1. If you wager that only the dealer or you have a blackjack, and you guess right, the odds increase to 15:1. The house carries a big edge—close to 10 percent—on all bets, as there is only a 4.73 percent chance of a blackjack showing up.

Perfect Pairs

This multideck game (usually eight decks) asks players to wager on whether their first two cards will be a pair. A perfect pair, which is a pair of the same rank and suit, pays 30:1. Colored pairs, which are pairs of the same rank and color, pay 10:1. A mixed pair (black and red) pays 5:1. Perfect Pairs gives the house a 3.45 percent advantage over players, which puts it into the category of games to be avoided. Pair Square, a variation of Perfect Pairs, pays off when the first two player cards are of the same rank. Payoffs vary, but the house edge is around 6 percent, and can be more.

Suited 6-7-8

If your first three cards are 6-7-8 of the same suit, you win this simple side-bet game. Play it right, which means hitting a 6-7 when the dealer shows a 2 (yes, it goes against basic strategy, which is why you have to learn the strategy variations for these games), and you will have a slight edge over the house. It's only about 0.01 percent, which equates to a penny for every $100 you bet, but it's something.

Super 7s

This isn't one of the more popular variation games, as its odds are simply too long for players to embrace, but it still crops up from time to time. It calls for making a side bet on whether you'll be dealt consecutive 7s. If you get two 7s, you'll be dealt another card, even if the dealer has blackjack. Payoffs depend on the cards you get and vary from casino to casino. They start small and increase significantly from there:

- First card any 7. Typical payoff: 3:1.
- First two cards any 7. Typical payoff: 50:1.
- First two cards 7s same suit. Typical payoff: 100:1.
- First three cards any 7. Typical payoff: 500:1.
- First three cards 7s same suit. Typical payoff: 5,000:1.

This game carries an astronomical 11 percent house edge. Avoid it like the plague.

Bust Out

This older side-bet game is a little like taking insurance, and makes about as much sense as that player option does. Here's how it works: After the dealer turns over his hole card, but before he finishes his hand, players bet on whether the dealer will have a stiff hand (hard 12 through hard 16). If the dealer draws a 10, you win. The payoff is 2:1. This game is a cakewalk for card counters. As such, it crops up very rarely. You might never see it.

Five-Card 21

A very simple side-bet game, Five-Card 21 pays 2 to 1 if a player gets a five-card hand that totals 21. The odds of this happening are pretty good, which makes this side-bet games one of the better ones you can play.

21+3

This game adds a poker-like element to blackjack, which may seem a bit odd at first. How can these two games go together? Here's how: players bet that their first two cards, when combined with the dealer's up card, will make a flush, a straight, a straight flush or a three of a kind. A win pays 9:1.

Rule-Variation Games

Rule-variation games are exactly what the term implies—they're blackjack games with very different rules than what you'd typically find in a standard blackjack game. As such, they require learning a different set of basic strategy rules if you're going to play any of them.

Super Fun 21

Single-deck games are rare, but this is one that you'll find at some Las Vegas casinos. The rules go like this:

- Players can double down on any number of cards. Doubling is also allowed after hitting and after splitting aces. Aces can be split.
- Cards of equal value, including aces, can be split up to three times.
- After the dealer checks for blackjack, players can surrender half their bets on any number of cards as long as the total is less than 21. Surrender is also allowed after hitting, splitting, or doubling down. The only exception is when the dealer has blackjack, in which case the surrender option is null.
- Hands totaling 20 or less with six cards are instant even-money winners unless players double down.
- Hands totaling 21 with five or more cards instantly pay 2:1 unless players have doubled down.

- Player blackjacks always win, even if the dealer also has blackjack. If the blackjack is suited in diamonds, it pays 2:1.

This is a great looking set of rules, definitely designed to give players the edge over the casino. Remember, though, casinos always have the edge. So where is it here? Here are the house-favorable rules:

- Dealers hit on soft 17.
- All blackjacks other than suited diamonds pay even money.

Of these rules, the second is particularly onerous. The chances of your getting a diamond-suited blackjack are about 1 in 16. This means that you have to settle for even-money payoffs on 15 of every 16 blackjacks you get. Is that worth giving up the 3:2 payoff that standard blackjack games offer? You do the math.

This game has at least a .77 percent edge over basic strategy players (some experts put the edge at 0.8 percent), which is higher than lots of multideck blackjack games with so-so rules. If you're serious about protecting your bankroll, this isn't the game for you. Plus, the long list of rule variations makes it difficult to learn basic strategy for this game.

Spanish 21

This multiple-deck game (usually played with six decks) is one of the oldest blackjack variation games. It's also one of the most player favorable of the batch, with a house advantage of just under 1 percent.

Spanish 21 is played with a Spanish deck, which is simply a regular fifty-two-card deck that has had its 10s removed. All face cards remain in the deck. Since the deck contains a greater percentage of low-value cards, and there are fewer chances of players getting blackjacks, it favors the house. Depending on other rules in place, the house edge typically ranges from 0.4 percent to 0.8 percent on this game.

To compensate players for the disadvantage of playing with four fewer 10s than they typically would, Spanish 21 offers more liberal rules than standard blackjack does. It's a long list of rules, though, which makes this game hard to play and even harder to learn basic strategy for:

- Player 21 always beats dealer 21.
- Five-card 21 pays 3:2.
- Six-card 21 pays 2:1.
- Seven- or more card 21 pays 3:1.
- 21 consisting of 6-7-8 of mixed suits pays 3:2.
- 21 consisting of 6-7-8 of matching suit pays 2:1.
- 21 consisting of 6-7-8 of spades pays 3:1.
- 21 consisting of three 7s of mixed suits pays 3:2.
- 21 consisting of three 7s of matching suits pays 2:1.
- 21 consisting of three 7s of spades pays 3:1.
- Dealer usually hits a soft 17 and stands on hard 17.
- Players may double after splits.
- Players may re-split up to three times, including aces.
- Players may draw and double down to split cards.
- Players may double on any number of cards.
- A form of surrender called double down rescue lets players take back the doubled portion of their bet and forfeit their original wagers. Late surrender is also offered.
- Three suited 7s in addition to the dealer having any 7 face up pays $1,000 for bets between $5 and $25, and pays $5,000 for bets of $25 and over. All other players get a $50 bonus when these bets are paid. Bonuses aren't paid on hands that are doubled.

Seven and One-Half

This game is actually an old vingt-et-un derivative that developed in Italy quite a while ago. Since it's similar to blackjack, it can be considered a rule-variation game. Seven and One-Half is played with a standard fifty-two-card deck from which the 8s, 9s, and 10s have been removed. Aces count as 1; face cards count as ½. Pairs of 3s, 2s, or aces can be split.

The goal of the game is to get as close as possible to seven and one-half without busting. Dealers and players each get one card dealt face up. Players can hit, stand, surrender, or double down, just as they would in blackjack. The dealer must draw to 4 and one-half and stand on 5. He wins all ties.

New Games

As previously mentioned, casinos are always coming up with new blackjack game variations. These games use the same strategies as the other variation games do to lure people to the tables. Like the other games, the new black-jack variation games typically don't offer much beyond some twists to the basic game of blackjack. Some are more player friendly than others, though, and might be worth checking out if you're looking for a new game to play.

Double Exposure

This game takes all the guesswork out of blackjack, as the dealer's cards are both dealt face up. The basic game calls for dealers to win all ties, except on natural blackjacks. Player blackjacks pay even money, and players can only split pairs once.

Other rules vary depending on the casino. Some require dealers to stand on soft 17. Blackjack ties might go to the player. Some let players double after splits, others don't. Players *might* be allowed to double on any two first cards, split more than once, or split unmatched 10-value cards.

The house edge on this game typically ranges from 0.6 percent to 0.7 percent, depending on house rules. However, it can go down to as low as 0.3 percent. This makes Double Exposure one of the better variation games, especially if you learn the basic strategy plays for it.

Blackjack Switch

You're more likely to see this game at online casinos, although it's also becoming a popular offering at land-based casinos. You play it two hands at a time, placing equal bets on both hands. You can trade cards between the hands, but you can only switch the second card. This increases the chances of hitting a blackjack and getting better hands in general. For this reason, casinos offset the player advantage by applying other rules that make the game friendlier to the house.

Here's how Blackjack Switch works: Players must make two equal bets. Cards are dealt face up. Players can switch the second card dealt between both hands. As an example, let's say you're dealt a 5-3 and a 7-6. Neither are great hands, and the second—13—is terrible. But since you're playing Blackjack Switch, you can put the 6 on the 5, and the 3 on the 7, and you've got two great hands, both of which put you in double-down territory. What's more, players can double on any two cards and after a split. Players can also place an extra bet if they get two matching cards out of their first four cards.

Here are the rules that turn the advantage back toward the house:

- No resplitting.
- Dealer hits soft 17.
- Blackjack pays 1:1 instead of 3:2.
- If dealer gets 22, all bets are pushed except for player blackjacks.

Multiple-Action Blackjack

As this game's title suggests, Multiple-Action Blackjack lets players place more than one bet—in this case, two or three. Special tabletops for this game display three betting boxes at each position. Players must place bets in at least the first two boxes. Multiple-Action is basically standard blackjack with a few interesting—and tricky—rule variations. The dealer doesn't get a hole card, just an up card. Players then make their playing decisions. After they're done, the dealer deals himself three additional cards. Each card is paired with his up card to make three dealer hands. All player hands stay exactly the same.

As an example, let's say you place three bets. You got a pat hand of 10-7 for 17. The dealer's up card is a 9. His three cards are 7, 8, 10, which makes his three hand totals 16, 17, and 19. He hits the 16 and busts. His 17 pushes yours. He wins with the 19-value hand. You win one hand.

Double down and split bets are placed in the same number of betting boxes that you cover with your original bet. Insurance bets go in the usual spot and are resolved on each hand.

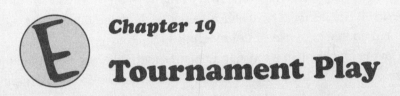

Chapter 19

Tournament Play

If you're serious about playing blackjack, and you play it consistently, you might want to play in a blackjack tournament at some point along the way. Tournaments are lots of fun and a good test of your skills, even for novice players. Chances are you'll meet some neat people at them, too. Best of all, if you play your cards right, you might even come away a winner!

Basics of Blackjack Tournaments

The gaming world is full of tournaments. You'll find tournaments for slot players, tournaments for poker players, and, of course, tournaments for blackjack players. Because of the amount of space it requires to put on a blackjack tournament, you won't find as many of them as you will slot tournaments. It isn't as easy for casinos to put aside game tables as it is to section off a couple of banks of slot machines for a tourney.

Playing blackjack in a tournament isn't much different from playing anywhere else. While there are some different strategies to tournament play, which you'll learn more about later in this chapter, the basic game is still the same. It is still you against the dealer. However, there is a second layer of competition in tournaments that doesn't exist in table games. Unlike table play, when you play in a tournament, you play against other players. You have to. Otherwise, it wouldn't be a tournament.

This one aspect—the chance to pit your playing skills against those of other players—is one reason why many people like to play in tournaments. In addition to the challenge of beating other players at their game, it adds a layer of excitement that you simply can't get when you're playing against the house.

Are there other advantages to playing in tournaments? You bet. Beyond the obvious—the chance to win a nice amount of money—tournaments have some very intriguing aspects, including:

- **No house edge.** For once, you don't have to worry about what you might be giving up to the house.
- **Player perks.** Tournaments are marketing gimmicks that casinos use to bring players through their doors. As such, they typically include special offers such as free meals, discounted room rates, and promotional items such as mugs, t-shirts, caps, and so on. Large tournaments might kick off with a player party where contestants can meet and greet, food is plentiful, and beverages flow freely.
- **The opportunity to compare your play to others.** Tournaments are great places to see how your blackjack abilities stack up to those of other players. You might fall by the wayside in the first few rounds. Or you might be very pleasantly surprised and end up in the final rounds of play.

- **The chance for casino personnel to get to know you a little better.** When you decide to play in a tournament, you instantly set yourself apart from about nine-tenths of the people who walk through a casino's doors. Don't think for a moment that casinos don't know this. While playing in a tournament doesn't ensure preferential treatment, don't be surprised if the perks you're offered suddenly ratchet up a notch or two after you compete in one.

ALERT!

If you enter a blackjack tournament, plan to play in it. While things can and do happen, and casinos realize this, don't pull out of a tournament unless you have a very good reason for doing so. If you can't make it, call the casino and let them know—popular tournaments often have waiting lists, and casinos would rather have all chairs filled if possible. Empty spots at the tables are very noticeable, especially at limited-entry events that cap contestants at a fixed number. If it's an invitation-only event, you might not be asked back in the future.

Inside a Blackjack Tournament

Tournaments vary so much from place to place that there's really no single description that fits them all. They come in all shapes and sizes. They can be big or small, single or multiday, held during the week or over a weekend. During the off-season, you'll find more tournaments on weekends than you will during periods when crowds are larger and space is at a premium.

That said, there are some common aspects that all tournaments share:

- **Entry fees.** Virtually every tournament charges them. The amount varies, and typically reflects the type of tournament and its duration. One-day tournaments are often held during the week to bring players into the casino, and are often fairly cheap to enter—maybe $20 or so. Weekend tournaments usually carry higher entry fees. Mega-tournaments, such as the multiday events held in Las Vegas and Atlantic City, can cost as much as $500 or more to enter.

- **Prizes.** Casinos use contestant entry fees to set tournament purses, which can range from a few hundred dollars or so to $100,000 or more. The best tournaments return all player entry fees in prizes, and you definitely want to play in ones that do if at all possible.
- **Table assignments.** When you play in tournaments, you typically don't get to choose where you sit. Most tournaments assign contestants to specific tables. This might be done on a first-come, first-served basis, with players of all levels mixed together at the tables. You might also come across tournaments that sort player tables based on playing level or experience, such as novice, intermediate, and advanced, and offer prizes for each category.
- **Bankrolls.** Unlike table play, where everyone gets to determine the amount of his or her own bankrolls, everyone starts with the same amount in tournament play. Depending on the tournament, you might have to put up your own cash. This is often the case at large tournaments that offer big cash prizes. Others use special tournament chips to represent bet amounts, so you're not playing with your own money.

QUESTION?

If I enter a tournament with a friend, can we sit at the same table?
Probably. However, should you be separated for some reason, don't switch seats without first checking with tournament organizers. There might be a specific seating arrangement that you don't know about, and making a change without approval could disrupt it.

All tournaments require players to compete over a specific period of time. It could be a few hours on a single afternoon, or multiple rounds of play spaced out over several days. Some tournaments require players to complete a specific number of hands. At the end of play, the contestant (or contestants) with the most money wins. Keep this point in mind. Tournaments aren't about the number of hands you win. The only thing that determines the eventual winner is how much money that person has after all is said and done.

Tournament Formats

Do some checking around on blackjack tournaments and you'll see that there's not much difference in their playing formats. Elimination tournaments are the most popular and the most widely offered. These tournaments are organized by heats or elimination rounds. After a certain period of time, or after a certain number of hands are played, the player with the most money is declared the table winner. The other players are eliminated. Depending on the size of the tournament, more than one heat or elimination round might be necessary.

The table winners from the preliminary rounds compete against each other in a semifinal round. Again, each table declares a winner or winners. These individuals go on to compete for the top prize. The number of finalists varies depending on the tournament. Most tournaments crown the same number of finalists as there are spots at a blackjack table—typically six or seven.

Blackjack tournaments can also be played in a nonelimination format. These aren't common, mostly because the format isn't as popular with players. Nonelimination tournaments group all contestants into a large pool. There might be multiple competition sessions, but they're for convenience sake, not to eliminate players. Everyone stays in competition.

Some nonelimination tournaments pull the top players together after a certain period of time and have them play a final round at one table. At others, competitors just keep playing for the duration. As in elimination tournaments, the player or players with the most money at the end of all playing sessions wins.

Chip totals do not carry forward from round to round. Each round starts with each player having an equal amount of chips. Plus, some tournaments will let players rebuy or put additional money of their own into the pot so they can get back in the tournament.

Picking the Right Tournament for You

Since tournaments come in all shapes and sizes, it's important to find the kind of tournament that best suits you. Some people like the excitement and glitz that accompany big multiday events. Others prefer the more casual and intimate atmosphere of smaller events. There really isn't a right or wrong about this, just what you prefer.

First, however, you have to track down some tournaments to play in. If you belong to the player's clubs at the casinos where you like to play, you probably receive a monthly casino newsletter or special mailings with casino promotions. If you've expressed a particular interest in blackjack, the mailings you get will reflect your preferences, which means you will likely get notifications of tournaments when they're scheduled.

If by any chance you don't get casino mailings and you are a player's club member, call the casino and ask to be placed on the club's mailing list. Don't assume there isn't one just because you don't receive it.

Some casino tournaments are by invitation only, so you won't know about them unless you're on the invite list. These tournaments are often restricted to qualified players. Casinos vary on the qualifications for these tournaments, but they typically sort out players based on betting levels and ability. Other tournaments are organized to reward loyal players or members of player's clubs who reach certain comp levels. But sometimes all you have to do is ask to be put on the invitation list. It all depends on the casino, so it never hurts to ask. Both types of tournaments usually offer contestants other nice perks such as free or reduced-rate lodging and free meals.

Other tournaments are open to anyone who wants to play, regardless of skill level, how long they've been playing, how much money they typically gamble with, and so on. These tournaments are often advertised in local newspapers as part of casino marketing programs. Ads can appear any day of the week, but you'll usually see more of them as the weekend approaches.

Which type of blackjack tournament is right for you? If it's your first tournament, you might find an open tournament more to your liking. These events typically attract average, regular players like yourself who enjoy the game but don't live and die by it. And they're usually cheaper to enter.

Let's say you've found a tournament that you want to play in. It's at your favorite casino, and a couple of your friends want to play, too. Everyone's really excited and you're ready and raring to go. But hold your horses! Your selection process isn't done yet. You've got a few other things to think about before you sign on the dotted line, such as:

- **Prizes.** As mentioned, tournament organizers use entry fees to determine what prizes will be. The best tournaments usually return 100 percent of entry fees to tournament players in the form of prizes, but they don't all do this. Before you enter, be sure to take a look at the tournament's prize structure so you can figure out what the player return is. An easy way to do this is simply to get a copy of the tournament brochure or flyer from the casino's marketing department. Add up the prize amounts. If the total prize money equals the number of players times entry fees, you've got a 100 percent return tournament.
- **Rules.** These include minimum and maximum bets, number of rounds, and other rules pertaining to how the tournament will be run and what players can do at the tables. Again, it's a very good idea to avoid any surprises by checking out tournament rules in advance.
- **Bankroll.** Will you be required to put up your own bankroll, or will players use tournament chips? If you have to bring your own money to the table, what is the buy-in? Will players be allowed to rebuy— that is, put additional money of their own into the pot so they can get back into the tournament?

FACT

Some tournaments return less than 100 percent of entry fees. However, they make up for the difference in various ways, typically by offering contestants free rooms, meals, and special tournament gifts, which you might want to take into consideration when choosing the tournaments you want to play in.

Once you've checked everything out and found it to your liking, go ahead and sign up. Larger tournaments might require advance registration of anywhere from a day to a week or more. Smaller, more informal events typically start registration a couple of hours before the event. Be sure to ask. Don't miss out on the fun because you didn't get your name in on time.

Tournament Day

Well, you've done it! You've entered a tournament, and the great day is here. You're at the casino, and you're ready to play. Now what happens? If you're playing at a large tournament, there will probably be a registration table. Here you check in, pay your fee, and pick up your table assignment and time slot. Smaller tournaments sometimes have registration tables, too, or you might be told to check in at the player's club desk. In some casinos, you simply check in at the tournament tables. Don't be late! Many tournaments disqualify late players, so give yourself enough time to get there. Doing so will also give you some time to catch your breath and compose yourself before you hit the tables.

After you register and/or check in, go into the tournament area and find your table. Some tournaments assign table positions randomly. At others, you'll have to draw for position. Some tournaments will let you choose where to sit. If the tournament is open seating and spots are open at your table, simply pick one. If there are other players at the table, introduce yourself. As you do so, you'll probably meet a variety of different personality types. You also might notice that some of your fellow competitors look a little jittery. Others might appear to be cool, calm, and collected, but don't fool yourself. Just about everyone gets a little nervous—or very nervous—at these events. Even the small, low-key ones. There's just something about competition that fires folks up.

Once tournament play begins, you'll be required to stay at your table until the end of each round unless you really need to leave. Rounds typically don't last very long—usually anywhere from 20 to 100 hands or so—so schedule your bathroom breaks for between rounds. There might be some people—friends, loved ones, assorted hangers-on and kibitzers—milling about the tables before the tournament starts. For security reasons, and to eliminate any possible cheating schemes, they'll be asked to leave before play starts.

Tournament Gear

You don't have to bring much with you to the tables. Nor should you. When it comes to tournaments, it's best to keep your attention focused on playing. Keep your accoutrements to a minimum to avoid distractions.

> If the tournament you're going to play in is following different rules than what you're accustomed to, generate basic strategy charts based on these rules and learn them well in advance of the event. Don't put yourself at a disadvantage by using strategies that don't match rules and conditions where you are.

That said, a bottle of water is a nice thing to have, especially if you tend to get parched when you play, but you'll be offered beverages during play. Along these lines, even if you typically like to have an alcoholic drink or two when you play, skip them during tournaments. It's best not to ingest anything that could impair your abilities or judgment, even if you think it might calm your nerves. Other things you might want to bring along include:

- Breath mints, gum, or throat lozenges. Dry mouth is a common tournament malaise.
- If you're a smoker, bring your cigarettes unless smoking is prohibited. If you usually use a lighter, if it's a reflective metal lighter you might be asked to pocket it as it could be used for cheating (you wouldn't dream of this, of course, but others do, and have). You'll be given a book of matches to use instead.
- A jacket or sweater. Casino air conditioning can kick in, and usually does, at the most inopportune times.
- Lip balm or lip gloss. People tend to lick their lips a lot when they're nervous. If you're really anxious, you could end up with a bad case of chapped lips by the end of the tournament.
- If you have one, a lucky charm, amulet, or talisman. No one will think you're odd, so don't feel embarrassed about this. You might, however, be asked to keep it in your pocket. Casinos typically

discourage players from placing extraneous items on the felt, especially during tournaments, again because of security issues and cheating concerns.

The one thing you don't want to bring with your are basic strategy charts. If you're playing in a tournament, you shouldn't have to use them anymore. If you still need them, you probably shouldn't be playing.

Let the Games Begin!

At the appointed time, the casino will announce the opening of play. As is the case in any blackjack game, the dealer at your table will distribute two-card hands to all players and himself. But here's where things go a bit differently than normal table play. Betting might not start at the traditional spot, which is to the dealer's immediate left. It could start somewhere else.

FACT

Some tournament players play close attention to the fact that first base rotates around the table. Being able to figure out exactly where play will begin could make a difference in how the final round of betting plays out, as the person who goes last will be able to see how everyone else bet, and can structure his or her bet on this knowledge.

Here's why: In tournaments, players advance through rounds based on how much money they have at the end of each round. To even the playing field as much as possible, and ensure that everyone at the table plays an equal number of hands, first base usually rotates around the table. The opening first base location might be determined by drawing numbers or by playing a quick hand of poker. Or it simply might start in the traditional spot, and after each hand, the dealer will use something called a button to indicate who goes first on the next round. Each player will have the chance to open a couple of betting rounds, or more, depending on the tournament, by being "on the button."

Strategies for Tournament Blackjack

There are whole books on this subject, and a couple of tournament trainer programs as well. You'll find some suggestions for both in Appendix C.

Regardless of the approach you choose to take for tournament play, there is one basic fact to keep in mind about it: the player with the most money wins. You may lose a lot of hands along the way. But if you make smart bets, you can come away a winner. How you play is important, but in tournaments, how you bet is even more so. Luck can and often does play a role in these events as well. All things being equal, a player who is having a lucky day will score the win.

Betting Strategies

Players take many different approaches based on this one very important factor. They're all variations on the same theme: doing what it takes to make it to the next round. Some players like to establish an early lead by betting big from the start. Others bet more conservatively and wait until later on to place bigger bets.

A good betting approach for tournament newbies is to get a feel for the table by betting the minimum for the first few hands. Always keep an eye on how the other players are doing chip-wise, especially as the end of the playing round draws near. If you're behind the leader, you want to have enough time to alter your betting strategy before the round ends. You might need to bet more, less, or the same, depending on what you think might happen. If you are in the lead, your best strategy will be to match the bets that other players place in hopes of catching up to you. Regardless of whether all players win or all players lose, you'll still be in the lead. Most players have to catch up to the leaders at some point during each round. If you have to, the best way to do so is by placing one large bet instead of multiple smaller bets. Your chances of gaining the lead, or regaining it if you had it and lost it, are substantially better with one large bet than a bunch of little ones.

If things look hopeless, don't be afraid to bet everything you can if you're still within a reasonable distance of the leaders. In blackjack tournaments (poker tournaments too, for that matter), the outcome of one hand can and often does swing the lead.

Playing Strategies

The fact that blackjack tournaments are all about the money also governs some interesting basic strategy variations. Depending on which round you're in, and your betting position, you might choose to make a very risky move, like doubling down on 17, simply to get more money on the table. Players have even been known to double down on blackjack hands, which means they treat the ace as a 1 instead of an 11. If the next card up is a 10, they're golden. If not . . . well, you can't say they didn't gamble.

Other gutsy plays that go against basic strategy include:

- **Splitting 10s.** Yes, basic strategy says never to do this. In tournament play, however, it's another way to get more money on the table.
- **Doubling down on questionable hands**, such as 12 or 13.
- **Doubling for less.** Again, you never want to do this in regular play. However, it can make sense in tournament play. Doing so can help you gain the edge over your opponents without having to risk more money than you have to.

Down to the Last Draw

The last five hands or so in every round are the most important. How you bet in the final moments of a round depends a lot on your table position and your chip position. Most players take an all-or-nothing approach and bet everything they have, or everything they can, given maximum bet limits. If you have to bet first, and you're in a position where another player can catch you by betting everything he has, then you have to bet the maximum, too. If you're so far ahead that no one can catch you, you'll have nothing to lose by betting the minimum. Being last up on the final hand is the best spot. You'll be able to see how everyone else bets, and adjust your strategy accordingly.

Chapter 20

Blackjack in Cyberspace

Today, there are tons of online casinos—Web sites that run computer simulations that offer real-time wagering on casino games. Lots of blackjack players are taking their action to cyberspace and hooking up with online games. If you'd like to join them but you're unfamiliar with the world of cybergambling, this chapter will tell you what you need to know to play safely and legally.

Gambling on the Internet

Various forms of gambling have been available online since the mid-1990s. Things started relatively small, and the first online games were fairly rudimentary, as gaming software and computers weren't as advanced as they are today. As new technology made possible better and faster game simulations, online gaming became hugely popular. Today, some of the games you find in cyberspace rival the action you'll find in land-based casinos. They also look and sound very realistic. Many have 3-D graphics. Others offer chat via instant messaging so you can talk to other players at your table.

FACT

It's hard to know for sure just how large the online gaming industry is, as it truly stretches around the globe and the numbers change by the second. In 1997, some thirty-two online gambling sites took in an estimated $300 million. By 2000, those figures jumped to 1,400 casinos with an annual take of $2.2 billion. In 2003, some 1,800 Internet gambling operations took in $6 billion, and this figure is expected to climb to $7.6 billion in 2004, according to Christiansen Capital Advisors, a New York consulting firm that analyzes the gambling and entertainment industry.

From the beginning, blackjack has been one of the most popular gambling games in cyberspace, and it's one of the games most closely associated with online gaming. In fact, it's hard to find a gaming site that doesn't have it.

A Powerful Force

With almost 2,000 gaming sites offering the chance to play casino-style games, bet on sports, or play lottery or bingo any time, day or night, online gambling has become a powerful force in the e-commerce world. Not only are there billions of dollars being exchanged online; gaming sites also play a huge role in online advertising, placing some 2.5 billion ads in 2002 alone.

Americans are the biggest gamblers in cyberspace, with more bets coming from the United States than any other country. One estimate has U.S.

players accounting for half of the revenues that run through offshore gambling sites. Some sources place figures even higher.

Against the Law?

A fair number of state and federal lawmakers have taken steps to make it against the law to gamble online. Depending on where you live, and how you interpret existing laws, you may or may not be breaking the law if you play casino games, bet on the ponies, choose lotto numbers, or wager your money on other games of chance on the Internet.

FACT

Due to the murkiness of existing legislation regarding online gambling, there are no online casinos based in the United States. While some United States-based companies own online casinos, or have ownership interests in them, these "virtual casinos" are instead located in parts of the world where online gambling is legal. Many are in countries such as Costa Rica, Antigua, the Dominican Republic, and several Caribbean islands.

The Law

Online gaming is a big part of Internet commerce, or e-commerce, which some consider the last great financial frontier. Even today, it is still relatively unexplored, and there are great riches to be mined in it.

Like all of the Internet, e-commerce is also relatively free of regulations. To some people, the lack of laws regarding what can and can't happen on the Internet isn't a concern. For the most part, they have found the Internet to be a pretty safe place, and they want to keep things the way they are. For others, especially some lawmakers, not having regulations in place regarding what can and can't happen on the Internet is a grave concern. They worry about such problems as shadow companies taking and running with people's money, rigged games, illegal bookmaking, and shady characters using the Internet for money laundering. And many lawmakers would like to figure out a way for the government to get a part of the billions of dollars annually flowing through the Internet.

The Wire Communications Act

Legislators have taken several approaches to imposing laws on Internet gambling. One is to apply a federal law established many years ago for a different purpose. Adopted in the early 1960s, the 1961 Wire Communications Act prohibits placing sports bets over phone lines. It calls for fining or imprisoning (or doing both to) anyone caught "engaged in the business of betting or wagering knowingly" using a "wire communication facility." Since many bettors connect to the Internet via the same lines they use for voice communications, some authorities argue that placing sports bets—wagering on horse races, prize fights, and what have you—over the Internet is also illegal. By extension, it could be argued that other forms of online gambling are also against the law.

However, many legal experts believe that the Wire Communications Act, in its current form, only applies to betting on sporting events, not to card games or other games of chance. And since the legislation only prohibits transmissions over wires, it has no jurisdiction over transactions taking place via wireless Internet access.

The federal government hasn't had a great deal of success enforcing the Wire Communications Act. The biggest problem is that it's an old act, and it doesn't specifically mention the Internet. But there have been a few notable prosecutions—and convictions—of individuals affiliated with online wagering sites under this law.

Regulating Internet Gambling

In 1995, U.S. Senator Jon Kyl (R-Ariz.) mounted the first attempt to regulate Internet gambling with his Crime Prevention Act. This act called for punishing bettors with fines and jail time. It came under fire from many corners, and especially the Justice Department, which argued that the legislation would be virtually unenforceable, and that federal agents had better things to do than spend their time trying to track down cyberbettors.

Saying that laws against sports betting and Internet gambling advance important social policy, and that failing to adapt the 1961 law to include the Internet leaves unchecked a "dangerous and growing addiction," Kyl attempted to get an amended version of his bill through Congress in 1997. It passed in the Senate, but the House never voted on it.

Since then, members of the House and the Senate have introduced other legislation that would amend the Wire Act and other existing laws that could relate to Internet gambling, and that would create new legislation that would regulate various facets of online gaming. None have passed, but this doesn't mean that lawmakers will abandon the issue.

FACT

According to Christiansen Capital Advisors, consumer spending on Internet gambling could increase to as much as $10 million in 2005.

The States Get in on the Act

In addition to federal laws banning Internet gambling, some states have also passed similar legislation making it illegal to gamble online. Interestingly, two states that have a heavy interest in land-based gambling—Nevada and Louisiana—led the way, obviously to protect their land-based casinos from competition.

In 1997, Nevada lawmakers passed a bill that banned any entity not licensed by the state from taking bets via any communications medium, including the Internet. Later the same year, Louisiana became the first state to specifically prohibit Internet gaming, and to penalize bettors for gambling online. Other states in which land-based casinos are located, and some that didn't have them, followed suit. By 2004, the following states had various laws prohibiting online gambling: California, Florida, Indiana, Illinois, Kansas, Louisiana, Michigan, Missouri, Nevada, South Dakota, Tennessee, Texas, and Wisconsin.

What does this mean for bettors? It should be obvious by now that the legalities of online commerce are murky, to say the least, and they are particularly muddy when it comes to online gambling. However, it's pretty clear that depending on where you live and the country that you're a citizen of, if you gamble online you're technically participating in an illegal activity. It's important to keep in mind, however, that there are no federal laws on the books, or pending legislation, which call for prosecuting online bettors. Instead, they target the companies that run online casinos and make it illegal for them to accept bets from U.S. citizens. Laws in the states have generally taken the same approach.

FACT

In March 2004, online casinos based overseas won a major victory when the World Trade Organization ruled that U.S. laws prohibiting online gambling violate international trade law. The Bush administration vowed to appeal the decision, which was seen by some as a possible first step in liberalizing U.S. laws on online gambling.

It's hard to predict where things will go with efforts to regulate online gambling. Many government officials realize it's impractical to monitor Internet activities, which makes laws that govern them almost impossible to enforce. Monitoring online activities also raises the often sensitive and controversial issues of privacy and free speech, which many officials would rather avoid. While some lawmakers are firm in their beliefs that Internet gaming should be banned, others are more open-minded and are willing to look at alternatives, such as allowing states to license, oversee, and collect taxes from online casinos. The best way to keep up with the legalities of playing online is regularly checking the status of legislation regarding it. There are Web sites that track this information; two to know about are *www. profreedom.com*, operated by the Internet Consumers Choice Coalition, and *www.thestandard.com*, a news site that reports on issues related to the Internet and other technologies.

Advantages to Playing Online

If you decide to play blackjack online for money, you'll be joining a huge crowd of people who are already doing so. That said, unless you decide to gamble at a multiplayer site, which offers live games instead of (or in addition to) computer-simulated games, and allows you a certain amount of interaction with other players, the chances of your meeting any of your fellow bettors are slim. This can be an advantage or a disadvantage, depending on your point of view. Some people like not having to deal with distractions that other players might cause. For others, having other people around to talk to, and perhaps commiserate with, is essential to having a good time at the tables.

Other advantages to playing blackjack online include:

- **It's private.** If you don't want people to see you gamble, what better way to do it than in the privacy of your own home?
- **It's readily available.** Yes, there are casinos just about everywhere these days, but you might not have one nearby. With online casinos, you can play blackjack twenty-four hours a day, any time you like, day or night.
- **No transportation costs.** Or transportation hassles, either.
- **It's a smoke-free environment** (if you want it to be!). And, of course, if you're a smoker, if you play online you won't have to suffer disparaging looks from nonsmokers.
- **You can practice or play for real.** One of the neatest things about online gambling is that most sites offer practice games. They're a great way to test the site, and a good way to hone your playing skills.

Disadvantages to Playing Online

As many things as online blackjack has going for it, there are some disadvantages as well. As with the advantages to playing online, some of them depend on your point of view. Some, like the potential for being taken for a ride by a fly-by-night site operator, are fairly obvious. Others aren't.

A couple of the biggest drawbacks to online blackjack relate to the technology itself. There's something about computer games, which online gambling is at its most basic level, that can be mesmerizing. While it's certainly possible to lose track of time when you're playing in a land-based casino, it's often a bigger problem for players in cyberspace. Zone out for too long, or too often, and it can spell financial disaster.

Many people find online games addictive. Having them at their fingertips is simply too alluring. This can also lead to big trouble, and not just financially. Spending too many hours playing online can isolate you from family and friends. It can also lead to circulation problems from sitting too long and repetitive motion injuries from working the keyboard, mouse, or trackball. Other disadvantages to playing online are:

- **You're isolated from other players.** Even the best simulation games in the world aren't the same as playing live.
- **You can't adjust your play** as easily as you can at a real table.
- **You lose out on real-life ambience.** There are no free drinks, no roving casino hosts handing out spot coupons, no people to chat with.
- **Differences in rate of play.** In real casinos, you have to wait for the dealer to shuffle and pass out cards, and for the actions of the other players. In cyberspace, games move amazingly fast, as dealing is done electronically. And unless you're playing a multiplayer game, it's just you against the dealer. Online blackjack can move so fast that it sometimes feels as if you've barely finished a hand before you have to place your next bet. In a game where strategy is so important, playing fast can pull you off your game, and cause you to make decisions before you've had the chance to think them through.

Discipline and good money management are essential when you're playing online, as it's very easy to hit your credit card and ante up more money if things aren't going your way. Set limits for your play online, just as you would in land-based casinos, and don't go beyond them, even if the computer tempts you to.

- **You can't get your winnings right away.** Depending on the casino's policies, it can take as much as a month before you can receive your money.
- **Safety concerns.** Land-based casinos are heavily regulated, which makes them safe places to play. Plus, they're typically owned by major corporations with established reputations. In cyberspace, it's pretty easy to make a company look credible when it's not, and there are no laws to protect you, just the integrity of the company operating the site. For the most part, however, it's safe to gamble on

the Internet, especially if you do your homework and play at solid, secure sites. While it's possible that something can go wrong, there are things you can do to minimize your risks and make your play safe and enjoyable.

Before you jump into online blackjack, give it some thought. It's not for everyone. If you think any of the downsides listed here might be problematic for you, consider limiting your play to land-based casinos.

Finding a Site to Play

One of the first things you'll need for online play is a casino at which to play. As previously mentioned, there are thousands of online gaming sites to choose from, and they're just waiting to welcome you with open arms. Some are places you'll want to play at. Others might look great, but may actually be places you should avoid like the plague.

You can use either a PC or a Mac for online gambling. Both are more than capable of handling anything a gambling site can throw at it. However, most gaming software is developed on a PC platform, which means it runs best on these computers.

Start Your Search

Wading through all online gambling sites—good and bad—would take a long time. Fortunately, you don't have to. There are some tried and true alternatives that can make fast work out of picking a place to play. Most people take a couple of different approaches to finding a site to play at, including:

- **Following an ad.** Many players get their first introduction to online gambling by clicking on banner ads that pop up when they're surfing the Web. This isn't a bad way to go, but you'll probably start seeing fewer of these kinds of ads in days to come, as several major Internet companies no longer accept ads from casino sites.

- **Searching the Web.** Enter just about any gambling term you can think of into the Web browser of your choice, and you'll get a list of hundreds of sites to look at.

- **Going through online gaming portals.** These are specialty sites that provide links to online gaming sites. Many contain lots of other information for online gamblers; some even offer site ratings. You'll find some listed in Appendix C.

- **Ask others.** If you have friends who play online, ask them which sites they like. There are online discussion groups, message boards, and chat rooms where players meet to discuss sites and other online gaming topics. Again, doing a search will bring them up. Some gaming portals sponsor these as well. You'll also find a list of some of them in Appendix C.

ALERT!

Downloading files and software from the Internet makes computers vulnerable to viruses, which are software programs or bugs in programs that can destroy all or part of the files on your computer. To protect your information from corruption, and keep things running the way they should, install a virus protection program on your computer and run it regularly.

Surfing the Sites

Now that you've identified some sites to look at, it's time to check them out. As you do, you'll notice that they vary quite a bit as far as appearance goes. Some are pretty simple. Others look a lot like real casinos. What you'll find on the sites can also vary quite a bit. Here's what you want to look for, and what any site you're interested in playing at should have:

- **A sign-in or registration page.** These typically contain fields where you enter a player name and password. It might be the first page to pop up. Sometimes you'll see a general entrance page first.

- **A list of featured games**, both ones to play for fun and ones to play for real. Playing for fun lets you see if you like the site's gaming software.
- **Information on gaming software.** Good gaming software is expensive, and it's the mark of a quality site if they're using certain types. Look for logos from companies like Microgaming, Cryptologic, or Boss Media. They'll typically appear on the site's entrance page.
- **A list of rules and policies.** These should spell out the rules governing games played. There should also be information on how the site operator handles disputes and conflicts.
- **Betting guidelines.** You want to know things like how much it takes to open an account, what the betting limits are, and when and how payouts are made. You might also see information here about bonus programs, which are special spiffs that sites offer to keep you playing at them.
- **An "About Us" page.** Companies that are willing to tell you about themselves are typically the ones that are going to stay in business. You want to see information such as when they started up, how long they've been in business, whether the site is licensed, where they're actually located, and who they're owned by.
- **A privacy policy.** Don't overlook this. You want to know exactly what the site's policies are. If they're not to your liking, move on.
- **Audit information.** One of the best ways to check the legitimacy of an online casino is to see if they're regularly audited. Those that are generally post the reports on their sites so players can compare the payout rates for various games, or they make the information available on request.
- **A customer service/tech support area.** Good features here include a twenty-four-hour toll-free service number and e-mail addresses for customer support. A good way to test customer support is to call the toll-free number and send them an e-mail. See how long it takes to get through on the phone, how long it takes to respond to e-mail, and how they word their response.
- **An area that tracks your purchases and payouts.** The best sites keep running logs that track every move players make.
- **A security statement.** It's essential to play at a site that offers top-notch security.

When you've located some sites that look good, take some time to explore them in depth before you begin playing for money. If they offer an online tour, take it. Go to the practice area and play some games to get a feel for how they operate.

Establishing Your Player Account

The last step in getting ready to play online is establishing your player account. You'll need to pick a user name and password. Different sites have different guidelines for this; just follow the instructions at the site where you've chosen to play. Choose a name and password that you can remember, but not so easy that someone else can guess them and hack into your account. When you decide what you're going to use, write the information down somewhere and keep it in a safe place, away from prying eyes.

One sign of a good site is membership in the Interactive Gaming Council, a not-for-profit organization that represents the global interactive gaming industry. It provides a forum for addressing online gaming issues, works to enhance consumer confidence by establishing fair and responsible guidelines and practices for the industry, advocates public policy related to online gaming, and serves as an information clearinghouse for the industry.

You'll also need to fund your play. The fastest and easiest way is by using a credit card, but you may not have this option. Many financial institutions, including such industry giants as Citibank and PayPal, no longer process gambling-related transactions. If you can't use your credit card, there are alternatives. You can send a personal check, cashier's check, or money order to the company that operates the site. However, these options can take up to two weeks or more before your money hits your account. If you're anxious to play, the wait can be excruciating.

There are also Internet-based banks, which will accept transfers from your credit card, personal check, or via wire transfer from your bank.

Some will also take transfers from bank accounts. Not only are they safe and secure, many offer bonuses for using them. You'll find a list of them in Appendix C.

If you decide to use an Internet bank, be sure to check out its terms and conditions. Things to ask about include transaction fees and withdrawal policies. Some might charge transfer fees if you move money from one account to another, and might not reimburse you for things like wire transfer fees, if your bank charges them. You also want to know how many days it will be before you can access your money. Are funds sent by cashier's check, or are they deposited to your home bank?

What's a good starting amount for funding your player account? It's a good idea to start small, maybe $50 to no more than $100. Until you know for sure that the site is legitimate, don't plunk down large amounts of money.

Playing Sanely (and Safely)

As previously mentioned, the dynamics of online casinos are different from those of land-based casinos. For this reason, getting used to online play can take a little time. Start out slow. You might want to play at tables with lower betting limits and increase your lowest betting level until you feel comfortable in the online environment.

Keep in mind that the basics still hold. Stick to what you know about betting and playing strategies. If you have the choice between one-on-one and multiplayer games—many casino sites offer both—consider playing one on one. As is the case in land-based casinos, it's the ideal blackjack game, as it's just you against the dealer. Especially when you're first starting out with online play, it's a good idea to minimize distractions until you are comfortable with it. Plus, multiplayer games really don't add that much to the online experience. There's a big difference between sitting next to other players in land-based casinos and playing with virtual players in cyberspace. The flavor that other players might add to land-based games simply doesn't translate that well to playing online.

Online blackjack can be a little tricky to get a handle on at first. Many factors can affect play, and it's a good idea to determine what they are before you put any money down. Some casinos shuffle decks after each hand, which makes it useless to count cards. Others shuffle after the deck is dealt. Online casinos also vary in the number of decks they use. Some will let you play more than one hand, and there are some that will even let you play up to five hands at a time.

ALERT!

Many online casinos use software programmed to detect huge betting swings. For this reason, the odds at many online casinos don't favor players who sharply increase the amounts of their bets from one hand to the next. To avoid a massive table turn, stick to a conservative betting strategy.

Internet gambling has been around for some time now, and, for the most part, it's pretty safe. Millions of people have wagered money online, and have received payouts with no problems. But it can still be a little disconcerting—even scary—to ante up your money to a faceless entity. That said, there are things you can do to ensure your safety if you decide to play online:

- **Do your research.** Play at reputable gambling sites that have been in business for a while.
- **Guard your privacy.** Make sure any site you play at has solid privacy policies in place. Don't give out personal information to anyone you meet in cyberspace, and don't offer up any more information than is absolutely necessary at casino sites.
- **Play at sites that have transaction logs** that track your deposits, wins, losses, and payouts. Having an electronic paper trail is one of the best ways to avoid problems.
- **Look for sites that belong to the Internet Gaming Council**.

Cashing In

If you're successful at playing online, the time will come when you'll want to get your hands on your winnings. To do this easily, you need to know the casinos' cash-out procedures, and you need to follow them carefully.

In fact, to avoid surprises, it's a good idea to know what they are before you start playing.

The cashing-in process typically starts by going to the site's cashier area and following the instructions there. As part of the cashing-in procedure, you might be asked to complete and fax in release forms, a copy of your credit card, and some other form of identification to prove you are who you say you are.

To avoid possible problems claiming your winnings, do a screen capture every time you win. You can do this on a PC by pushing the Print Screen button, which is usually located just to the right of the function keys (F1, F2, etc.) at the top of the keyboard. Having a picture of the screen that shows your winnings makes it easier to claim them should there be a dispute over what you've won.

Casinos follow various cashing-in procedures, but just about all of them will only credit your original deposit back to your credit card, if that's what you used to fund your account. Additional funds are usually sent via wire transfer or check. One last point: never assume the casino received your information. Make sure it gets there by following up with a phone call or e-mail to make sure casino management has everything they need to process your claim. And always, always, keep track of all your communications. Save copies of all correspondence, and keep notes of all phone calls, including the time you made the call and the person you spoke with.

If Something Goes Wrong

While no one likes to think about problems, it's a good idea to prepare for what you'll do if you run into trouble when playing online. Problems happen less frequently these days, but they still can happen, and for a variety of reasons. Sometimes it's a matter of simple miscommunication. Or there may have been a software or hardware glitch. Regardless of the situation, it's important to approach things as calmly as possible. Most problems related to online play deal with payouts, which is another reason why it is a good idea to keep track of your winnings independently of the tracking that is done at the site.

Assess the problem, and determine your best plan. Typically, it starts with contacting the casino. This is when you'll be glad you decided to play at a site that has twenty-four-hour customer support lines. When you reach a customer support person, stay calm. Don't yell or make threats. State the problem clearly and succinctly. These problems are usually resolved quickly, and most often in the player's favor. Like land-based casinos, online casinos are intent on keeping players happy so they will come back to play often.

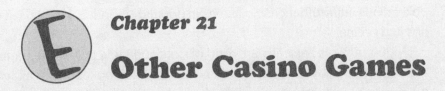

Chapter 21

Other Casino Games

At times, you simply have to get away from the blackjack table. If you're getting tired, or if you're counting cards and the count goes negative, getting up and away from the blackjack table is a very good thing to do. Fortunately, there are many other games to choose from. Some are good tests of your skills and knowledge, others are simply fun to play. A couple of casino games even have odds that are fairly favorable to players.

Video Poker

Video poker, first introduced in the 1970s, began as a low-stakes game that people played while waiting for drinks at casino bars. Since then, the stakes have increased—it can be hard to find a nickel poker machine these days, although they do exist—along with the game's popularity. These days, video poker rivals many other casino games in popularity, both at land-based casinos and online.

Video poker is basically a hybrid of slots and table poker. But there is a big difference between it and table poker. In video poker, it is you against the machine—you're not playing against other people. Therefore, instead of trying to beat your opponents in various ways, such as bluffing if you don't have a good hand and raising when you do have one, your only objective is to get the best hand you possibly can.

FACT

Many blackjack players also like video poker—and with good reason, as the games have some basic attributes that are very similar. They are both games of skill, and they have a low house edge. Like blackjack, there is a basic strategy for playing video poker. If you master it, you can play at close to 100 percent payback.

Video poker machines look a lot like slot machines. You'll see them in two basic shapes: tabletop or upright. Like slot machines, they offer play in various denominations, ranging from nickels to $1 or more. Quarter and dollar machines are the most common, and the most popular.

Types of Video Poker

Most video poker machines offer games that are variations of the classic five-card draw poker game called Jacks or Better. Just like table poker, however, there are many different variations on the basic game. For the most part, they fall into two basic categories:

- **Wild card games,** such as Joker Wild, Joker Poker, Sevens Wild, Deuces Wild, and so on. In these games, various cards serve as wild cards and can count as any value. In Joker Poker, for example, a joker can be used to make a winning hand, such as a high pair, two pair, three of a kind, and so on.
- **Non–wild card games.** These are games such as Tens or Better, Aces and Eights, Bonus Poker, etc. They're all variations on Jacks or Better, with various twists to keep players interested.

Video poker is one of the better casino games you can play, as the payouts are better than most of them. Some variation games, such as Joker Wild, can yield even better than 100 percent payback with optimal play, which makes them very attractive. **TABLE 21-1** shows payouts on some of the better-known, more common games, beginning with the best:

TABLE 21-1: Video Poker Payouts	
Video Poker Game	**Payout (with optimal play)**
Deuces Wild	100.75%
Joker Wild	100.6%
Double Bonus	100.17%
Double Joker Poker	99.96%
Aces and Faces	99.85%
Triple Bonus	99.8%
Jacks or Better	99.54%
Tens or Better	99.1%
Deuces and Joker Wild	99%
Sevens Wild	98.8%

Rules of the Game

All video poker games play in the same way. The machine deals five cards. You choose to hold or discard as many as you want to. When you're done deciding what to hold or toss, you hit a button marked "draw." This tells the machine to replace your discards with new cards. If they line up as you hoped, you'll be a winner. If not, you'll bust.

Unlike regular table poker, there is no bluffing, calling, or raising. You only get one draw, which means you have only one chance to improve your hand. Some casinos, however, offer the chance to double your winnings after you win a hand. If you take this option, the machine will deal five additional cards. The first will be face up, the rest face down. You then pick one of the face down cards. If it is higher in value than the up card, you double your winnings. If it is lower, you lose the hand and your winnings. In some casinos, a tie is a push; in others, you lose. If you win the double, you can usually keep doubling.

Winning Money at Video Poker

As in regular poker, video poker payoffs are based on hand values. Winning hands range from as low as a pair of 10s or jacks all the way up to royal flush, which is a hand of 10 through ace, suited. The amount you win is based on each possible winning combination. Hand values are the same no matter what game you play. From the best hand to the worst, they are:

- **Royal flush.** This is the best hand you can possibly hold in poker. It consists of an ace, king, queen, jack, and 10 of the same suit.
- **Straight flush.** The second-highest hand possible, it consists of five cards of the same suit, in order, such as A, 2, 3, 4, 5 (as in blackjack, the ace can be counted high or low).
- **Four of a kind.** This is four cards of the same value, plus one card that isn't.
- **Full house.** A hand containing three cards of the same value and two of another value, such as 10, 10, 10, king, king.
- **Flush.** All cards in the hand are of the same suit.
- **Straight.** All cards in the hand are in order, but are not of the same suit.
- **Three of a kind.** This is three cards of the same value, plus two cards that aren't.

- **Two pair.** Two sets of two cards of the same value or rank, such as two 4s and two 8s.
- **One pair.** Any two cards of the same value.

Video poker payoff tables can vary from machine to machine, depending on the odds set by the manufacturer. They can range from 91 to 100 percent, and even higher in some cases. If a machine has an expected payoff level of 99.54 percent, you can expect to get $99.54 back for every $100 you put in if you play perfectly. This means making the correct play every time. If your moves aren't perfect, your expected return will be lower.

How can you tell what the payoff is on a particular machine? You have to read the entire pay table. However, unless you know how to interpret the information on the pay table, you still won't know what the payoff is. The easiest way to figure it out is to compare this information to a standard pay table that you already know has a certain payback.

Always play maximum coins in—typically five. This is the only way you'll be eligible for the premium for the best hand of all—a royal flush.

TABLE 21-2 represents three different pay tables for one game—Jacks or Better. Note how the percentages change depending on how the machine is set up. The numbers at the top represent the type of machine. In each case, they represent what the machine pays on a one-coin wager for a full house and a flush. For example, a 9/6 game pays nine coins for a full house and six for a flush.

TABLE 21-2: Payouts for Three Variations of Jacks or Better			
Machine Type	**9/6**	**8/5**	**6/5**
Royal flush	250	250	250
Straight flush	50	50	50
Four of a kind	25	25	25
Full house	9	8	6
Flush	6	5	5
Straight	4	4	4
Three of a kind	3	3	3
Two pairs	2	2	2
Pair of jacks or better	1	1	1
Payout	**99%**	**97%**	**95%**

TABLE 21-3 compares common payouts for two more popular games—Deuces Wild and Jokers Wild. Here we're looking at payouts based on maximum coins in (five).

TABLE 21-3: Number of Coins Paid for 5 Coins Played		
Hand	**Deuces Wild**	**Jokers Wild**
Royal flush	800	800
Four deuces	200	n/a
Five of a kind	15	200
Wild royal	25	100
Straight flush	9	50
Four of a kind	4	20
Full house	3	7
Flush	2	5
Straight	2	3
Three of a kind	1	2

Hand	Deuces Wild	Jokers Wild
Two pair	n/a	1
Kings or better	n/a	1

TABLE 21-3: Number of Coins Paid for 5 Coins Played (continued)

Just as you can beat blackjack by learning basic strategy, you can be a winner at video poker by learning optimum play. This means matching your play to the game you're playing. Which cards you choose to keep and which hands you try to make (keep that pair? or toss it and try for a flush?) are determined by the payouts for various hands. There are tons of different game variations, and a strategy to match every one, so it's impossible to list them all here.

Pai Gow Poker

Pai gow poker is a cross between a Chinese gambling game called pai gow, which is played with dominoes, and poker. It is similar to blackjack and baccarat in that players compete against the banker to make the best possible hands. In Chinese, pai gow means "make nine."

ALERT!

When you want to play pai gow poker, be sure you're sitting down at a pai gow poker table, not at a pai gow table. The two games are very different. Pai gow poker is played with a standard fifty-two-card deck, plus a joker. Players are dealt seven cards, which they arrange in two-card and five-card hands. While pai gow also calls for players to arrange two hands, it uses dominoes instead of cards.

Some gamblers find pai gow poker enjoyable because it tends to move more slowly compared to other casino games. It's also less nerve-racking than some games, as it often ends in a push with the dealer. Given these characteristics, bankrolls can last a lot longer when you're playing pai gow poker than with some table games. And it's more relaxing than many casino games.

Finally, there's no hidden house edge in pai gow poker. Instead, players are charged a 5 percent commission, or vig, on winnings. Some casinos charge a flat fee per hand instead.

Basic Rules

As mentioned, pai gow poker uses a standard deck of fifty-two cards plus one joker. Two to seven people can play. The objective is to beat the dealer. When you're the dealer, the objective is to beat the players at your table.

Here's how it works: Players place their bets. The dealer, or banker, then makes seven stacks of seven cards each. Next, he shakes three dice in a little cup. The resulting number determines how stacks are distributed. (In some casinos, this order is determined by a randomly generated number, not by dice.) Each spot at the table—even those where there are no players—receives a stack of cards. The cards dealt to empty places are called "dragon hands." Another player can play a dragon hand, and play two positions instead of one, but isn't required to do so.

When players get their cards, they arrange them into two poker hands—a low, or back hand, which contains five cards, and a high, or front hand, which contains two cards. The five-card hand *must* have a higher value than the two-card hand, which can be confusing to new players. If you happen to mess up, and set a higher value on your front hand, it's called a foul and you'll automatically lose both hands.

FACT

In pai gow poker, high and low hands refer to where the hands are placed on the table, not to their value. To help keep them straight, think of them as front and back, not high and low.

After players set their hands, the dealer arranges his, using a set of fixed rules called the "house way." From here, there are four possibilities:

- **A win**, in which each hand beats the dealer's hands—front must beat front, back must beat back. The probability on this outcome: 28.55 percent.

- **A tie**, in which one hand wins and the other hand loses. The probability on this outcome is 41.47 percent.
- **Both hands lose to the dealer.** The probability on this outcome: 29.98 percent.
- **One or two hands with equal value to the dealer's hand.** These are called copies. When they come up, the dealer wins.

Winning combinations are paid even money, minus the vig or commission. Pai gow poker hands are valued exactly the same as poker hands are, with the following exceptions:

- An A, 2, 3, 4, 5 straight is the second-highest straight.
- The two-card hand can be a pair or two individual cards.
- The highest two-card hand is a pair of aces. The lowest is a 2, 3.
- The joker can be used to complete a straight, a flush, or a straight flush. If not used to complete any of these hands, it counts as an ace.

Banking the Table

In pai gow, banking goes around the table. The dealer can do it, and players can do it, too. Any player can choose to be the banker when it comes time for him or her to do so. Since the bank has a slight edge, thanks to ties, being the banker can be a profitable move. However, it can also cost a lot, especially if the other players are lucky and the banker isn't. Depending on the number of players, the banker risks up to six times a normal bet on one hand. For this reason, the banker must have enough money to pay off all the winning bets of the other players and the dealer. Some casinos will let players co-bank with the house.

To keep players from banking too often, most casinos have rules that require the bank to rotate evenly among players, or that limit players to how many hands they can bank.

Pai Gow Poker Strategy

Pai gow poker can be a fun game to play, but not necessarily an easy one to learn. For example, it might make sense to you to load all your high cards in your back hand. However, depending on the other cards you're holding, this might not be a good idea. Remember, both hands have to win for you to win your bet. As such, there are many different ways that hands can be set. If all else fails, you can ask the dealer to set your hand for you.

Caribbean Stud Poker

This hybrid poker game was invented on the island of Aruba in 1988. It can be a fun game if you like poker but don't want to get into the mental gymnastics required when you're playing against a table of gamblers. In Caribbean Stud Poker, as in blackjack, it's just you against the dealer.

Rules of Play

Caribbean Stud Poker is played at a standard blackjack-sized table. Each player places an ante, which is a bet of at least the table minimum. Players can also place optional side bets on a progressive amount, which shows on a meter displayed above the table. After all bets are placed, the dealer gives each player five cards, dealt face down. He then deals himself five cards. Four are face down; one is face up. Players then check their cards. At this point, there are two options:

- **Folding**, in which case you lose your ante bet.
- **Calling.** This requires an additional bet of twice the ante amount. As an example, if your ante was $10, a call would require $20, for a total bet of $30.

After everyone is done with this round, the dealer reveals his cards. If he isn't holding ace-king or better, he folds. Players are paid even money on their ante bets and push on their call bets. If he is holding an ace-king or better, his hand is said to qualify, which means he's "qualified" to play against you and the other players.

If the dealer's hand is better than yours, the house gets your ante and your call bet. If his hand is worse than yours, you are paid even money on the ante bet and a certain amount on your call bet, depending on what you're holding (see **TABLE 21-4**).

TABLE 21-4: Win Payouts in Caribbean Stud Poker	
A-K or pair	1:1
Two pair	2:1
Three of a kind	3:1
Straight	4:1
Flush	5:1
Full house	7:1
Four of a kind	20:1
Straight flush	50:1
Royal flush	100:1

Strategy

Since the dealer usually qualifies more than half of the time, Caribbean Stud Poker is a game with a fairly strong house edge. Because of this, it's important to learn the strategies for playing this game well. They're a bit complex, so we won't present them here. But we can give you some betting strategies to keep in mind:

- Bet when you hold A, K, Q, J or better, including any pair or better.
- Bet when you hold A, K, Q when any other card in your hand matches the dealer's up card.
- Bet when you hold A, K, Q and your two unsuited cards have a higher value than the dealer's up card.
- Bet when you hold A, K, J when any other card in your hand matches the dealer's up card.
- Bet when you have a four-card flush of the same suit as the dealer's up card as long as at least one of the cards is either an 8 or better or a higher value than the dealer's up card.

- Bet when you have A, K when any of your unsuited cards match the dealer's up card.

Caribbean Stud Poker also offers a $1 side bet on a progressive jackpot, which you can win if you draw a flush or better. You can win a progressive bet even if the dealer doesn't qualify to play, or if you lose your hand. However, the odds are so long on this bet—about once in 500 hands, even for the lowest payoff—that it's really not worth playing.

Baccarat

Baccarat is a very elegant-looking French card game. It is a derivative of blackjack, and it resembles blackjack in a number of ways. Because of this, many blackjack players enjoy playing it.

Baccarat has a "big player" allure to it, which casinos enhance by positioning the game in special areas, which are often roped off to keep onlookers out. They're also often elaborately decorated, and the cast and crew might even be dressed in formal evening attire. All of this makes baccarat seem mysterious and a bit off-putting. That's too bad, because it's actually a simple and fun game to play.

Basically, baccarat consists of two hands—a player hand and a bank hand. All you have to do is bet on whether the player's hand or the house's hand—the bank hand—will come closer to the total of 9. You don't even have to touch the cards. The dealer does all the work.

FACT

The house edge in baccarat is very low—about 1.36 percent if you bet on the payer, and about 1.17 percent if you bet on the bank, or the house. (The house makes money by taking a percentage from bank wins, typically 4 to 5 percent.)

You'll find two styles of baccarat in American casinos. First there's the traditional, full-pit version, which is played on a long table with twelve to fourteen players and a team of elaborately garbed house personnel.

Mini-baccarat is less formal (less intimidating, too) and is played on a standard blackjack-sized gaming table that accommodates six players and one dealer. If you play baccarat's more formal full-pit version, you'll be playing in an area of the casino that's set apart from the rest of the place, which can also be very calming. However, the stakes in the formal full-pit version aren't. Full-pit baccarat has higher table limits than mini-baccarat, typically starting at $25 to $100 per hand.

How to Play Baccarat

Baccarat is a simple game. There are no complicated strategies or rules to follow. In fact, the only decision you have to make is where to place your bet. The rest is done for you. In baccarat, 2 through 9 carry face value. Tens, jacks, queens, and kings are counted as 0, and aces count as 1. You don't even have to count the cards—the dealer does it for you.

Each player position at a baccarat table has three spots in front of it. One is marked player, one is marked banker, one is marked tie. This is where you'll place your bets. Next, the dealer, or croupier, will deal two cards to each hand. Strict rules dictate how the cards are played once they're dealt. For this reason, only the croupier makes playing decisions. The rules are the same whether you're playing full-scale baccarat or mini-baccarat. First, the croupier checks the hands for an instant winner, which is a two-card total of either 8 or 9. This is called a natural. An 8 is le petit natural; 9 is le grande natural. Le grande beats le petit. If both hands are equal in value, a tie is declared. These hands are pushes, and neither side wins.

If neither hand has a natural and there is no tie, both hands are played out. Each hand can receive no more than a total of three cards. The player hand always goes first, regardless of what the banker's hand is. The rules of play for the player hand and the dealer hand start fairly simply and get more complex as they go:

- If the first two cards total 0 through 5, the player must draw another card.
- If the first two cards total 6 or 7, the player must stand.
- If the player hand does not draw a third card, the banker hand always does.

- When the banker hand's first cards total 5 or less, the banker will draw.
- If the banker hand's first cards total 6 or more, the banker will stand.

Here is where things start to get tricky. Depending on what the player's third card was and what the hand's total is, the banker will either draw or stand. Since you don't make the decisions, however (remember, the croupier does everything), you really don't have to know the intricacies of play at this level.

When both hands have played out, the hand that comes closest to 9 wins. The croupier will then pay those who bet on the winning hand. Winning banker and player hands are paid even money. If there is a tie, banker and player bets are a push, and you get your money back. If the hands tie, the payoff is either 8:1 or 9:1, depending on the rules where you are playing. This sounds great, but the odds are really against a tie. Because of how baccarat rules are set up, the odds of any hand resulting in a tie at this point are 9.5 to 1.

FACT

Baccarat's setup resembles blackjack in many ways. All cards are dealt from a shoe, just as in blackjack. And, as in blackjack, the shoes hold multiple decks, which are shuffled before each round of play. Players are asked to cut the cards. The cut card is inserted back into the deck, and the first card is burned.

Because baccarat is such a simple game, basic strategy is simple for it. Stick with banker and player bets. Ignore tie bets. The payoff for these bets looks great, but the odds are against you winning them.

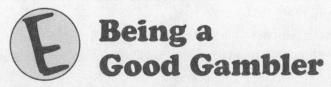

Chapter 22

Being a Good Gambler

Etiquette and good manners go a long way in the casino world. While being a turkey—a casino slang term for a player who doesn't know or chooses not to abide by casino etiquette—might not get you thrown out of a casino, if you're new to casino gambling, you might not know what proper casino comportment is all about. That's understandable, as much of what you need to know is experience-driven. This chapter shows you the ropes.

Table Manners

Proper behavior at gaming tables is a mixture of the old adage of "doing unto others as you would have them do unto you" and knowing the general etiquette and customs that govern table play. It is important to remember that there are certain rules and regulations specific to blackjack and the casino environment that people on both sides of the table are expected to know and follow. If you're not familiar with them, you might react inappropriately to something that is perfectly normal and routine but came as a surprise to you.

Casinos aren't fond of bouncing people out on their ears for simply being rude or obnoxious. This doesn't mean, however, that it doesn't happen. If you're playing at a table where someone's behaving so poorly that it's disrupting your game, casino management will most likely know about it, and will step in and do something if they feel such action is warranted. If nothing happens, it might be more your problem than theirs. If so, your best bet might be to move to another table.

Minimize Distractions

One of the best things you can do as a player is help keep the action going at your table. This means not doing things that distract other players and cause game delays, including:

- **Buying in excessively.** Some players like to keep their beginning buy-in small as part of their approach to money management. That's okay, but having to stop the action repeatedly for additional buy-ins is a hassle for the dealer and irritating to other players. It's best to buy enough chips to stake your play for an entire session. If it's necessary to buy more, buy what you think you'll need for the remainder of your play.
- **Fumbling the equipment.** Help casinos keep cards and chips in good condition by washing your hands before you play, and not eating

while you play. If you drop a card or chip, don't retrieve it yourself. Let the dealer know instead. He or she will call someone over to pick it up.

- **Losing focus.** Yes, casinos are fascinating. Yes, the people-watching is great. Save your fascination and gazing about for when you're not playing.
- **Phoning home.** Like good restaurants and theatres, gaming tables are places where cell phones aren't welcome. Turn off your phone when you're playing. The same goes for pagers, beepers, and watch alarms. Casinos are noisy enough. You don't need to add to the din.
- **Coming and going.** If you're going to play, stay and play. Don't disrupt the game by taking excessive breaks. It's okay to take a bathroom break or a short walk to stretch your legs. Just do it judiciously. Along these lines, if you're going to be away for longer than few minutes, free up your spot. Collect your chips and let someone else have your chair.
- **Excessively checking basic strategy charts.** It's okay to use these, but try not to consult them on every hand.
- **Celebrating excessively.** If you win a big hand or hit the jackpot in some other way, it's hard not to let everyone know about it. A quick whoop or yahoo is fine, and will probably earn you some "attaboys" or "way to goes." If you don't get them, don't go chumming for them by continuing to draw attention to your win in some way. You know you did well. It isn't necessary for the entire casino to join in on your celebration.

Zipping the Lip

It's also a good idea to keep table chatter down. Yes, it's okay to talk a little when you're playing. Going into long political diatribes or involved, detailed orations about your latest bunion surgery isn't.

Along these lines, as tempting as it might be to offer advice to other players, especially if they're making blatant mistakes, don't do it. Even if your advice is the best in the world, you're going to take the blame if the player you offer it to follows it and loses. It always happens. Do yourself a favor and just don't give advice even if it's solicited. If people try to give it to you, you can simply ignore it, and them. If this isn't possible—it's amazing how pushy some people can be about offering advice—a simple "Hey, I really appreciate it, but I've got my own strategy" usually works.

QUESTION?

How can I tactfully tell someone who is asking for my advice that I'd rather not give it?

This can be a sticky situation, especially if you're doing well and the other person isn't, but a little tact can go a long way. One way is to side-step the question with a little humility, such as saying, "Geez, I'm really not an expert. I guess I just hit a lucky streak. You will, too." And just keep on playing. If you're the forthright type, just come right out and say that you'd rather not offer any advice as you'd hate to see the person lose if they followed it and it didn't work for them.

If a player at your table makes an amazingly poor move, don't berate him or her for it. No dirty looks, either. Remember that what other players do doesn't affect your outcomes. Typically, these people balance any moves that might go against you with ones that are in your favor. Just let them play.

Eat, Drink, and Be Merry?

Gambling is a leisure-time activity—for most of us, anyway—so it only follows that we want to have fun when we do it. The good news is that casinos want us to have fun, too, and they make it pretty easy for us to do so. That said, gaming isn't a free pass for abandoning all good sense and going crazy the second you come through the door.

Drinking and Gambling

Virtually every casino offers complimentary drinks to players. Many casinos offer alcoholic and nonalcoholic beverages at the tables; some limit table service to nonalcoholic beverages only.

For many people, gambling and drinking go hand-in-hand. For them, a game just isn't the same unless they can play while tossing back a couple of cocktails or quaffing a few beers.

Knowing what you now know about blackjack, you've probably realized that drinking and gambling isn't a good mix. It's especially not a good combination when you're playing games such as blackjack that require skill and concentration, but it's also not a good idea regardless of the game or games you enjoy playing.

Using perfect basic strategy and keeping count of cards simply requires a clear head. Even one drink can significantly impair your playing ability. It's easy enough for the house to have an edge over you. Why give them an even greater advantage by playing when your judgment is clouded?

QUESTION?

Why do so many casinos offer free drinks to players?
They know that alcohol loosens up inhibitions and can make players more reckless when they play, which often results in making decisions that are bad for them and good for the house. Simply put, have a few drinks, and you're more likely to fork over more of your bankroll to the house.

It can be extremely tempting to take advantage of a casino's hospitality and enjoy those free drinks while you're playing, especially if you're on a budget. And it's easy for one drink to turn into two, or many, when you're concentrating on the action and not paying much attention to what's going on around you. But it's definitely wise to wait until after you're done playing to imbibe. Yes, you'll have to pay for those drinks—the freebies are only available to players when they're actively gambling—but you'll be money ahead. The price you'll pay for them won't come near what you'll spend when you drink and gamble.

Casinos don't like to see people who have had too much to drink. Beyond having to deal with drunk and belligerent gamblers, they might face legal ramifications if they serve them. There are certain legal implications in various gaming areas concerning serving players too much alcohol. One player sued a casino for overserving him and causing him to lose his money.

He won, and the casino had to reimburse him. In South Dakota, for example, dealers cannot deal to players who are visibly inebriated.

Smoking and Gambling

Casinos have always been smoker-friendly, and most still welcome smokers throughout their establishments. For the most part, however, smoking is restricted to cigarettes or cigarillos. Some casinos allow cigar smoking but might restrict these smokers to certain areas. Some casinos designate these areas with signs, but it's always a good idea to ask if you're not sure.

If you are going to smoke when you're playing, be sure there's an ashtray on the table. Don't use a plastic gaming cup—you could melt it. If you need an ashtray, ask for one and wait until it arrives before you light up. If you use a reflective metal lighter, keep it in your pocket and ask for matches if they didn't accompany the ashtray. Mirror-finish lighters could be considered cheating devices, and casinos typically discourage their use.

Eating and Gambling

Many casinos offer complimentary light buffets to their guests. If there is one where you play, enjoy the goodies from them away from gaming tables. For convenience, buffet items are often finger food. As such, they make for sticky, grimy fingers. Dirty fingers result in sticky, stained or smudged cards. Cards in this condition must be replaced, which causes game delays. No one likes those, not the casino, and not your fellow players. If you must eat while gambling, do it during a planned break from playing. Get away from the tables and go have a bite. Take a walk, do some stretches. The game will still be there when you get back. Chances are you won't be asked not to eat when you're playing, but it's a common courtesy not to do so.

Flirting and Gambling

This last point is somewhat of a sticky subject, but we'd be amiss if we didn't address it. Casinos offer an environment where people can let down their inhibitions and have fun. As such, flirting is part of the action for some, especially when they've had a few drinks (another reason to keep tabs on how much you imbibe).

A little flirtation is fairly harmless, and it can be fun. However, if you come on heavy to another player at the tables, or to a dealer, you could be asking for big trouble. Plus, such behavior can be very irritating to other players. You might think it's cute. They might, too, to a point. Surpass that point, and they'd just as soon you took it somewhere else. If you get positive signals from another player at your table, keep your desires on hold until there is a break in the action. Then, definitely take it somewhere else.

Money Talk

Casinos put a big emphasis on how money is handled, and for good reason: they deal with lots of it every day. For this reason, casinos have strict policies governing how dealers and players should handle their cash.

Handling Your Money

We also covered this subject in Chapters 14 and 15, but it's important enough to recap here:

- Never hand money or chips directly to a dealer. Always place both on the table, and allow the dealer to pick them up.
- Don't touch your bet after the deal starts or the dealer stops accepting bets.
- Always exchange cash for chips at the table. Casinos prefer chips to cash, as they're easier to track.

Protecting Your Stash

Casinos hire people whose sole responsibility is to keep things safe for players and staff. This doesn't mean, however, that you can afford to be lax when it comes to keeping your money safe.

Most people who come to casinos carry more cash on them than they typically would. People who are interested in taking it away from them know this. While it doesn't happen that often, people do get robbed both in casinos and outside of them.

Here's how to protect yourself, your bankroll, and your winnings:

- Always stash extra cash, jewelry, and any other valuables in the hotel safe. It's also a good idea to put any credit cards you've brought in there, too, or leave them at home if you don't think you'll use them.
- If you're going to carry a purse, make it one with a long enough strap so you can wear it across your chest. Good purse choices also include bags that close with flaps and buckles or zippers. If your purse has outside pockets, don't store any valuables in them, even if the pockets zip.
- Wear a fanny pack. Casinos are about the only place where they aren't a fashion faux pas. Instead of wearing the pack the way you typically would, with the sack part nestled into your back, turn it around so the sack is in front of you. You defeat the purpose of wearing a fanny pack if you can't see the pouch.
- Don't keep large amounts of money in your wallet, and don't take it out of your pocket any more often than necessary. Keep it in an interior pocket if possible.
- Always keep an eye on what's going on around you. It's the best way to stop suspicious behavior before it becomes a problem. If you're too tired to do much more than stare at the table in front of you, it's time to stop playing.
- Keep an eye on your chips. If you need to leave the table for any reason, the dealer will keep an eye on things, but it's a good idea to tote up what's there before you go. If it's a lot, take the majority of it with you. Leave enough to reserve your seat.
- If you hit the jackpot, ask to have your winnings dispersed as a check, or have it deposited at the cashier's cage and collect it when you're done playing. If you take your winnings in cash, ask for a security escort to your car or room.
- Don't give out your address indiscriminately. The fewer people who know where you live, the better. If there's an address tag on your keys, keep them in your pocket or purse.
- Cheating doesn't happen that often, but it does happen. If you see it, or you suspect you're a victim of it, immediately report it to casino security.

All About Tipping

Although you might not think of it as such, gambling is a service industry. The people who facilitate your gaming experience and make it enjoyable as you play are performing a service to you. Therefore, it's appropriate to tip them.

FACT

Tipping casino staff isn't necessary or required, but it's a common practice, and a common courtesy. What's more, people who tip, and tip appropriately, typically receive better service, whether it's in a casino or anywhere else where tipping is customary.

Knowing how to tip—both the appropriate amounts and to whom they should go—is somewhat of an inexact science. There really isn't any one set of guidelines to follow, and appropriate amounts can vary quite a bit. There are also some people in a casino whom you shouldn't tip.

While it may seem as if you should just go to the experts about this, it's also inappropriate for casino staff to solicit tips from you, or to tell you how much or when you should tip, so you really can't ask them. But we can tell you.

The following suggestions cover most standard tipping situations and procedures. They're not engraved in stone, however, so feel free to modify them as you see fit and as the situation warrants. It is always appropriate to tip wait staff. An appropriate tip for a drink is $1 or so, which you can offer via paper money, coin, or chips. If you're ordering drinks for more than two people, or asking for some sort of special consideration, such as a special drink or a pack of cigarettes, it's appropriate to up this amount a little.

It's appropriate to tip the casino cashier when you're exchanging chips for cash. Since these people are stationed on the periphery of a casino, it's easy to forget about them, but they also provide an important service. A dollar or two, depending on how much you're exchanging, is always appreciated.

Dealers are the people you'll tip the most in casinos. Of everyone a casino employs, they'll spend the most time serving you, so it's a good idea to learn the procedures and amounts that you should follow when tipping them. They include placing tip or token bets from time to time. This is basically the same as tipping, although if your hand loses the dealer loses, too. You place a tip bet—also called a "toke"—by putting a chip in front of your own wager. A reasonable amount is at least 10 percent of your bet amount—$1 if you're betting $10. You can also do this after a big win, or after you win a hand the dealer helped you on. If you do so after a big win, consider placing small amounts on a few hands instead of one big toke on one hand. This way, the dealer won't be out the entire amount should your next hand be a loser. Here, tip what you are comfortable with. If it was a big win, 10 percent of the win might seem a bit too much, but if you split it up over several hands, it will probably be about right.

You can also hand the dealer a chip (or chips) as a tip. Unlike a tip or token bet, this money is not wagered. A good time to tip is when you're done playing and you've colored up your chips. Just lay a chip or two on the table. Say thanks, or "this is for you." It's appropriate to do this even if you lost, and you should definitely do so if you haven't placed tip bets for the dealer during the game, or you feel you didn't do so often enough. Tip an amount you're comfortable with. While there are no rules of thumb for this, many people feel comfortable with $5 a playing session.

ALERT!

Never offer a tip to casino management. This includes pit bosses on up. They're not allowed to accept tips, and it can be embarrassing to both them and you should you offer one. Save yourself an awkward moment and express your appreciation with a simple thank you. Keep your cash in your pocket.

Clothes and the Gambler

Back in the day, people dressed up to gamble. Look at photos from Las Vegas in the 1950s and 1960s, and you won't see a pair of jeans or shorts anywhere. Times have definitely changed, and it's okay to be comfortable when you gamble, but don't be sloppy. Dress the part of a responsible gambler and you'll get treated better. It's almost guaranteed.

Dressing the Part

What does dressing the part mean when it comes to gambling? It always means wearing clean clothes in good repair. A small hole or a ragged hem in a pair of jeans is okay, especially when they're part of the design. Jeans that are held together with threads instead of cloth aren't appropriate. Dressing the part also means wearing clean clothes. It's easy enough to sweat through a shirt when you're playing, especially if you're nervous. Don't distance yourself from other players by wearing clothes that should have hit the Biz bag before you hit the casino.

Leaving Inhibitions Behind

As previously mentioned, casinos are places where people feel comfortable cutting loose a bit. If you're one of them, you should definitely take advantage of the setting and have some fun. If you live a buttoned-down life outside of a casino, it can be lots of fun to vamp it up a bit (or a lot) when you're inside them. And that's fine. (Within reason.)

Keep in mind that flashing a lot of jewelry, even if it's costume jewelry, can be distracting to other players. Bangle bracelets that clank together and jingly charm bracelets are especially irritating. If you want to wear them, fine. Just take them off or leave them in your room when you play.

Good Gambling Habits

Throughout this book, we've emphasized the importance of being a smart gambler. These are individuals who know and set their limits, and they quit when they reach these limits. Adopting these behaviors and making them into habits when you're a newcomer to gambling is one of the best things you can do. Adhering to them throughout the course of your gambling career will make you a winner in the long run, regardless of how much money you take away from the tables.

Going beyond your limits and continuing to play when you should quit doesn't put you in good stead for winning back what you've lost, or turning nice amounts into mega-jackpots. What's more, it sets a dangerous precedent that can turn gambling into a problem.

Gambling with Gambling

No one gambles with the intention of becoming addicted to it. However, it's no secret that gambling can and does cause problems for some people. As gaming continues to grow in popularity, the number of people who develop problems with it is on the increase as well. Recent studies show that gambling addiction is on the rise in every state where gambling is legal. Since that's forty-eight out of fifty states, this is a problem that can't be ignored.

FACT

According to researchers at the University of Connecticut, online gamblers might have more problems with addictions than other gamblers do. Investigators found that of those who have gambled on the Internet, 74 percent could potentially have gambling problems, compared with 22 percent of those who play in land-based casinos. Researchers added that more studies are needed to determine whether the Internet attracts people with gambling problems, or it if causes the problems.

Both winners and losers can develop gambling problems. People who have addictive personalities are simply at a greater risk than those who don't, regardless of which side of the equation they fall on. This doesn't necessarily mean that these individuals should stay away from gambling. But it does mean that they need to be aware of the risks gambling poses for them. Like alcoholism and drug abuse, gambling addictions are recognized as a disease. As such, it's no longer a dirty secret that must be kept behind closed doors. There are programs in place to treat and support people with this disease.

Recognizing the Signs

Recognizing the signs of gambling addiction is a good way to stop potentially problematic behavior before it escalates into full-blown addiction. The following questions from Gamblers Anonymous will increase your awareness of what the signs of gambling addiction are, and are a good way to measure your own behavior.

If you answer yes to at least seven of these questions, you might have a problem:

1. Did you ever lose time from work or school due to gambling?
2. Has gambling ever made your home life unhappy?
3. Did gambling affect your reputation?
4. Have you ever felt remorse after gambling?
5. Did you ever gamble to get money with which to pay debts or otherwise solve financial difficulties?
6. Did gambling cause a decrease in your ambition or efficiency?
7. After losing, did you feel you must return as soon as possible and win back your losses?
8. After a win, did you have a strong urge to return and win more?
9. Did you often gamble until your last dollar was gone?
10. Have you ever borrowed to finance your gambling?
11. Have you ever sold anything to finance your gambling?
12. Were you reluctant to use "gambling money" for normal expenditures?
13. Did gambling make you careless of the welfare of yourself or your family?
14. Did you ever gamble longer than you had planned?
15. Have you ever gambled to escape worry or trouble?
16. Have you ever committed, or considered committing, an illegal act to finance gambling?
17. Did gambling cause you to have difficulty in sleeping?
18. Do arguments, disappointments, or frustrations create within you an urge to gamble?
19. Did you ever have an urge to celebrate any good fortune by a few hours of gambling?
20. Have you ever considered self-destruction or suicide as a result of your gambling?

Seeking Help

If you feel you're at risk, or you think a friend or loved one has a gambling problem, it's important to seek help as soon as possible. For many people, the first step is a support group or twelve-step program such as

Gamblers Anonymous. GA has local chapters in many U.S. cities, and maintains a Web site at ✍*www.gamblersanonymous.org.* It's important to remember that there's no reason to be ashamed of gambling problems. The only shame is in not doing something about them.

Keeping Things in Perspective

Gambling has been around as long as there have been people on earth. The ability to weigh the potential benefits of risk is an innate part of human behavior. While people vary greatly on the amount of risk they're willing to take on, or enjoy taking on, everyone is born with a willingness to take some level of risk. What's more, we're born with a certain desire to do so. We might satisfy this desire in the boardroom, on the golf course, or in a casino.

Playing casino games such as blackjack is just one way to satisfy the need to put things on the line. However, they're far from the only way. Life itself is full of gambles, and we take on risk every day in some way or another. Gambling can be part of our risky business, or it could be none of it. Either way, casino gambling should be an adjunct to the life we lead, not life itself. Approach it as such, and you'll come away a winner each and every time you play.

Appendix A

Glossary of Terms

action:
The amount of money being wagered.

anchorman:
The person who sits immediately to the right of the dealer. Also called the anchor, or third base.

ante:
An opening bet.

banked games:
Games where players play against the house, as opposed to playing against other players.

bankroll:
The total amount of money that a player sets aside for gaming. Sometimes called a betting handle.

basic strategy:
A mathematically proven system that determines the optimal play for all hands, based on the dealer's up card and the value of the player's cards.

bet:
The money you put up, wager, or risk in a gambling game in hopes of winning an award.

break:
Drawing cards that exceed a total of 21 points. Also called bust.

break down a bet:
Separating a stack of chips into separate stacks, each of a single denomination. Performed by dealers to make it easier to pay off the bet, and to prevent cheating.

breaking hand:
A hand of two cards that total 12 through 16 points, which is a total that can easily be pushed over 21 with a single card.

burn card:
The card that is removed from the beginning of a new deck or shoe, or when a new dealer comes on duty.

button:
A small round marker used in tournament play to indicate the player who starts a betting round.

buy-in:
The amount of money you start a game with; the amount of money exchanged at a table for chips before beginning play.

cage:
Where the casino cashier is located.

candy store:
Sometimes used to describe a casino where blackjack rules and conditions are favorable to the player.

coloring up:
Exchanging smaller denomination chips for larger-value chips.

comp:
Abbreviation for complimentary. Casinos bestow comps such as meals, free or discounted lodging, and entertainment on players who either bet enough money or spend enough time in the casinos (or both) to earn special consideration from them.

croupier:
Another term for dealer, often used in baccarat.

cut:
Offered by the dealer to the player just after the shuffle and before the first hand. The cut tends to split the deck or shoe into a different order.

discard rack:
The tray in which discards are held until the next shuffle.

double up:
Increasing a bet by the same amount. Also called a press.

dump:
To lose a large amount of money very quickly. Casinos use it to describe tables where players have been winning a lot, too.

edge:
The advantage held by the house or the player. Also called house advantage and player advantage.

expectation:
The amount that a player can expect to win or lose, based on statistical advantages and disadvantages.

face card:
A jack, queen, or king.

felt:
The playing surface on the table.

first base:
The first player spot at a blackjack table, located on the dealer's far left.

george:
Dealer's term for a generous tipper.

hard hand:
A hand without an ace, or one with an ace that can only be counted as a one.

hard count:
The value of a hard hand.

head-up game:
Playing a game alone with the dealer. Also called one-on-one.

high card:
Typically refers to a 10-value card, although 9 can be considered a high card, too. Ace can be considered a high card for betting purposes and a low card for playing purposes.

high roller:
Someone who plays for lots of money.

hit:
Drawing additional cards after the first two cards.

hit and run:
A playing strategy that calls for entering a game, playing a hand or two, and then leaving.

hole card:
The face-down card that the dealer deals to himself.

insurance:
A side bet offered by most casinos when a dealer shows an ace.

low roller:
A low-income player, or a player who doesn't play for lots of money. Also known as a grinder.

natural:
Blackjack achieved by a 10 and an ace.

odds:
The mathematical probability that an event will occur.

pat hand:
A hand with which nothing more needs to be done.

payoff:
The amount you collect if your bet wins. Some times called a payout, especially when referring to slot and video machines.

payout schedule:
How much a winning hand, roll of the dice, or combination on a slot machine will pay.

penetration:
The amount of a deck or shoe that is dealt out to players.

push:
What results when the total of both the player and the dealer is the same. Also referred to as a tie or a stand-off.

shoe:
A plastic device that holds the cards being dealt.

side bet:
A separate bet, such as insurance, placed before or during a regular blackjack game.

tap out:
To lose all your money.

third base:
The last seat at a blackjack table, located to the dealer's right.

tokes:
Short for token of gratitude or gratuity. Also called zukes.

turkey:
A slang term for a player who is unfamiliar with the social and situational etiquette of the casino.

up card:
The dealer's card that is dealt face up.

vingt-et-un:
The French game that blackjack was derived from.

win rate:
Another way of stating player expectation, in this case over the long run.

Appendix B

Blackjack
Strategy Charts

Basic Strategy—Multiple Deck										
Dealer	2	3	4	5	6	7	8	9	10	Ace
Player										
17	S	S	S	S	S	S	S	S	S	S
16	S	S	S	S	S	H	H	H*	H*	H*
15	S	S	S	S	S	H	H	H	H*	H
14	S	S	S	S	S	H	H	H	H	H
13	H	H	S	S	S	H	H	H	H	H
12	H	H	S	S	S	H	H	H	H	H
11	D	D	D	D	D	D	D	D	D	H
10	D	D	D	D	D	D	D	D	H	H
9	H	D	D	D	D	H	H	H	H	H
8	H	H	H	H	H	H	H	H	H	H
A8	S	S	S	S	S	S	S	S	S	S
A7	S	D	D	D	D	H	H	H	H	H
A6	H	D	D	D	D	H	H	H	H	H
A5	H	H	D	D	D	H	H	H	H	H
A4	H	H	D	D	D	H	H	H	H	H
A3	H	H	H	D	D	H	H	H	H	H
A2	H	H	H	D	D	H	H	H	H	H
AA	P	P	P	P	P	P	P	P	P	P
TT	S	S	S	S	S	S	S	S	S	S
99	P	P	P	P	P	S	P	P	P	P
88	P	P	P	P	P	P	P	P	P	P
77	P	P	P	P	P	P	H	H	H	H
66	H	P	P	P	P	H	H	H	H	H
55	Always treat as 10, never split									
44	H	H	H	H	H	H	H	H	H	H
33	H	H	P	P	P	P	H	H	H	H
22	H	P	P	P	P	P	H	H	H	H

*Surrender if offered

S = Stand, H = Hit, D = Double, P = Split

Basic Strategy—Multiple Deck, Double Down Allowed After Splitting										
Dealer	2	3	4	5	6	7	8	9	10	Ace
Player										
17	S	S	S	S	S	S	S	S	S	S
16	S	S	S	S	S	H	H	H*	H*	H*
15	S	S	S	S	S	H	H	H	H*	H
14	S	S	S	S	S	H	H	H	H	H
13	S	S	S	S	S	H	H	H	H	H
12	H	H	S	S	S	H	H	H	H	H
11	D	D	D	D	D	D	D	D	D	H
10	D	D	D	D	D	D	D	D	H	H
9	H	D	D	D	D	H	H	H	H	H
8	H	H	H	H	H	H	H	H	H	H
A8	S	S	S	S	S	S	S	S	S	S
A7	S	D	D	D	D	S	S	H	H	H
A6	H	D	D	D	D	H	H	H	H	H
A5	H	H	D	D	D	H	H	H	H	H
A4	H	H	D	D	D	H	H	H	H	H
A3	H	H	H	D	D	H	H	H	H	H
A2	H	H	H	D	D	H	H	H	H	H
AA	P	P	P	P	P	P	P	P	P	P
TT	S	S	S	S	S	S	S	S	S	S
99	P	P	P	P	P	P	P	P	P	P
88	P	P	P	P	P	P	P	P	P	P
77	P	P	P	P	P	P	H	H	H	H
66	P	P	P	P	P	H	H	H	H	H
55	Always treat as 10, never split									
44	H	H	H	P	P	H	H	H	H	Ace
33	P	P	P	P	P	P	H	H	H	H
22	H	P	P	P	P	P	H	H	H	H

*Surrender if offered.

S = Stand, H = Hit, D = Double, P = Split

Basic Strategy—Multiple Deck, Double Down on 10 and 11 Only										
Dealer	2	3	4	5	6	7	8	9	10	Ace
Player										
17	S	S	S	S	S	S	S	S	S	S
16	S	S	S	S	S	H	H	H*	H*	H*
15	S	S	S	S	S	H	H	H	H*	H
14	S	S	S	S	S	H	H	H	H	H
13	S	S	S	S	S	H	H	H	H	H
12	H	H	S	S	S	H	H	H	H	H
11	D	D	D	D	D	D	D	D	D	H
10	D	D	D	D	D	D	D	D	H	H
A9	S	S	S	S	S	S	S	S	S	S
AA	P	P	P	P	P	P	P	P	P	P
99	P	P	P	P	P	S	P	P	S	S
88	P	P	P	P	P	P	P	P	P	P
77	P	P	P	P	P	P	H	H	H	H
66	H	P	P	P	P	H	H	H	H	H
55	Always treat as a 10, never split									
44	H	H	H	H	H	H	H	H	H	H
33	H	H	P	P	P	P	H	H	H	H
22	H	H	P	P	P	P	H	H	H	H

*Surrender if offered.

S = Stand, H = Hit, D = Double, P = Split

Basic Strategy—Single Deck										
Dealer	2	3	4	5	6	7	8	9	10	Ace
Player										
17	S	S	S	S	S	S	S	S	S	S
16	S	S	S	S	S	H	H	H	H*	H
15	S	S	S	S	S	H	H	H	H*	H
14	S	S	S	S	S	H	H	H	H	H
13	S	S	S	S	S	H	H	H	H	H
12	H	H	S	S	S	H	H	H	H	H
11	D	D	D	D	D	D	D	D	D	D
10	D	D	D	D	D	D	D	D	H	H
9	D	D	D	D	D	H	H	H	H	H
8	H	H	H	D	D	H	H	H	H	H
A8	S	S	S	S	D	S	S	S	S	S
A7	S	D	D	D	D	S	S	H	H	H
A6	D	D	D	D	D	H	H	H	H	H
A5	H	H	D	D	D	H	H	H	H	H
A4	H	H	D	D	D	H	H	H	H	H
A3	H	H	D	D	D	H	H	H	H	H
A2	H	H	D	D	D	H	H	H	H	H
AA	P	P	P	P	P	P	P	P	P	P
TT	S	S	S	S	S	S	S	S	S	S
99	P	P	P	P	P	S	P	P	S	S
88	P	P	P	P	P	P	P	P	P	P
77	P	P	P	P	P	P	H	H	S*	H
66	P	P	P	P	P	H	H	H	H	H
55	Always treat as a 10, never split									
44	H	H	H	D	D	H	H	H	H	H
33	H	H	P	P	P	P	H	H	H	H
22	H	P	P	P	P	P	H	H	H	H

*Surrender if offered.

S = Stand, H = Hit, D = Double, P = Split

Basic Strategy—Single Deck, Double Down Allowed after Splitting										
Dealer	2	3	4	5	6	7	8	9	10	Ace
Player										
17	S	S	S	S	S	S	S	S	S	S
16	S	S	S	S	S	H	H	H	H*	H
15	S	S	S	S	S	H	H	H	H*	H
14	S	S	S	S	S	H	H	H	H	H
13	S	S	S	S	S	H	H	H	H	H
12	H	H	S	S	S	H	H	H	H	H
11	D	D	D	D	D	D	D	D	D	D
10	D	D	D	D	D	D	D	D	H	H
9	D	D	D	D	D	H	H	H	H	H
8	H	H	H	D	D	H	H	H	H	H
A8	S	S	S	S	D	S	S	S	S	S
A7	S	D	D	D	D	S	S	H	H	H
A6	D	D	D	D	D	H	H	H	H	H
A5	H	H	D	D	D	H	H	H	H	H
A4	H	H	D	D	D	H	H	H	H	H
A3	H	H	D	D	D	H	H	H	H	H
A2	H	H	D	D	D	H	H	H	H	H
AA	P	P	P	P	P	P	P	P	P	P
TT	S	S	S	S	S	S	S	S	S	S
99	P	P	P	P	P	S	P	P	S	S
88	P	P	P	P	P	P	P	P	P	P
77	P	P	P	P	P	P	P	H	S*	H
66	P	P	P	P	P	P	H	H	H	H
55	Always treat as 10, never split									
44	H	H	P	P	P	H	H	H	H	H
33	P	P	P	P	P	P	H	H	H	H
22	P	P	P	P	P	P	H	H	H	H

*Surrender if offered.

S = Stand, H = Hit, D = Double, P = Split

Basic Strategy—Single Deck, Double Down on 10 and 11 Only										
Dealer	2	3	4	5	6	7	8	9	10	Ace
Player										
17	S	S	S	S	S	S	S	S	S	S
16	S	S	S	S	S	H	H	H	H*	H
15	S	S	S	S	S	H	H	H	H*	H
14	S	S	S	S	S	H	H	H	H	H
13	S	S	S	S	S	H	H	H	H	H
12	H	H	S	S	S	H	H	H	H	H
11	D	D	D	D	D	D	D	D	D	D
10	D	D	D	D	D	D	D	D	H	H
A9	S	S	S	S	S	S	S	S	S	S
AA	P	P	P	P	P	P	P	P	P	P
TT	S	S	S	S	S	S	S	S	S	S
99	P	P	P	P	P	S	P	P	S	S
88	P	P	P	P	P	P	P	P	P	P
77	P	P	P	P	P	P	H	H	S*	H
66	P	P	P	P	P	H	H	H	H	H
55	Always treat as 10, never split									
44	H	H	H	H	H	H	H	H	H	H
33	H	H	P	P	P	P	H	H	H	H
22	H	P	P	P	P	P	H	H	H	H

*Surrender if offered

S = Stand, H = Hit, D = Double, P = Split

Blank Basic Strategy Chart										
Dealer	2	3	4	5	6	7	8	9	10	Ace
Player										
17										
16										
15										
14										
13										
12										
11										
10										
9										
8										
A8										
A7										
A6										
A5										
A4										
A3										
A2										
AA										
TT										
99										
88										
77										
66										
55										
44										
33										
22										

Appendix C

Blackjack Resources

Web Sites

✐*www.profreedom.com*
Site on legalities of playing online, operated by the Internet Consumers Choice Coalition.

✐*www.thestandard.com*
News site that reports on issues related to the Internet and other technologies.

✐ *www1.cs.columbia.edu/graphics/courses/ mobwear/resources/thorp-iswc98.pdf*
This is the paper on the first wearable computer that Edward Thorp presented in 1998 to the Second International Symposium on Wearable Computers. An interesting read, largely thanks to Thorp's droll humor.

✐*www.casinomeister.com/casinos.html*
A good site for choosing online casinos to play at. In most cases, the site master meets face to face with the people managing the casino before it is listed on the site. At ✐*www.casinomeister.com/ rogue/index.html*, there is a list of questionable casinos (rogues), and casinos not recommended.

✐*www.igcouncil.org*
Web site for the Interactive Gaming Council. Place to go for information on regulations and legislation regarding online gambling, current news. Has a complaint section where, if you feel you've been treated unfairly by a member, you can complete a consumer complaint form and their mediation department will look into it and try to get it resolved.

✐*www.gambling.com/grumbles/front/*
Site where disputes are resolved between players and online casinos.

✐*www.onlineplayersassociation.co.uk*
Web site for The Online Players Association. Another place to look for casinos to play and to avoid.

✐*www.blackjackinfo.com*
Great information-packed site on all aspects of playing blackjack. Includes an engine for generating basic strategy charts.

✐*www.wizardofodds.com*
Site for generating blackjack strategy charts.

✐*www.blackjackinfo.com/blackjack-tournaments .php*
Information on blackjack tournaments and strategies for playing in them.

✐*www.casino.com*
Billed as "your one-stop Internet center for gambling," this site is a portal to online gaming and information on the top casino games.

✐*www.neteller.com*
Online banking site.

✐*www.prepaidatm.com*
Online banking site.

✐*www.hitorstand.net*
Blackjack trainer site.

✑*www.blackjackinfo.com*
Blackjack trainer site.

✑*www.bju21.com*
Free basic strategy and counting drills, a basic strategy engine for generating charts, and casino reports, which recap rules of play at casinos in the United States and abroad.

Gambling Newsgroups

✑*News:rec.gambling.blackjack*

✑*News:rec.gambling.blackjack.moderated*

✑*News:rec.gambling.misc*

✑*News:alt.gambling*

✑*www.qfit.com*
Blackjack software and calculator site.

✑*www.deepnettech.com*
Blackjack training and counting software developed by DeepNet Technologies.

Books

Wong, Sanford. *Casino Tournament Strategy*. La Jolla, Calif.: Pi Yee Press, 1998.

Mezrich, Ben. *Bringing Down the House: The Inside Story of Six M.I.T. Students Who Took Vegas for Millions*. New York: The Free Press, A Division of Simon & Shuster Inc., 2002.

Thorp, Edward O. *Beat the Dealer: A Winning Strategy for the Game of Twenty-One* (revised edition). New York: Vintage Books, 1966.

Index

THE EVERYTHING SERIES!

BUSINESS & PERSONAL FINANCE

Everything® Budgeting Book
Everything® Business Planning Book
Everything® Coaching and Mentoring Book
Everything® Fundraising Book
Everything® Get Out of Debt Book
Everything® Grant Writing Book
Everything® Homebuying Book, 2nd Ed.
Everything® Homeselling Book
Everything® Home-Based Business Book
Everything® Investing Book
Everything® Landlording Book
Everything® Leadership Book
Everything® Managing People Book
Everything® Negotiating Book
Everything® Online Business Book
Everything® Personal Finance Book
Everything® Personal Finance in Your 20s & 30s Book
Everything® Project Management Book
Everything® Real Estate Investing Book
Everything® Robert's Rules Book, $7.95
Everything® Selling Book
Everything® Start Your Own Business Book
Everything® Time Management Book
Everything® Wills & Estate Planning Book

COOKING

Everything® Barbecue Cookbook
Everything® Bartender's Book, $9.95
Everything® Chinese Cookbook
Everything® Chocolate Cookbook
Everything® College Cookbook
Everything® Cookbook
Everything® Dessert Cookbook
Everything® Diabetes Cookbook
Everything® Easy Gourmet Cookbook
Everything® Fondue Cookbook
Everything® Grilling Cookbook
Everything® Healthy Meals in Minutes Cookbook
Everything® Holiday Cookbook
Everything® Indian Cookbook
Everything® Low-Carb Cookbook
Everything® Low-Fat High-Flavor Cookbook
Everything® Low-Salt Cookbook
Everything® Meals for a Month Cookbook
Everything® Mediterranean Cookbook
Everything® Mexican Cookbook
Everything® One-Pot Cookbook
Everything® Pasta Cookbook
Everything® Quick Meals Cookbook
Everything® Slow Cooker Cookbook
Everything® Soup Cookbook
Everything® Thai Cookbook
Everything® Vegetarian Cookbook
Everything® Wine Book

HEALTH

Everything® Alzheimer's Book
Everything® Anti-Aging Book
Everything® Diabetes Book
Everything® Hypnosis Book
Everything® Low Cholesterol Book
Everything® Massage Book
Everything® Menopause Book
Everything® Nutrition Book
Everything® Reflexology Book
Everything® Stress Management Book

HISTORY

Everything® American Government Book
Everything® American History Book
Everything® Civil War Book
Everything® Irish History & Heritage Book
Everything® Middle East Book

HOBBIES & GAMES

Everything® Blackjack Strategy Book
Everything® Brain Strain Book, $9.95
Everything® Bridge Book
Everything® Candlemaking Book
Everything® Card Games Book
Everything® Cartooning Book
Everything® Casino Gambling Book, 2nd Ed.
Everything® Chess Basics Book
Everything® Crossword and Puzzle Book
Everything® Crossword Challenge Book
Everything® Cryptograms Book, $9.95
Everything® Digital Photography Book
Everything® Drawing Book
Everything® Easy Crosswords Book
Everything® Family Tree Book
Everything® Games Book, 2nd Ed.
Everything® Knitting Book
Everything® Knots Book
Everything® Motorcycle Book
Everything® Online Genealogy Book
Everything® Photography Book
Everything® Poker Strategy Book
Everything® Pool & Billiards Book
Everything® Quilting Book
Everything® Scrapbooking Book
Everything® Sewing Book
Everything® Woodworking Book
Everything® Word Games Challenge Book

HOME IMPROVEMENT

Everything® Feng Shui Book
Everything® Feng Shui Decluttering Book, $9.95
Everything® Fix-It Book
Everything® Homebuilding Book
Everything® Landscaping Book
Everything® Lawn Care Book
Everything® Organize Your Home Book

All Everything® books are priced at $12.95 or $14.95, unless otherwise stated. Prices subject to change without notice.

EVERYTHING® KIDS' BOOKS

All titles are $6.95

Everything® Kids' Animal Puzzle & Activity Book
Everything® Kids' Baseball Book, 3rd Ed.
Everything® Kids' Bible Trivia Book
Everything® Kids' Bugs Book
Everything® Kids' Christmas Puzzle & Activity Book
Everything® Kids' Cookbook
Everything® Kids' Halloween Puzzle & Activity Book
Everything® Kids' Hidden Pictures Book
Everything® Kids' Joke Book
Everything® Kids' Knock Knock Book
Everything® Kids' Math Puzzles Book
Everything® Kids' Mazes Book
Everything® Kids' Money Book
Everything® Kids' Monsters Book
Everything® Kids' Nature Book
Everything® Kids' Puzzle Book
Everything® Kids' Riddles & Brain Teasers Book
Everything® Kids' Science Experiments Book
Everything® Kids' Sharks Book
Everything® Kids' Soccer Book
Everything® Kids' Travel Activity Book

KIDS' STORY BOOKS

Everything® Bedtime Story Book
Everything® Bible Stories Book
Everything® Fairy Tales Book

LANGUAGE

Everything® Conversational Japanese Book (with CD), $19.95
Everything® French Phrase Book, $9.95
Everything® French Verb Book, $9.95
Everything® Inglés Book
Everything® Learning French Book
Everything® Learning German Book
Everything® Learning Italian Book
Everything® Learning Latin Book
Everything® Learning Spanish Book
Everything® Sign Language Book
Everything® Spanish Grammar Book
Everything® Spanish Phrase Book, $9.95
Everything® Spanish Verb Book, $9.95

MUSIC

Everything® Drums Book (with CD), $19.95
Everything® Guitar Book
Everything® Home Recording Book
Everything® Playing Piano and Keyboards Book
Everything® Reading Music Book (with CD), $19.95
Everything® Rock & Blues Guitar Book (with CD), $19.95
Everything® Songwriting Book

NEW AGE

Everything® Astrology Book
Everything® Dreams Book, 2nd Ed.
Everything® Ghost Book
Everything® Love Signs Book, $9.95
Everything® Meditation Book
Everything® Numerology Book
Everything® Paganism Book
Everything® Palmistry Book
Everything® Psychic Book
Everything® Reiki Book
Everything® Spells & Charms Book
Everything® Tarot Book
Everything® Wicca and Witchcraft Book

PARENTING

Everything® Baby Names Book
Everything® Baby Shower Book
Everything® Baby's First Food Book
Everything® Baby's First Year Book
Everything® Birthing Book
Everything® Breastfeeding Book
Everything® Father-to-Be Book
Everything® Father's First Year Book
Everything® Get Ready for Baby Book
Everything® Getting Pregnant Book
Everything® Homeschooling Book
Everything® Parent's Guide to Children with ADD/ADHD
Everything® Parent's Guide to Children with Asperger's Syndrome
Everything® Parent's Guide to Children with Autism
Everything® Parent's Guide to Children with Dyslexia
Everything® Parent's Guide to Positive Discipline

Everything® Parent's Guide to Raising a Successful Child
Everything® Parent's Guide to Tantrums
Everything® Parent's Guide to the Overweight Child
Everything® Parenting a Teenager Book
Everything® Potty Training Book, $9.95
Everything® Pregnancy Book, 2nd Ed.
Everything® Pregnancy Fitness Book
Everything® Pregnancy Nutrition Book
Everything® Pregnancy Organizer, $15.00
Everything® Toddler Book
Everything® Tween Book
Everything® Twins, Triplets, and More Book

PETS

Everything® Cat Book
Everything® Dachshund Book, $12.95
Everything® Dog Book
Everything® Dog Health Book
Everything® Dog Training and Tricks Book
Everything® Golden Retriever Book, $12.95
Everything® Horse Book
Everything® Labrador Retriever Book, $12.95
Everything® Poodle Book, $12.95
Everything® Pug Book, $12.95
Everything® Puppy Book
Everything® Rottweiler Book, $12.95
Everything® Tropical Fish Book

REFERENCE

Everything® Car Care Book
Everything® Classical Mythology Book
Everything® Computer Book
Everything® Divorce Book
Everything® Einstein Book
Everything® Etiquette Book
Everything® Great Thinkers Book
Everything® Mafia Book
Everything® Philosophy Book
Everything® Psychology Book
Everything® Shakespeare Book

RELIGION

Everything® Angels Book
Everything® Bible Book
Everything® Buddhism Book
Everything® Catholicism Book

All Everything® books are priced at $12.95 or $14.95, unless otherwise stated. Prices subject to change without notice.

Everything® Christianity Book
Everything® Jewish History & Heritage Book
Everything® Judaism Book
Everything® Koran Book
Everything® Prayer Book
Everything® Saints Book
Everything® Torah Book
Everything® Understanding Islam Book
Everything® World's Religions Book
Everything® Zen Book

SCHOOL & CAREERS

Everything® After College Book
Everything® Alternative Careers Book
Everything® College Survival Book, 2nd Ed.
Everything® Cover Letter Book, 2nd Ed.
Everything® Get-a-Job Book
Everything® Job Interview Book
Everything® New Teacher Book
Everything® Online Job Search Book
Everything® Paying for College Book
Everything® Practice Interview Book
Everything® Resume Book, 2nd Ed.
Everything® Study Book

SELF-HELP

Everything® Dating Book
Everything® Great Sex Book
Everything® Kama Sutra Book
Everything® Self-Esteem Book

SPORTS & FITNESS

Everything® Fishing Book
Everything® Fly-Fishing Book
Everything® Golf Instruction Book
Everything® Pilates Book
Everything® Running Book
Everything® Total Fitness Book
Everything® Weight Training Book
Everything® Yoga Book

TRAVEL

Everything® Family Guide to Hawaii
Everything® Family Guide to New York City, 2nd Ed.
Everything® Family Guide to RV Travel & Campgrounds
Everything® Family Guide to the Walt Disney World Resort®, Universal Studios®, and Greater Orlando, 4th Ed.
Everything® Family Guide to Washington D.C., 2nd Ed.
Everything® Guide to Las Vegas
Everything® Guide to New England
Everything® Travel Guide to the Disneyland Resort®, California Adventure®, Universal Studios®, and the Anaheim Area

WEDDINGS

Everything® Bachelorette Party Book, $9.95
Everything® Bridesmaid Book, $9.95
Everything® Creative Wedding Ideas Book
Everything® Elopement Book, $9.95
Everything® Father of the Bride Book, $9.95
Everything® Groom Book, $9.95
Everything® Mother of the Bride Book, $9.95
Everything® Wedding Book, 3rd Ed.
Everything® Wedding Checklist, $9.95
Everything® Wedding Etiquette Book, $7.95
Everything® Wedding Organizer, $15.00
Everything® Wedding Shower Book, $7.95
Everything® Wedding Vows Book, $9.95
Everything® Weddings on a Budget Book, $9.95

WRITING

Everything® Creative Writing Book
Everything® Get Published Book
Everything® Grammar and Style Book
Everything® Guide to Writing a Book Proposal
Everything® Guide to Writing a Novel
Everything® Guide to Writing Children's Books
Everything® Screenwriting Book
Everything® Writing Poetry Book
Everything® Writing Well Book

We have Everything® for the beginning crafter!
All titles are $14.95.

Everything® Crafts—Baby Scrapbooking
1-59337-225-6

Everything® Crafts—Bead Your Own Jewelry
1-59337-142-X

Everything® Crafts—Create Your Own Greeting Cards
1-59337-226-4

Everything® Crafts—Easy Projects
1-59337-298-1

Everything® Crafts—Making Cards with Rubber Stamps
1-59337-299-X

Everything® Crafts—Polymer Clay for Beginners
1-59337-230-2

Everything® Crafts—Rubber Stamping Made Easy
1-59337-229-9

Everything® Crafts—Wedding Decorations and Keepsakes
1-59337-227-2

Available wherever books are sold!
To order, call 800-872-5627, or visit us at *www.everything.com*.
Everything® and everything.com® are registered trademarks of F+W Publications, Inc.